MW01027775

JUST LOVE 2

JUST LOVE 2

The Essence of Everything

A COMPILATION OF TALKS

'The great journey from the mind to the Heart'

SRI SWAMI VISHWANANDA

The words spoken herein contain everything, the entire universe. They describe a Love that has been addressed before – after all there is essentially nothing new to add to the wisdom of the Holy Scriptures of both East and West – yet the way this Love is addressed is new. They are expressed by someone who not only knows about the all-pervading, all-life sustaining Divine force that forms the creation of the Universe, but who is completely one with it.

His message is simple: Just Love. Yes, just love. Love is all there is. Love is all you have to do. The rest will take care of itself. Those who have inner ears will hear. The words are like a sweet love song that if you allow it to touch you – will change your life forever. Because it will change you, and make you want to become again that which you already are, always have been, always will be - just Love.

JUST LOVE 2 is part of a series of books, written with words directly from Sri Swami Vishwananda. It contains 59 talks which he gave between 2005 and summer 2011 in various parts of the world with the goal of enabling each and everyone to attain the Divine Light in a simple way.

JUST LOVE 1 (released Christmas 2010): Love, Divine Names, Humility, Devotion, Surrender, Guru

JUST LOVE 2 (released Gurupurnima 2011): Mind & Pride, Willpower & Faith, Sadhana & Service, Awakening & Transformation, Grace

JUST LOVE 3 (planned release date Christmas 2011)

JUST LOVE 2

PREFACE

Welcome to the second volume of JUST LOVE, which is again about – what else could it be – Love. However it has quite a different taste, as it takes on another angle than its predecessor. In the first volume of JUST LOVE themes such as *humility*, *devotion* and *surrender* constituted the core, whereas volume 2 deals with the "harder" side of spirituality, such as *ego*, *pride*, *willpower* and *sadhana*.

JUST LOVE 2 lays out a path of how to travel from the mind to the heart and ends with the final, most crucial "ingredient" in the recipe for complete transformation: *Grace*.

Without Divine Grace, all our efforts are in vain; all sadhana, all determination, all longing for the Divine to help us transcend our mind & ego will not lead to lasting success. Here the reader will receive some invaluable advice of how to be smart on his spiritual journey. Not that we can outsmart God - Grace is not to be obtained by a system or a plan. It is given by Divine blessing, and yet, we can make use of our brain in a good way to reach the sanctum of our heart. God likes it when we are "smart" in that way and He also likes to play. Rather than putting on too much of a grim face as we walk through the sometimes dark valley of our existence, He encourages us to see through the scheme of Divine Mother, and to enjoy the ride that we call Life with a smile. Life is too beautiful to be sneered at.

May this book help us to develop the most positive outlook on life.

Let us cultivate a joy and positivity that springs from deep inside us without end. Let us share it with all those of us who have not yet found the key that unlocks the door of their heart. Let us give! and receive the joy that comes from giving - ourselves. As Saint Francis expressed in one of his most known prayers: It is in Giving that we Receive. This is what Bhakti truly means. To give yourself, completely, because of Love.

So may we unmask this ego that our mind creates, and that envelops us with pride, negativity, limitation, judgement and fear.

May we find the willpower and faith, that permits us to patiently purify ourselves enough to develop a deep longing for Divine union, accepting with positivity everything that comes along before we reach the final goal.

May we build up the discipline to persist in our sadhana long enough to obtain the fruits of our puja, japa, meditation or any other means through which we express our Love for God.

May we awake and transform ourselves on our spiritual journey, and may we see the Light that we are by listening to our inner voice that leads us to lasting freedom.

Most importantly, may we obtain the Grace of the Guru, Divine Mother & God, to find our way back Home at last.

Springen, Germany, 9 July 2011
S.K. on behalf of the Publishing Team

You give but little when you give of your possessions.
It is when you give of yourself that you truly give.
Kahlil Gibran

JUST LOVE 2

Mind&Pride

Ego / Negativity / Limitation / Ignorance /
Insincerity / Judgment / Fear

One cannot see the sun when the
clouds cover the skies. That does
not mean that it is not there.

Sri Ramakrishna

JUST LOVE 2

THE POWER OF THE MIND

Darshan, Steffenshof, Germany, 31 January 2008

Yesterday, we were talking about humility and also about the Love of God. Like I said yesterday, many people tell me "Swamiji, it's very difficult; it's very difficult to be humble." It's true. Some people told me again today it's difficult. Actually, *all* of you want to Realise God and to Realise God one also has to develop the qualities of the Divine.

So for God nothing is difficult and everything is possible, but for the human mind, with human limitations, everything is impossible. If you transcend this mind and yourself, everything will be easy. It all depends on how you think of things. If you think it is difficult, it will become difficult. Like I have always said, God is the Creator, but part of this Creator is present inside of us. When we create the barrier and think that it's difficult, when we become the creator of this big barrier, then it will become difficult. But when we say "Yes, I can transcend everything" we become positive towards ourselves. We develop the qualities and we make it happen.

Look, when you *so* want something – let's say you want to eat something nice – what would you do? You would do anything to have it. No matter what people think, would you bother about what people think? No, you just want to have it; you don't think about what people would think of what you want to eat! Or would you bother about what people think? No, you wouldn't. If you want to eat something, you will eat it – no matter what! Whatever your neighbour thinks about you, you will not bother about it. So why do you bother about other people, what they think or what they do or how they act? Bother about you! If *you* develop the qualities, people will learn from you; you will become an example.

You are spiritual people, yes? So you have to act in a certain way; you have to have the quality of the Divine within you. This quality has to reflect on the outside as well. The quality of the Divine is not to gossip around; the quality of the Divine is not to criticise; the quality of the Divine is not to curse others. No! The quality of God is to Love everybody. No matter what way a child is behaving, a mother always loves the child, no? So if God says "OK my children, you are all very bad, you have acted very badly today. I shall punish all of you" what will happen?

Yet, we who call ourselves spiritual, we let these qualities govern us. We forget about our real qualities, the Divine qualities within us. If little by little you get rid of your negativity – firstly, the negativity of the mind – and if the mind is transcended and the mind becomes pure, everything that you do will be pure. There will be no negativity present inside of you. The power of the mind is so great that you will create what you want. That's why when you read something, instantly you go into the image of that which you are reading.

> If little by little you get rid of your negativity – firstly, the negativity of the mind – and if the mind is transcended and the mind becomes pure, everything that you do will be pure.

You become identified with that. So what you are reading is very important. If you are reading positive things, you are becoming positive too; you're creating this positive energy. If we train our mind to be positive at *all* times, we will create positive things. If we just say "Yes, I want peace in the world. I want to change the world.

I want to make a big impact on the world," and when it comes to ourselves, our self is negative, then what in the world do we want to change, when we can't even change ourselves? If you want to change the world, if you want to have peace in the world, change your *mind*. When the mind is changed, everything becomes pure.

Let me tell you about the power of the mind. You know, a few years ago, some scientists made an experiment about the power of the mind. There was one man who was under a death sentence, so the scientists went to him and said "My dear man, you know very well you will die, so only if you accept, we would like to make a certain experiment with you." So the man thought for a while and said "Yes, look, I will die anyway, so it doesn't matter what I do. I will die." So he agreed.

Then the doctors said to him "Listen, before you agree, we will show you how we will kill you." So they took the man to show him a horse and a snake. The horse was bitten by the snake and the horse started to tremble, to shiver and foam started coming out from his mouth and he died. The man saw that and said "Yeah, well, I will die, whether here like this or in the electric chair, still I will die." Maybe it was in Texas, somewhere – probably.

So, what happened was, on the day of the sentence, they brought the man to the laboratory. Inside, the man was thinking "Yes, I will be bitten by a snake." The doctors said to him "We will cover your head." So they covered the head of the man. The man could not see anything. They took, in place of a snake, a rat. They made the rat bite the man. So what happened? He died; he died in the same way he saw the horse die. He started to tremble and then the foam started to come out, then he fell down dead. The most amazing thing is, when the doctors analysed his blood, inside of him was no rat venom, but there was the venom of a snake. Such is the power of the mind, that it can change the venom of a rat into the venom of a snake and that it can make the person die in the same way he had seen. So we programme everything the way our mind functions.

We can create, also. Like it is said, human beings use only 5% of their brain and the rest is dormant. So imagine if everybody transcended the mind and transformed everything which is negative into Divine wisdom. This can be done only if you become positive. Lots of illnesses can be cured just by changing the way Man thinks. If you think of yourself as being ill, strongly, you will get sick, but if make yourself strong and say "Yes, I want to transcend this illness, I want to transcend this mind," you will get cured.

How is this done? Of course, the grace of God is there, yes, but this also depends on *you*. When *you* say "Yes, I want to take the first step" then you will have the grace of the Divine. However, if you just sit around and say "Yes, OK, I will meditate, I will not do anything else, God will do it for me" then the nice food you want to eat will not come to you. Then you will always wait.

Whereas when you make your effort, you will see that even with just a thought – you want to eat something – you just need to think about it and God will provide. So many times it happens in your life that when you are in a certain state you have so much connection with the Divine that you just think "Oh, you know, today I would like to eat this" and during the day somebody brings it and gives it to you. How do you think it's possible? It's coincidence, but I don't believe in coincidence, it's you and the Divine Will together. In a light bulb you have two electrical charges – the positive and the negative. The negative charge is like the human being and the mind and the positive charge is like the Divine Will, the Divine Grace. When both of them join together, the light happens. So it's the same way when you are attuned to the right frequency; He will know about it and He will send.

So you see, my dears, that spirituality is very simple. Even when I talk about it, it seems so simple, but *you* have to take the first step. This is up to you to do. Like yesterday, I said I will help a little bit, but

I will not take all the steps for you, so for the first step it's you who has to say "Yes Swamiji, I want to change." Like in Mauritius, there was somebody's parents who always came to me saying "Swamiji, you know, my son, he always drinks. He will drink, drink, drink, always, but he doesn't want to change. We have done *everything*. We went to pray in *all* the temples we have ever heard of, but yet, it's like God never heard. God doesn't hear our prayers." They didn't know to which Saint to pray. So I asked them "Tell me something, does your son really want to change? Have you ever talked to him?" They said "Yes, Swamiji, we talk to him all the time." Then I said "Call your son. Tell your son to come and see me."

The first thing was, when he came he was late. So if somebody really wanted to change, he would never be late. This was the first sign that he didn't really want to change. I spoke with him. The poor guy, since the age of 12, he had been drinking secretly – now he's 35. He can't change. He doesn't want to change, because everybody around him is pushing him to change, change, change, but it's not coming from him. So I said to him "Listen, I can help you, yes, but only if *you*, from *your* side, come to me and tell me 'Swamiji, I want to change'", but yet, I'm still waiting for him to come. Well, I know he will come. So *you* have to take the first step, you know. You have to say "Yes, God, I want to change; I want to be positive." When you say that to yourself, every thought that comes, the moment it comes, you will change it. Let's say my mind says something like "She is bad. Look at how she's laughing; she's very wicked." Of course, before it comes out, you think about the thought inside, but what if, when you think about it, you challenge the mind, saying "No" to it; "No, it's not like that. This person is not the way I'm thinking."? You change it, but if you listen to the mind, of course, you go into the game of it. It all depends on the moment when the thought is happening in the mind. If just at the beginning, you change it, it will go away, instantly, but if at the beginning you listen to it, the negativity will come, again. If you go deeper with it, if you listen and listen, of course, it will grow. If the first time you don't notice it, but the second time you say "No" to it, it will come a third time and if you say "No" to it then, it will vanish away.

Such is the power of the mind and such is the power that *you* have to control the mind. But no, we like to listen. Like I always say, I don't understand one thing about humans, you know, well I am human, also. We like to listen to the mind, we like to suffer and we like to complain. Three good qualities: listening to the mind, enjoying the mind and suffering and complaining – four!

You see, God has given the mind to Man for a reason. Of course, each part of the body, each aspect that is inside this body, God has given. He is the master engineer of everything, you know. He is so perfect that He created human beings perfectly. The mind has been given for the right reason and if we use it for the right thing, it will always be constructive. If we use it in a negative way, it will be destructive to ourselves, firstly, and also to others.

Each one wants to change, so let's see. Be positive in your mind and change. Let the Divine Love that is inside your heart take control of you. The more you want this Divine Love, the more the Divine qualities will be present inside of you and the more you will feel the Love of God. You will feel how much He loves you.

Look, when a child makes a mistake, of course, the mother will slap the child – a small slap – but the mother's heart stays the mother's heart, no matter how many mistakes you make. His heart also stays the same, even if sometimes He has to slap you a little bit. When you sit down with God and talk to Him, you will see. He will say "I slapped you, but my Love inside is stronger for you." Look, when a mother beats a child, what happens? The mother showers more love afterwards. So no matter what comes along the way, even a small slap, you know, later on His Love will be much more and in more abundance. It's for your own good!

DEEP DIAMONDS

Darshan, Steffenshof, Germany, May 4 2008

It's nice to be here with all of you – everyone outside, also. So yesterday in *Darshan*, I was talking about the most worthless thing. I told a story about how a Guru asked his disciple to offer as *Dakshina* the most worthless thing he could get. As the disciple was going to pick up some earth, some soil, he heard Mother Earth saying "How can you consider me worthless? Look at all the greenery and the beautiful flowers. All that you see around you comes from me, so I cannot be worthless."

The next thing that he saw was a stone. He said "Oh, a stone is nothing." So as he was going to pick up the stone, he heard a voice saying "How could you consider me worthless? All the buildings, all the temples, are built with me. All the Deities are carved from me." Then he thought for a while and said "Yes, of course, it is worthy." So after thinking for a while, he realised what the Guru was asking for as *Dakshina*. It was his ego, his pride. So he went to his Guru and said this and offered to the Guru the most worthless thing, which is the pride, the ego in Man.

Actually, what stops one on one's spiritual advancement is the pride of thinking that one knows everything. The pride and ego always stop one, because they are a creation of the mind. A creation that always wants for selfish reasons and is always, even when we are aware of it, jumping to put himself in front, saying "Here, I am in front, you should look at me. Here, I am in front, you should consider me. Here, I am in front, you should feed me", but once you fall in the trap of it, what happens? You are lost. That's what Christ said "The first will be last and the last will be first, because that which is always in front is always the pride and when you feed the pride, you are gone."

It's done because the pride wants you to look at it. The pride wants you to flatter yourself, but how can pride reach Divinity? It's only through humility that one can reach God. It's only through humility that you will shine the light that you have inside of yourself. In front of God everybody is equal, whether it is a saint or not a saint, whether it's a rich person or a poor person, whether it's a white person or a black person, for God is Love and he just knows how to love. In your true aspect, deep inside your heart, you are Love.

Why is it difficult for you to just love? You know why it becomes difficult to love unconditionally? It's because of this pride. Whether pride is big or small, as long as you have a little, it will always be an obstruction. Like it is said, a small pebble can make a huge building fall, but a small pebble which is fixed properly can hold the whole building. A small stone, a corner stone, can hold the whole building if it is fixed properly, but the same stone can make the whole building fall if it is not fixed properly.

It's the same thing if you have your ego under control. You will rise, but if your pride is visible and extravagant in front of your eyes and you enjoy it, don't think you will advance. You know, especially in spiritual people, I see that very often. Not in other people, because other people don't bother about that.

Spiritual people very often bother more about their pride. They forget about the Love of God, but they think more about the ego and the pride – how much they are advancing, where they are, how much brilliant light they are seeing – optical illusion. But if one is humble, one will keep it and introvert it. Whatever you experience, any experience has to help you advance, not retrogress. When you treasure it inside of you, you will see that you will advance faster.

When you like to publicise it, just to make your fame great, it becomes difficult.

Once there was a boy, who was studying sculpture. His father was his teacher and he was a well-known sculptor. He was studying and after some time the father said "My son, now it's time for you to go and study further in the school." So he went to a college to study and he became very, very, good in the art of sculpting and everybody was flattering him – everybody. Whenever he would make a beautiful statue, everybody was flattering him, saying "Oh, your statue is so perfect, so good, but when he showed the statue to the father, the father would always find something negative in the sculpture. Even if those people would say it's perfect, it's very beautiful, the father would say "No, it's wrong."

After years and years, the son started to think "Why does my father always say that I have some defect in the statues?" So, one day an idea crossed his mind. He said to one of his close friends "Here, I have sculpted this beautiful statue. I would like you to bring it to my father and say that *you* have sculpted this statue and I will hide and I will listen."

So the friend brought the statue to the father of the boy and when the father saw the statue, such beauty, such finesse in the statue, he started praising the sculpture and also the sculptor. He said for sure whoever had sculpted this statue should be a very great artist. As he was praising, the son came out from hiding and said "Father, I sculpted the statue. I am the sculptor of this statue. I sculpted it. This is my statue. You always find defects in my statues yet right now you are praising this statue. Tell me, now what do you see as a defect in the statue?"

Then the father said "OK, my son. Now, it's time for you to know the truth." He said "The statues you have carved were always perfect, but I have never told you. From the beginning they were perfect, they were very good, but I have never told you that it is very good, so that your ego and pride would not stop you. Today who you are is because every time I have said there was a defect, you have tried to improve yourself. If from the beginning I had told you 'Yes, you are right', what would have happened? You would have stopped progressing. The ego would have taken place. You would have stopped everything." Hearing that, the son fell at his father's feet and said "Really, you are a great teacher" and from that moment he didn't stop progressing.

The same thing is so in spiritual life, also. You see, when a little thing happens in one's life, very often one puts it on such a big pedestal, forgetting the greatness of the true identity. Who can show off such a little thing? There is much more to give. So if one forgets about the tiny thing – the ego, the pride – and becomes humble, one will attain the Supreme. One will attain His Love and one will get a greater thing. You know how beautiful, how great a thing you have inside of you? You think only of the body and the mind as being one's self. The beauty of your soul is even more beautiful than whatever you see with these physical eyes. That is what you have to attain!

The greatness of the Love that you have in your heart is even more, much more beautiful than the nature that you see on the outside. One looks at nature and says "Wow! How wonderful it is!" Even today I was looking and I said "How beautiful it is." It's true. Look at nature; it's beautiful! If nature is beautiful, then the Creator of this nature, how much more beautiful It will be – no?

That's what we have to try to gain. Not only a small experience. I don't say it's not nice because it is nice. This builds up faith inside of Man, when you see a ball of light or you see a saint walking around, but there is a much greater thing. These are there to help you to advance. Don't get stuck by the pride and ego. Whenever something happens to you, whenever you see anything, whenever you feel something, say "there is more", always say "there is more."

As always, while talking to you about something, I was remembering a story that I actually told a year ago.

Once, there was a woodcutter in a forest, a very hard-working man. As he was cutting wood one day in the forest, a saint was passing by and as he saw the saint, he bowed down to the saint. The saint said "My dear man, I see that you are very hard-working. You are cutting this wood and you go to the market and sell it. I am very proud of you, but you know one thing, go deeper into the woods, just go deeper into the woods." So he listened to the saint. The next day he went deeper into the forest and as he went deeper into the forest, he discovered a forest of sandalwood.

The diamond is what the saint will guide you to, but if you see the sandalwood forest and stop, what will happen?

So, very happily he cut some sandalwood trees. He took them to the market and he got more money for that. After some time he didn't stop. He said to himself "The saint told me to go deeper into the forest, but he didn't tell me how deep I should go." So he started again, he went deeper inside the forest past the sandalwood and as he went even deeper into the forest, he discovered a silver mine. Very happily he took as much as possible. He went to the market and sold it and he became very rich.

Again he said "The saint told me to go deeper. I didn't need to stop." So as he went deeper once more, leaving the silver mine behind, he discovered a gold mine and again he took the gold and sold it. He became extremely rich, but yet, he didn't stop. He said "The saint told me to go deeper." He went deeper, deeper and deeper into the forest until at the end he found a diamond mine. Then, as he found the diamond mine, he said "Look, the saint told me to go deeper. I have found all this: the sandalwood forest, a silver mine, a gold mine. Now look, I find a diamond mine." Then he realised that the saint guided him to the diamond mine.

The diamond is what the saint will guide you to, but if you see the sandalwood forest and stop, what will happen? You will not advance. If you see the silver mine and stop, you will not advance. If you see the gold mine and stop, you will not advance. But when you have the diamonds, then you can stop; then you are rich enough.

It's the same thing, on the spiritual path you will experience many things, but don't let these experiences stop you. Always look forwards, there is a much greater thing awaiting you. I have seen now through travelling many spiritual people. Just by getting the silver mine or the sandalwood forest they stop and their level of consciousness stops at a certain level. If you want to Realise the ultimate, cross over everything. Only then will you Realise the Unconditional Love. Then you will be your True Self. You will attain Narayana; you will attain God's Love.

So don't let anything stop you on your spiritual progress. If you take a path, go deeper into it and don't lose time, because the more time you lose, the more difficult it becomes. The sooner you enter into the deep forest, the quicker you shall Realise your Self.

THE LIMITS OF KNOWLEDGE

Darshan, Shree Peetha Nilaya, Germany, 19 December 2009

I was asked a question a few days ago, actually. Somebody asked me "Swamiji, you always say, as also Christ said 'Blessed are the poor in Spirit, for they shall inherit God.' The person said to me "Shall we be ignorant?" Well, it's not what I said, you see, blessed are the poor in the mind. Christ, actually, didn't mean that you have to be completely ignorant to realise God, but what He means is one has to have knowledge about God, because if you are ignorant, you will not know anything.

Very often, with knowledge arises pride and we get so attached to our knowledge that even the reality gets covered. When you are in ignorance, of course, it's not good but actually, it's good when they are both in balance. At the same time if you want to Realise God fully, you have to put aside both of them. Knowledge is in the mind and if you want to understand the Divine with the mind, it's futile. You will never be able to understand. We want to grasp something, which is ungraspable, which is not physical.

Our mind understands, even our heart understands only what is physical, what we can grab and handle. Like I have given this example before – when a thorn enters your foot, what do you do? You try something. You procure another thorn to take it out but then do you keep them both with you or do you throw them away? You don't treasure it! In the same way, to take out the thorn of ignorance, you need the thorn of knowledge. The more you advance towards the Divine, the more you advance towards your Self, you have to put aside both of them, because it becomes an obstruction. *Lakshmana*, the brother of Rama, once asked a question to Rama, while looking at Vashishta, who was crying bitterly at the death of his son. Vashishta is considered one of the great Saints who is so knowledgeable about the *Vedas*, who is so knowledgeable about the Consciousness, everything. So *Lakshamana* said "How is it possible?" Rama smiled and said "My dear brother, where there is knowledge, there is also ignorance. If one is aware of knowledge, one has to be aware of all the knowledge, not only certain knowledge.

So it's the same thing if you are aware of light, you have to be aware of darkness. This is the duality of life; but are we limited to this duality or are we beyond this duality? In reality, who are we? We live life on Earth. Are we bound by this duality? In a certain way yes, we

Knowledge is in the mind and if you want to understand the Divine with the mind, it's futile.

are bound by it, because we are here, in the physical world. If we identify ourselves with the true Self, our true Self is not bound by this duality.

It all depends on what we identify with. That's what your spiritual path or your spiritual growth is about – to cross over the duality of things and attain the non-duality state. For this non-duality state, you can't attain it with limits that you put on yourself. Only when you cross over beyond that limit, then you will be your true Self. What is this Self that we always talk about, the Spirit? What is the Spirit? We know it as a word. Have we experienced it? The answer is "Yes", from day one that you are on the Earth, until the end, you do experience the Self, but you are not aware of it. Have you paused for a moment and asked yourself "What is giving life in this body?" It's God and the Self is part of that. Probably, it's just a small part, but in this small part is the whole.

This is the mystery of the Divine. Even in the one molecule of the Divine, of God, is the whole inside. That's what we are; we are not just human beings. When we take the Bible, what is said – even in the *Vedas* it is said – "God created human beings in His own image". The *Vedas* talk about it by explaining that we all emerge from the Oneness and we all will go back into the Oneness.

It doesn't matter how long we want to spend here, we will go back into the Oneness. This is our true Reality, only His Reality. At the end it's only Him that stays. The quicker we Realise it, the quicker we will reach Him. This is the choice that we have, this choice of making it faster or slower. This is in each one's hands. So do you know what to do? Do you know what you want? So, it's up to you to work a little bit.

THE SWAMP THAT IS A JUDGING MIND

Liturgy in the Chapel of Shree Peetha Nilaya
Springen, Germany, 20 March 2010

Today as we were in the Chapel for prayer, they were reading the *Gospel*. It was beautiful. I'm sure all of you know about this passage from the *Gospel* where Jesus was sitting and they brought a prostitute to Him and said "Master, this woman has sinned, what should we do?" They said "We should, according to the Law of Moses, lapidate her." So Jesus said "Fine, you can lapidate, you can throw stones at her, but let the one among you who has not sinned, throw the first stone." So no one threw any stones. As they were reading about this today, I was thinking "Oh, that's a good thing to talk about."
You see, often we think of ourselves as being too perfect, without any sin. We are white, pure white. That's how each one thinks of herself or himself. Then when they look to the outside, they have such great judgement. They think "Oh, you are wrong; I am right." Is that perfection? Is that what we are looking for?
If that is perfection, then one can forget about it! If you are continuously judging others and thinking yourself perfect, then you are wrong, my dear. I don't say that it is wrong to think that you are perfect. It's good to think you are perfect, that's how you will make yourself perfect. But if you analyse yourself, where would you situate yourself – with the people who would throw the stone or the people who would not?
This is about looking at oneself, about introspection, because it's so

easy to say "This is like this and this is like that", because everybody thinks that they know best. You think you know best, but what do you know? If you don't know yourself yet, what do you know of this world? You just pretend to know, when the secret of the world is hidden from you. That's how the world goes around. Until one has really searched for the truth, really searched for who they are, they will not know the world, because the world has so many secrets which are hidden from the eye of man. With your eyes you can only see the three dimensions. That's why you have so much judgement. If you can see beyond what your eyes can show you, there will be no judgement.

That doesn't mean that you should be just a fool and accept everything. There is a certain thing called common sense. You should use your common sense but your common sense is not about judging. It's about understanding. You have understanding in every part of your life. In everything that you do, there is an understanding behind it, because it's a learning process. You learn through every step of life and every lesson brings you closer to your goal.

You have to let go of this judging mind because that's the only thing that will always stop you. Like the great sages said "A judging mind is like a swamp in front of the mansion of the Lord." You will fall into it and drown yourself. If you can dry it, through faith, through Love, you will cross over and enter the mansion of the Lord. But many people would rather drown themselves in the swamp than Realise the Lord. They would rather drown themselves in judging and creating negativity in the mind than freeing themselves.

This is about faith, you know. If you have faith in the Lord who is seated in your heart, nothing can move you, but with lack of faith, you will move and you will be shattered. The lack of faith is pride, that's what makes one think of oneself as always greater than the other or knowing better than anyone else.

Once there was a devotee who had strong faith in his Master. His faith was so strong that by chanting the *Guru's* name, he could walk on water. So seeing that, the *Guru* started to say to himself "Wow, if my devotee chants my name and can walk on water, for sure, I am greater than that." So thinking this, the next day the *Guru* started chanting "I, I, I" and he proceeded over the water. Poor him, he sank and drowned.

This is what human beings always do. They chant "I, I, I" and they drown in it. They don't realise that they are drowning, because their mind is so focused on the outside even though the soul is calling for the Lord "Save me, save me, save me. When will you save me?" But here humans are a bit dumb.

They'd rather follow their stupid minds and let themselves be drowned than follow what the soul is asking, is praying for.

So as this time of Easter approaches, some people have been fasting, but Easter is a great time where the Lord has taught us humility. He has taught us to find the Kingdom

Like the great sages said "A judging mind is like a swamp in front of the mansion of the Lord." You will fall into it and drown yourself.

of God, the Kingdom of Heaven, not outside, but within ourselves. While you have not found this Kingdom of God, keep searching. Humble yourself. Once you find this Kingdom, once you Realise this Kingdom, then you can build up your ego if you want. But before that, why, for what? You know one thing, once you have reached there, there will be no point in building the ego. There will be no point in flattering yourself, because you will know, you will Realise that the actual Self is everything.

The actual Self and the Lord are One and the same. Then you can call yourself perfect, but I will tell you something – even somebody who has reached that stage will never call himself perfect, because he knows that perfection is not about this, it's not about this big I, but it's about Him, it's about God.

There was once a man who, for everything that he used to do, would remember the Name of the Lord. He would always say "Ram, it's the Grace of Ram" for everything. He was a shoemaker and when people came to him, he would make the shoes, return them and say "Whatever the Lord wishes, whatever Ram wishes, give it to me." So everybody knew that he was a very pious and devoted man.

One day someone accused him of stealing something. The King called him and said to him "My dear man, you have been accused of this and this and that, do you agree with it?" He said "By the grace of Rama, I have been accused, by the grace of Rama, they have put this charge on me, by the grace of Rama, I can't defend myself. Rama is my only witness." Every question that he would answer was not about him, it was about Ram. Such was his faith that the person who slandered him, the person who made the false accusation upon him, repented and asked for forgiveness and admitted that it was him who had said this. By the Name of Rama he was saved.

It's the same thing when we chant to ourselves our own glory. We will bring our downfall, we will drown ourselves in the swamp of egoism. But if we chant the name of the Lord, He will save us, he will free us and He will make us realise who we are. Like I said before, until you have realised your Self, until you have found your Self, don't praise your own glory, because this will bring your downfall. No one but your own self will cause it.

Even what you will not like to see, because you will always put the blame on others and say "It's because of that person I fell down." You don't know how to walk, but you blame the stone, which is along the way, saying "Because of the stone I fell down." How many say "I fell down because I didn't know how to walk"? The stone was there maybe for thousands of years!

This is how we have to change ourselves. We have to train ourselves to look within. Like we were chanting before *Sabse oonchi, prema sagai*, what we are looking for is this *Sagai. Sagai* means the union of Love. That is what we are looking for, that is what our soul longs for, that is what our soul is calling out to the Lord "Lord save me, make me realise the union between this (pointing to Himself) and you. Remove us from this illusion." This illusion can be removed only by Love, by pure Love, by Love from your heart. So strive to love the Lord with a one pointed mind, and He will come to you and He will save you.

THE MONKEY MIND AND THE VOICE OF THE HEART

Darshan, Shree Peetha Nilaya, Germany, 4 September 2010

Today I will talk about our mind, one subject that I like to talk about. The qualities of the mind are not the mind itself. The mind is very quick in creating different realities and different qualities. Like the first quality that the mind is very good with is making judgment. Experience comes afterwards, because throughout the judgment, throughout the worries, you are experiencing everything. The greatest quality of the mind is judgment, and from judgment come other qualities like criticising, pride and ego. These are all the qualities of judgment. Continuously, our mind is in a judging state. What happens when we analyse ourselves – I didn't say when we judge ourselves – when we say we analyse ourselves? Automatically, you look at all your bad things, all of your negativity. You never look at your positivity saying "This is good, let me put it in a corner", but the negativity, you will analyse it from different angles, from different facets and then you will feel sorry for yourself.

This is a quality of the mind, because you are not judging others, you are judging yourself. This is what Christ said. The judgment you see in others, in a little bit, is actually in yourself. That's why you can't accept this in others. Why should that person have it? I don't have it. You know this, because you would like to have everything and you would like that the neighbour doesn't have anything. This is the quality of the mind.

You know these three little monkeys – the ones that are covering the ears, the mouth and the eyes. These three senses are very needed to control the mind. We get influenced by what we see. We get influenced by what we hear. We get influenced by what we say. For example, if somebody is saying something nicely, people will say "It's boring; let's put it aside." Nobody wants to hear it, but when there is gossip, everybody would like to put in their bits and pieces, because these bits and pieces are not outside of you. They're inside of you. When you try to spice the gossip, actually you are expressing yourself.

A clever person will analyse himself and say "Hey, wait, what am I doing here?" The mind works differently though. The monkeys showed that you should not see, you should not hear and you should not speak evil, but that is what man does most of the time, because this creates sensation inside. Take the newspapers, take media everywhere – what do they create? Just sensation. Did you ever see anything good in newspapers? The first page of it is full with rubbish and why? Everyday it's the same thing, because your mind makes you perceive, makes you see only this negativity and the mind is attracted to this negativity.

Later on, when you see your life not progressing, not advancing, then you ask yourself "Why?" You say "I am the good one and the rest are the bad ones," but you don't see that just by analysing what you put inside of you – it is very important, also – but how you work with it inside of you is just as important. Like Krishna said "If the mind dwells on a certain object on the outside, one becomes similar to that." I will not say that if your mind dwells on a pumpkin, you will become like a pumpkin, but you will have similar qualities – you will be lazy and you will be heavy, you develop certain qualities. That's why it is said to let the mind dwell on the Divine. Let the mind be positive.

Of course one will say "Well, it's easy to say, but difficult to do." Actually, if you train yourself to think positively and be aware at each moment whether this is a judgment, this is a criticism, and analyse it - not outside of you, but in yourself, you'll be able to train your mind. It's very easy just to speak it out, isn't it? As the tongue doesn't have any bones, it's difficult to control. With training, with practice and with determination, if you really want to, you can change things. Otherwise, like the monkey, you will become the same. That's why the monkey shows "Don't do this thing. Don't become like me, otherwise there will be no difference between you and me."

This is where affirmation comes in, because if you want to be positive, if you want to achieve a life of a human being and finally attain the Divine, you have to act as a human being. You have to think like a human being, rather than like an animal, because animals don't think like that. Animals are bound very much with their intuition and they follow their intuition.

> When you are attentive to this inner voice, the more you listen to this inner voice, the more you will be directed into the right way, into the way of your heart.

Mankind is gifted with this great gift of knowledge, of using it in a proper way, but sadly they don't use it in that way. When they know that this will bring misery to them, still they do it much more, because afterwards they say, "We can change it." When is the afterwards? If you can't change now, afterwards it will be too late. Changes start now, when you are aware of yourself, when you are aware of how you are looking at things.

That's why the Scriptures said to chant the Divine Name. Let your mind submerge and transform itself through the Divine chanting, and let the real Love awaken inside of you, because this Love is not found by looking on the outside. It's by looking within you. This Unconditional Love is not about saying to somebody today "Yes,

I love you" and then saying "I hate you" tomorrow. It's the same person. Five minutes you love him and the other five minutes you say "I hate this person." Unconditional Love is the real Love, which mankind is looking for centuries. Through lives they look for it.

Now you are living in a time where you hear it often. You can hear it everywhere, you are living in a time where you can also put it into practice, if you close this mind, you utilise it in a proper way and you listen to your intuition. God has given you an intuition to follow. You have to learn to listen to the intuition in a calm way. You'll be able to hear your intuition only when you're calm, and then you will be able to accept what your intuition is telling you.

Often I've seen people listening to the mind and they say "Swamiji, I have been listening to my intuition," but actually, it's not like that. You see, the difference between the intuition and the mind; they are two different kinds of voices that you will hear. The voice of the mind will always be flattering you, will always say you are the best one, whatever you are doing is good, you should do more things like this.

The intuition, the intuitive voice inside of you is sharp and direct and it's not flattering. It often happens in your life that you have a certain decision to take. You feel it, but when you start thinking about it, you take the opposite. Then what happens? When it's done, the result comes, you say, "Oh, my goodness, I should have taken the other one. I was right; my intuition was right". Does this happen or not? Always!

Like that, you have to really be attentive to this inner voice. When you are attentive to this inner voice, the more you listen to this inner voice, the more you will be directed into the right way, into the way of your heart. This path is up to you. I can't come and tell you "You do this like that". You will say, "Oh, you can talk as much as you want, I will do what I feel!"

Somebody, like a month ago, told me "You know, Swamiji, I feel like coming and staying here." I said "Well, like you, there are a hundred people who feel the same." I said "No, you can't." Then she said "Well, I feel it inside so I will come." "Well," I said, "you can come, but you will not stay here." "But my brothers and sisters are here. I will be here." It's good to see this determination, but if one is not ready to listen, then it's just the game of the mind.

This is what will happen when you start to follow your intuition, not the mind, it will make you listen more. Nowadays, people are just talking, talking, talking, but very few people listen. It's like the control of the tongue, as I explained earlier, it's difficult. Because there are no bones in it, it's difficult to control it. How many people really listen? Yes, they listen, then they forget, but they're quickly talking, talking, talking. The tongue goes faster. Sometimes they start, they're still thinking what they will say, but the tongue has already said it. This is how quickly the tongue goes.

So watch yourself. Daily, analyse yourself – again, I said analyse – not judging, to see how you are functioning, how the mind is functioning. How many judgments have you put in? See if you see it as a judgment or a criticism, see it in you. "Where does this path lie within me? If I am seeing a fault in somebody else, it has to be inside of me. It's a mirror."

Like that, little by little, you will be able to change yourself, to change your mind, firstly, so that the Self can reveal itself to you. It's not a process of one month, it's a daily process throughout life. It depends on you to change now, to start it now. Like that, later on one day, when you hear your inner voice, you will be able to hear the Divine inside of you. You will be happy listening to this voice and following it.

BE CAREFUL WHAT YOU WISH FOR

Darshan, Steffenshof, Germany, 3 May 2008

Daily we do our *Sadhana*. We do our prayer, our meditation, our yoga practices. Why do we do it? We do our *Sadhana* to attain God's Love, to attain God-Realisation or Self-Realisation. Our daily *Sadhana*, actually, helps us and makes us ready to receive and beam this light of the Divine.

The Love of God is present in your heart always, but what covers it is the dust of arrogance, pride, ego. All these cover this light of God. When we do our daily *Sadhana* or our practices, we want to attain and let this light shine. That's why it is very important that we don't find excuses not to do our *Sadhana*. Humans are very quick to find excuses and they find excuses very quickly. If you tell them to meditate, they will say "Oh, my goodness," but if you tell them to do something else, they will skip their meditation to do something else.

In the temple of Dakshineshwar where the Divine Mother resides, Ramakrishna was a priest. In the temple, every day he would go and clean all the vessels there, which are used for prayer. Among the vessels, there was one very shiny pot. Every day he would give special attention to that pot and he would clean it until it shone. Every day it was very shiny. One day the people were wondering what's going on. "Why does he clean that vessel? He gives more importance to that vessel." They said "OK, let's go and ask him." So they went and asked "Swamiji, why do you clean like that?" He looked at them and he said "I clean this vessel specially every day and I clean it this way, so that it shines what I have inside, so that it brings forth what I have deep inside in reality."

So he said "What is brought out from deep within when I clean all the negativity from this pot, is like cleaning around the soul, removing all the negative qualities and letting the good thoughts shine." Let the purity of your mind shine, let the purity of your actions shine and let your True Self shine. In the same way we also have to purify daily and analyse ourselves, because we have a mind, a mind that continuously judges, a mind that continuously sees the faults in other people, sees the faults in whatever we don't accept, because humans do not accept their faults, humans like to put the blame on somebody else.

Doing our daily *sadhana* is also to self-analyse every day. The *sadhana* is not only in the morning, it's throughout the day. At night, when you go to bed, before you go to bed, just sit down and reflect on the day – what you have done well and what you have not done well. What you have done well will bring joy to you, and what you have not done well, there is a trace of un-calm inside of you. Try to rectify it.

When God sees that you are trying to rectify it, through His Grace and His Love, He will help. All the pride and the ego that you have, He will remove it. He is merciful, no? We say God is merciful, and if He is merciful, He will give you what you ask for, but only as long as you know what you are asking for, because sometimes you ask for things that will give you problems. You think you are asking for something good, but the result of it will be terrible.

Once there was a man, he was walking in the jungle and as he was walking, he felt tired. He saw a beautiful tree, so he said "Let me rest a little while." He lay down under the tree, not knowing that this tree was a wish-fulfilling tree. As he lay down – on the ground, he said "Oh my back is paining. How wonderful it would be if there was a soft mattress here now." As he had this thought in his mind, a beautiful mattress appeared next to him. Without thinking he just jumped on it. Then he said "Oh, how nice and soft," he started turning left and right, enjoying the mattress.

The next thought that passed through his mind was "Oh how beautiful is this mattress. How great it would be if there was a young girl pressing my feet, massaging my legs." As he thought of that, there appeared a young, beautiful girl massaging his legs. Then he started thinking, perhaps, whatever he thought would happen. At the same time he was feeling hungry. He said "Let me try." Then he thought "Oh, I wish there were many things to eat." As he was thinking that, lots of delicacies appeared in front of him and he started eating – very greedily, I would say. As he was eating, another thought passed through his mind "What if a tiger jumps on me and eats me?" So what happened? This wish was also fulfilled. At that moment, a tiger jumped out and ate him. The meaning of it is: Control the mind. Control your thoughts and always know what you are asking from God, because whatever you ask, out of His mercy, out of His grace, He will give you. Then don't complain to Him, because we like, as I said before, to complain. Like Christ said: "Don't try to remove the small splinter in the eyes of your brother when you have a big pole in your own eyes."

Control your thoughts and always know what you are asking from God, because whatever you ask, out of His mercy, out of His grace, He will give you. Then don't complain to Him.

We like to say "No, it's not me who is at fault." In place of analysing our own mistakes and changing and learning something, we like to say "No, it's not me, it's the other who did it" or "It's God who did it." He has the broadest shoulders, so put it on Him. I know what

Christ said, "Put your burden upon me; I shall carry it." We all put it on Him quite a bit.

Once there was a man. Always it happens to men, you know? There was a *Brahmin* who had a beautiful garden. Every day he would spend hours and hours in his garden. In it grew lots of beautiful trees and also fruit trees. One day, a cow was passing by and saw this beautiful mango on the tree. The cow just went and started eating the mangos. When the *Brahmin* saw that, he got very angry, he rushed toward the cow and started beating the cow. Poor cow; the cow is considered to be the mother.

The cow died from all this beating. When everybody heard that the *Brahmin* killed this cow, everybody rushed quickly to the spot where the dead cow was. They saw the *Brahmin* there and they started accusing the *Brahmin* with big, big words, you know. They said "You are a *Brahmin*? You killed this cow; you beat this cow and killed it." and the *Brahmin* said "No, I didn't kill it." Because he was very knowledgeable, he said "No, I didn't kill this cow, so don't blame me. It's my hand. My hand is governed by Lord Indra. He is the God of the hand, so blame Him."

Up in heaven, Indra was looking down and said "Oh my goodness! He killed the cow and I get the blame? Indra could not handle that anymore, so he came down on Earth in disguise, as a *Sannyasi*, as a *Sadhu*. He came there and as he was walking near the crowd of people, he started praising the beauty of the garden and said "Oh, what a beautiful garden." Then he asked "Who is the one who planted so many beautiful trees?" The man very eagerly said "Oh, I did it!"

Next he said "Oh, who laid this nice path?" and the man without thinking, said "I did it." very happily. He was getting more joyful, you know? Then the *Sannyasi* said "Who removed all the weeds from this garden and made it so clean?" The *Brahmin* was getting more excited and said "I did it." Then the *Sannyasi* said "Well, if you

did all of this, when you killed the cow, why did you put the blame on Indra?"
When good things come, everybody is there to receive, but when negative things come – one's own mistakes – nobody accepts them. So learn to accept it. Only by accepting whatever you have done wrong, you will be able to transcend it and change it. It's a learning process. Every time in life you go through learning processes. Every time in life you learn new things and if you have not learned something now, it's a cycle. It will come back to you and you will have to learn it again. Know one thing, sometimes one says "What should I learn from my mistake?" It seems like a worthless thing. We ask ourselves what can we learn from that? But we do learn, nothing is worthless.
Now I tell you a story. Once there was a man, who went to a *Rishi*, to a *Sadhu*, and wanted to get knowledge. He wanted to study under the Guru and he did. After some years, he succeeded in his study, and as you know, in the Hindu culture when you study under the Guru, at the end of your study you have to give a *Dakshina*. *Dakshina* is normally whatever you feel close to. So when he went in front of his Guru, he said "Guruji, I don't know what to give you as *Dakshina*. You tell me." The Guru said "My dear child, I want that you give me the most worthless thing." As the Guru said that, he bent down to pick up some earth, some soil and as he was doing that he heard a voice. Mother Earth said to him "You fool, you consider me worthless? Look around you. You walk on me, all this greenery, all these beautiful flowers, everything comes from me. How can you consider me worthless?" Then he started thinking "Yes, it's not worthless."
He put it down and as he was walking he saw a stone. He said "A stone – who cares about a stone?" He was going to pick up the stone, when the stone started talking to him and said "You consider me worthless? I tell you, all these big, big buildings that you see

around, they are all built from me. The statues, the Deities, are made from me and then you pray to those Deities, so how can I be worthless?" He thought for a while and said "Yes it's true." Then he started thinking "If the soil that we don't think too much about is not worthless, and if the stone itself is not worthless, what could be more worthless than my ego? That's the most worthless thing." He went to his Guru and bowed down to his Guru and said "Guruji, I offer to you as *Dakshina* my pride and ego." You always learn new things. Even from the smallest detail, you always learn.

REMIND YOURSELF OF YOUR GOAL

Darshan, Steffenshof, Germany, 23 April 2005

I would like to tell you a very sweet story with a great meaning in it. Once there was a master and his disciples. They were walking in a field, and while walking, the master stopped, looked at a rosebush and said to his disciples "Look how beautiful nature is!" The master was in ecstasy. The disciples looked at the roses, then at the bush, and then they looked all around, but they could not understand what the master was saying; they went on looking and looking. Finally the master said "You can't see, eh?" They were very confused. They looked at the roses again, looked at each other, then looked at their master. The master looked back at them, at their long faces, and he said to his disciples "Look at the flowers, look how beautiful they are. Look at them. They are living and acting now, without any hope for the future or any regret for the past. They are living and acting in the present moment, and finally, they are giving their fragrance, without any motive, without any expectation – freely. They are living their lives fully." Do you understand what is behind it? This is how nature does its work. Humans can learn so much from nature – even from a rose.

The rose did not expect anything, but what do humans do? Instead of putting their lives into right action, they are wasting time, always expecting and bringing misery on themselves. And then what do they say? "Oh God! Why do you send misery to me? I have always done good for you. I remember you always," but they are always expecting. In that game that they themselves start playing, they forget about their true nature. They forget about why they are here and they like it, you know. They like to say "Oh, I'm the poor one," they don't say "I am the Divine, I am the creator of everything." They like hanging around for the future, for what is to come in the future or what has been done in the past, they keep bringing it up all the time. Do you think this will bring happiness to humankind?

> Only when you let yourself say "God, I have tried everything! Now I abandon myself with all my expectations completely to you." Then you'll see the light, the light will reveal itself to you, because the light is yourself.

No! Only misery. Even when they sit for meditation, people expect to see some light, to see God in front of them. But I tell you, even this is an expectation, and with this expectation in the mind you will never see the light, you will never see the Divine. Only when you let yourself say "God, I have tried everything! Now I abandon myself with all my expectations completely to you." Then you'll see the light, the light will reveal itself to you, because the light is yourself. The mind always covers it with things, thinking this is the reality. So abandon yourself completely – body, mind and soul. Just let go of it! Let go of this small egoism that says "I" – I am this, I am that. What is this "I"? Have you known this "I"? Have you realised this "I"? No! As long as you have not realised it, you can't move forward. Why give much importance to something that you don't know? What is so great about this egoistic "I"? Thinking this is the whole. It's not. That's what the cross stands for. Cut the "I", and let only the Divine act. When this egoistic "I" disappears, what stays? The universal "I". The "I" without any identity of oneself. The "I" which is equal in each one of you.

This is the "I" that Jesus spoke of "I am the Way, I am the Truth, I am the Light" – the "I" of the consciousness, the "I" of the Christ consciousness that leads mankind. Yes, each one of you. This consciousness is in each one of you. It's waiting to become active. It's very good that you come for Darshan, very good that you sit for meditation, but you should not only do it now, you have to do it always! By receiving the blessing – prana hooti, it's called – you are receiving and activating the light within you. That's what I can do for you, the rest is up to you. I can take the food, crush it to purée and put it in your mouth, but I can't swallow it for you. Although I would be happy to do it for you, you know? But this part is up to each one of you. Your question will be "We keep trying yet nothing happens?" Remember what I said before, if you try with an expectation it can never happen. You have to empty your mind completely. The thought will pass by, let it pass – don't feed it. You are not the mind – you are not the thought, you are more than that. You are the Child of God. You are part of the Divine Creation. So make this your goal in life wherever you are, remind yourself of this goal. Whenever you think that you are doing something wrong or you're acting in the wrong way, close your eyes, drop inside, deep inside your heart and ask the Self and listen to it. Only when your mind is quiet will you hear the heart talking to you. So keep practising, I always say it, and I will keep saying it – maybe every time you come for Darshan you will hear the same thing. As long as you don't practise it properly I will keep saying it, I will bore you with it, because I'd love all of you to reach Divinity. I want all of you to realise the Love of God that is inside you, not only that – I want all of you to become an instrument of this Love and share it around, bring it to everybody. You don't need to go and hug the person to share the Love of God – just by the reflection of your face, this light will be passed on wherever you go; this light will be continuously with you.

DON'T BE AFRAID OF THE MIND

Darshan, Steffenshof, Germany, 24 April 2005

Today I would like to talk about the mind – a big subject. A subject that many people are scared of. Actually you don't need to be scared of the mind. The mind of its own is a great gift of God – because it is through the mind that you can achieve the Divine. But what is wrong with thought? It is said, the way you think, that's the way you are. If you think you are Divine you will become Divine, but if you think you're just a mere human being, you will always stay this mere human being. This is the power of thought. To control the mind is to control how you think, to control the thoughts. If the thoughts are good, the result outside will be good. But if the thoughts are wrong, do you expect anything good will come of it? This is how our thought – how our mind, how our thinking works. If you look at our mind as a gift that God has given us, how marvellous it is! Imagine: your brain can record 800 memories per second. Do you think a computer can do that? And it can last seventy-five years without getting exhausted – night and day. Imagine this storehouse that the mind has, imagine the storage – that the brain has, it's so small, isn't it? Like this, so small, maybe two pieces, one here, one there, can store about ten billion to a hundred billion memories in a life time. Even a computer can't keep such memories...only a few million, that's it.

So if scientists had to build a computer that could store that much – I think this building would be one of the biggest buildings in the world, storing so much information. How marvellous is this creation of God! That such a small brain can keep so many things inside! But people let the mind control themselves. They let themselves become the slaves of their thoughts, and they enjoy it. To control the thought – the thought will pass by. You know inside your heart whether it is constructive or destructive. It's upon to you whether you want to feed the thought with the right food or deny it.

If the thought is negative we keep feeding it with negativity, and we become miserable. You yourself create misery with unhappiness and problems. The thoughts

If you think you are Divine you will become Divine, but if you think you're just a mere human being, you will always stay this mere human being. This is the power of thought.

should be positive, then they will be more constructive. Then happiness, joy, peace will enter. Start thinking positively about yourself first, because you can't think positively of others unless you are positive yourself. You start with yourself. Sit quietly and start the conversation with the Divine within yourself. It's only through silence that you will be able to control the thought. Talk less – because people who keep talking and talking – they are just running away. They are just scared of seeing the truth, that's why they talk and talk. They talk without knowing what they are talking about.

If you want to start the communication with the Divine within yourself, be silent as much as possible. But if you want to start the communication with man, then keep talking! You know how beautiful it is to listen to the Divine inside you? It's the most beautiful thing, I can't even express it with words, because words are still limited. Like I said yesterday – from the form to the formless, from the name to the nameless. This is the Divine in each one of you, and to be always in this place, to be always in this awareness and find that you are not separate from the Divine! It's so beautiful, it's so fulfilling. Whenever you do something there is always a gap, something that is unsatisfied. But when you have discovered the reality in you – whatever you do, the satisfaction will be complete!

JUST LOVE 2

Faith & Willpower

Longing / Purification / Acceptance / Positivity / Patience

Faith is the bird that sings
when the dawn is still dark.

Rabindranath Tagore

REALISING OUR DIVINITY

Darshan, Dubai, 5 February 2006

I'm pleased to be among you today. The first thing we have to understand is that all mankind, in one way or another, is always on a search – a search for who we are, a search of what we are here for. So many times this clicks in your mind and you ask yourself "Is it just for this that I have been born here on Earth?" These searches can last for years and years. You can go around the world to look for what has depth, what will really satisfy you, because humans always have a desire for new things. You desire one thing, for example, a nice car. Once you have it, you enjoy it for some time and then the desire disappears. Then you desire something else. Always, you keep desiring something. You keep desiring, and as long as you desire material things, there will always be desires. One desire will lead you to another one, but do you think this is really the reason for the incarnation of mankind? No, it isn't.

Human beings are said to be *Satchitananda*. This is a Sanskrit word. *Sat* means Existence. *Chit* is the Consciousness and *Ananda* is Bliss. Everybody wants to be blissful, no? Everybody wants to be happy, but if you really, really want to be happy, you have to be sincere towards yourself. You have to be really truthful towards yourself firstly. Then, if you ask God "Lord, give me happiness," do you think He will refuse you? He will not. He will give it to you freely, but it's up to you to maintain the happiness. It's up to you to keep this happiness and let it grow.

God, for sure, has shown you that in your life. You have experienced *real* Love, *real* Bliss. Even if it was only for a few seconds, you have forgotten everything around you and you have felt that eternal Bliss, but the point is that it is very difficult for mankind to keep it. The mind, which is a big weapon, pride and so on, many other things keep people in delusion.

All Scriptures have said that Man is made according to the image of God. So, if Man is the image of God, Man is part of God. We have just to realise this Divinity within ourselves. Jesus said "I and my Father are one." First He claimed Himself to be the son of Man, purely human. Then he said "Who has seen the Son has seen the Father." One who has seen and realised that one is the child of God will come to the stage of realising that one is part of God. During these different stages, one firstly has to be really, really sure that one wants God, wants Realisation.

So *Satchitananda* – Existence, Consciousness and Bliss – this is your true Self. The body can`t exist without consciousness. If God didn't give consciousness to mankind, mankind would not feel joy, without experiencing Bliss. Even if you have forgotten it, these three can't exist separately. In direct language, the body, the mind and the soul, each one has to be an instrument of God and to reach that stage there are different ways.

The easiest way is if you look at God's Creation. God is so perfect. There is one thing, which all the living creation of God has in common and that is breathing. Through breathing everything lives - water, fish, animals, plants, human beings. So breathing is very important. We need to breathe with the conscious realisation of breathing. Your breathing is so normal that how many people consciously realise it? How many people think of their breathing state during the day? Not many do. It's very simple and very easy. Would you try a little bit?

A guided meditation

Just sit properly, so that you feel comfortable. In breathing there is the essence of all healing. It's through your breath that you will realise the Love deep inside you and the Love that crosses over all the barriers that the mind creates.

- Focus firstly, on the third eye. Forget about everything around you. For sure, the mind will think. Let it think. Don't try to stop it. Even if the thinking is not positive, it doesn't matter, but don't feed it.

- Focus all your attention just to the point of your third eye. With your creative power, – which you have, because you're created out of the Divine, so you are the creator also – create at the centre point a ball of light. Inside this ball of light, put any Divine aspect that you feel close with: OM, Cross, Krishna, Jesus, Allah.

- Listen to your breath. Breathe in slowly. Take your time. Do it in a relaxed way. Breathe in and breathe out. Don't forget to listen to your breathing and at the same time, to focus on it.

- Slowly let the light – with your willpower – let it increase in size.

- Let it become so big that it's covering your face completely.

- Growing more and more – covering the upper part of your body.

- Then covering your whole body.

- Don't let the light stop here. Let it keep growing. Let the light become brighter and brighter.

- Now, focus only on your hearing and keep looking at the ball of light.

- Listen to what your Self wants to tell you.
- Now, slowly, reduce the light and come back to yourself.

Whoever has heard deep inside them something should meditate on it and practice it whenever they have time.

To be good in meditation, to be good on your spiritual path, you have to be disciplined. It's not a pressure; it's not forcing. It has to come from deep within your heart. It has to be out of love. In the same way, if a child wants something, the child will do anything to get it. He will cry very loudly. When the mind has focused on something that the child wants, the child will want it.

All Scriptures have said that Man is made according to the image of God. So, if Man is the image of God, Man is part of God. We have just to realise this Divinity within ourselves.

It is the same way when Jesus says to enter the kingdom of God one has to be like a child. One has to be like the child who wants and who's screaming to the Father "God, give me Realisation. God, reveal Yourself to me. Reveal my purpose of being here." On this way you start but then you lose hope. Many people start, then in the middle they say "It's too long. It's taking a long time for God to reveal Himself." They lose hope in the middle of the way. Of course, they themselves stop the Realisation.

Love is a word that for generations, for years, for centuries, has been used and misused. In the name of Love, in the name of God, many things have been done. But it's up to each one of you to rectify that, to reflect the real Love, to reflect that you are part of

God, so that people see it. Love is not just a word. It's not just a sound, it's also visualised through the eyes of man. Show that you are who you say you are. If you are the child of God, prove that you are the child of God. Show that you are the child of God. Have this deep will of Realising God. Have this deep will of Realising who you are. You will have it. Let Love be the ultimate of your life.

Let God be the ultimate of your life, because in Him there is everything. Whatever you desire is in Him, is in your true Self. If you Realise who you are, just as when God commands and everything happens, the same way will happen for you also, but your willpower has to be really strong. You have to really want God. Otherwise you will only have the limitation that will make you always unhappy.

Try for real happiness and become really the *Satchitananda* that God has created. If you really want that, you will have it. It doesn't matter how long it takes. It can also happen right now! If you're a hundred per-cent sure of yourself, everything will be given to you.

WHY GOD GAVE US A HEART

Darshan, Steffenshof, Germany, 3 March 2007

You are all aware that human life is for something, and as you know, it is to realise the greatest goal, which is the True Self and which is Love. This Love, which seems far away with the mind and sometimes even inaccessible, actually, is closest. As you all know, you are an incarnation of Love, you are part of the Divine. We are all trying to become, to attain this Divine Love, to attain this bliss again, to become *Satchitananda,* that what in reality you are already. It's just that you don't let it out. You like the love on the outside. You think it's easy, but after sometime, you say "Headache". As you know, this Love is eternal. This Love is waiting to be awakened deep within you, this Love that you have been carrying for many lifetimes. Firstly, to have the chance, to have the grace of being spiritual, being on a spiritual path itself is an attribute to this Divine Love. Everybody is searching, but only when this Love comes to a point where it, firstly, starts to sprout out and grow and mature, then one realises one's Self, realises this Love.

The question comes to mind "Why every time, we come back, do we have to do the same thing over again? If we have already realised this Love, if we have already attained this Love, why don't we have it?" For that, if you look at a child, a child just goes with the daily flow. He doesn't bother to think how things have to be. But we older ones, I mean youngsters, we like questioning things, we like to doubt things, we like to put spice on it. So, when we have put too much spice on something, life has to change – it gets too hot! But this pure Love, this Divine Love is present at all times.

There was once, a Master, a Guru, traveling on his way with his disciples. They were tired. They stopped to relax a little bit and one of the disciples said "Master, you always talk about Love. You always say that Love is eternal. Love is the only thing that we have to attain. It seems that we take birth, we die, we don't realise this Love, but where is this Love?" The Master, for a while kept quiet. By his side there was a stone. He just picked up the stone next to him and he took one stone from the river beside him. He started tapping both stones – the one from the river and the one from the land. What happened after some time? Spark, fire came, no? The same stone which was in the water and the same stone which was on the land – both of them - had the spark. Even though the one from the water had stayed in the water for centuries, still it could produce this spark.

"Why every time, we come back, do we have to do the same thing over again? If we have already realised this Love, if we have already attained this Love, why don't we have it?"

The same with Man. No matter how many times you take birth, how many incarnations you will take, this spark of Divine Love is ever with you, is always there, but you have to want to let it out. It's simple, it's easy and it's just waiting. For that to come out, you have to want it, you have to let it out. When you put your mind aside and try not to listen to it, you will awaken this Divine Love. When you say "God, I surrender to You. I've tried my best, I did everything, every yoga, every meditation I did in my life but still, it is not coming." and you say "I'm tired of that; I surrender myself to You, now. You do what You have to do." In this deep surrender, you see how close God is to you.

Often we do lots of things, but we have an expectation into it. We pray; we expect something. We meditate; we expect God to jump into our meditation. This expectation will not lead you anywhere. Only when you don't expect anything from God and accept, like a child, whatever the Father is giving and you are happy with whatever He gives you, He will also give the full Realisation of His Divine Love.

Look deep within your Self and try your best to feel Him. God has given a heart, no? What is the heart for? To love and to feel – to feel He is present. When you love somebody, you feel the love, isn't it? You become blind with this love for some time, until your eyes open, until you realise that there is a greater Love that you want to achieve. It's not until you want to attain this Love, until you want to attain this real happiness that will never leave you, until you want to attain this real bliss that will never fade with time, that you finally will become this Love.

JUST LOVE 2

THE DETERMINATION TO REALISE GOD

Darshan, Friedrichshafen, Germany, 13 July 2008

It's nice to be here. Well, I was wondering what we can talk about, but there is one thing that I find very interesting. For all the *satsangs* that I have done lately, people always ask one question "What will happen in 2012?" I'm sure all of you have heard lots of predictions about 2012, no? That everybody will be enlightened, which is very good. Some people have heard that maybe the world will end in 2012, which is very bad. For the sporty people, they have heard that there will be the Olympics in London in 2012.

Above all this, I have seen the happy people who have heard they will be enlightened. I have seen people happy when they have heard that the world will end in 2012. I have seen people happy when they know that there will be the Olympics in 2012. In general, it is very good to be happy. There are a few people who got very scared that the world will end in 2012, they got very depressed. But when I say that it's true that there will be the Olympics, very good! It is true that people will become enlightened in 2012, because every day people become enlightened.

There is truth that the world is ending in 2012, because it is ending every day, little by little. I say to people that the world will not end the way people think – the end of all negative things you should see – and they are so depressed. When I say nothing will happen, they say "Why will nothing happen?" Should I say people are happy? You know I am not making publicity about the Olympics.

Enlightenment – don't think that it will just happen like that. You have to really work for it. I am happy to know that lots of people have the determination to reach God-Realisation by 2012. That is very good. This determination will make it happen, but don't think that by just sitting it will just happen. No, you have to do something. If you have determination, you have to do something; you have to act. It's the same thing as you having the determination to come here today. What did you do? You got in your car, you drove – some drove 500 km, some drove 200 km – you drove to be here. You had the determination to come; you have come here.

It's the same thing that you have the determination for God-Realisation or to get enlightenment, to become Self-Realised. It's now that you have to work – not waiting for 2012 when God will just say "OK, I love them so much that I will just give them all Self-Realisation just like that". Know one thing: Whatever God gives, He gives according to its time and according to whether you can handle things or not. He will not give you something that you will make a big mess out of. He will not give you Realisation until you can handle Realisation, because to just say "I am Self-Realised" is not just to put a label on yourself saying "Yes, I am Self-Realised." It's not like that. There is a big responsibility with that also, and you have to go through certain purification to attain that.

When you say that the world will end in 2012, of course, it will end, because all the negative qualities which are present inside of that person, will also end. This will be the end of it. But whether it will be 2012 or later, that determination depends on each one individually, because spirituality is an individual path. It's not upon the masses, it's not that just by eating something the stomach will get full.

Krishna did it. For the Divine Personality it is possible to do that. For the Master it's possible to do that, yes, but it is also, up to each individual to make the determination as strong as they want. Not only Krishna, many have given this Realisation. In the Bible, Christ even says "I will send My Spirit upon you." For Pentecost, the Spirit of God descended upon the Apostles. Of course, the Master can make it happen. The touch of the Master, when the disciple is sincerely ready, can give Realisation just like that. We have to have the determination for it. Like I just said, if someone eats something, his stomach will not get full, but in the spiritual realm it is possible.

In the life of Krishna, when the Pandavas were in the forest in exile, there was a sage, a *rishi*. He came to the house of Draupadi and the five Pandavas and said to them "I want to eat something, but first we will go and take our bath. Then, when we come, we would like to have lunch at your place." The Pandavas didn't have anything in their house. The only solution for Draupadi was to turn to Krishna. So she closed her eyes and called Krishna.

At that moment Krishna came and said "My dear sister, what do you have to offer me to eat? I am so hungry." Draupadi looked at Krishna and said "I don't have anything, my Lord. I don't have anything to give you." Then Krishna said "Are you sure you don't have anything? Show me the pot." Draupadi showed the pot to Krishna. There was just one grain of rice at the bottom of the pot and Krishna took it and ate it. As He ate it He said "Oh my stomach is full." What happened? When the *rishi* finished bathing in the Ganges, his stomach was completely full. So he didn't go to Draupadi. For Masters, to give Realisation is easy for them, but you have to be ready.

From your side, to make yourself ready, like I said, the goal is very important. It's not about 2012 or whatever year. The same thing was said about the year 2000 when everybody was expecting something to happen, but nothing happened. What did happen is that people had to become more spiritual. People are searching for the Truth, which is very good. To know about one's Self or to come to a point of realising one's Self is very important.

The determination has to be based on Love, not on fear. Often people say "I don't think I will have enough time to realise God in this life." Why do you think there is not enough time? It is said that even one second before you leave this body, if you have realised the Divine, you will be fully liberated. The foundation is Love that will make you liberated. The practice is now, not in the future, because often we say "We will see afterwards what happens," but what about now? If you want to realise your Self in 2012, start your practice now. Start your

> When you take a spiritual path, you have a certain goal and a certain determination. Nothing should obstruct you on your way and you should not allow anything to take you away from your spiritual path.

sadhana, start your spiritual way now, this moment. Find your path and really surrender to your path! Then by 2012, for sure, you will be Self-Realised.

The determination is like this. Once there was a drought in a certain country, so every plant was dying, every crop was dying. The farmers started digging a channel towards their field from the river, so they could have water to irrigate the field. There was one man who took a vow that he would not eat, he would not rest, he would not even think of taking a shower, until he had finished the channel. He started in the morning. Around 10 o'clock his daughter came and said "Father come. Wash your hands and have some breakfast," and he said "No, I don't want to eat anything until I have finished." A few hours later his wife came. The wife said "My dear husband, you have been working all morning, come now! Leave this spade aside. Come have lunch." Looking at his wife very angrily he said to her

"Go away; you are disturbing me. You are stopping me from doing my work. I have taken a vow that I will not eat or drink until I have finished my work."
Seeing such determination, the wife said "Let me try again to ask him" and she said "Please, come!" The husband got angrier and said "You better go!" He took the spade in his hand and started chasing after her. She was so scared that she ran away. At the end of the day, he reached the riverbank and the channel to his field from the river was finally connected. He sat down and listened to the water flowing to his field very happily. At that moment he felt a great peace, a great joy inside of him. Then he said to himself "Yes, I have succeeded."
There was another farmer who had the same problem. He also began digging a channel towards the river to get water, but the moment his wife came, he said "OK, for you my dear, I will leave it. I can carry on tomorrow." What happened? He never succeeded in reaching the river.
It's the same in life. When you take a spiritual path, you have a certain goal and a certain determination. Nothing should obstruct you on your way and you should not allow anything to take you away from your spiritual path. If you have set your mind towards your goal for God-Realisation, go for it. There will be lots of things on the way, but be strong. Never lose hope and know that the closer you are to your goal, the more tests there will be. But with each test, know that the Lord is next to you, know that He is there always supporting you. He is there always to guide you. The Divine Mother and He will always be with you. You know they are...
I will tell you something, they are like your guardians. They are always standing next to you. If They see that you really want it, They will be here to give you Their hands, you know? Hold tight! Hold so tight that when the first wind comes and starts blowing, you don't let go of the hand. If you let go of the hand you will go

back. Then you will have to go, again through the same thing. When you hold the Divine Mother's hand, She holds very tightly, I tell you, She doesn't give up easily, but we Her children, very often we give up easily. So hold tight and reach your goal!

Set a goal in your life. Set a determination in your life. Whatever you determine, whatever you focus on, you will reach it. Whether it takes many years – four years or whether it takes ten years – you will reach it. Stop worrying about the future. If you want to have a better future, it all depends on you. The past is finished, leave it behind. Don't bother about the past, as long as you hang onto the past, the past will hang onto you. The more you let go of the past, the more you are free, the more you are in the present.

I always say to people, in place of always thinking about what will be in the future or what has happened in the past, why don't you think of God, why don't you sing His Name continuously? It is said that in this time the easiest way to reach the Divine is to chant His Name continuously. Do *japa*. In this way you will not waste your time thinking negatively or waste your time becoming negative. You will start rising in God-Consciousness inside of you. You will start increasing the God quality inside of you.

Sri Chaitanya always said "In this age, chant the Name of Sri Hari. Chant the Name of God. God has given so many Names." He said *Harinama, Harinama, Harinama ewa kevalam Kalau nasteva, nasteva, nasteva, gatih anyatha*, which means *Sing the Name of Narayanaya, sing the Name of Sri Hari.* This will lead you to your determination, to your goal. *Harinama, Harinama, Harinama ewa kevalam.* All the Divine Names, as long as you sing, they will create happiness inside of you, so sing.

I will sing *Hari Haraya.* I always sing this *bhajan.* If you would like to stand and dance, you are free to do that also. I don't like people to just sit down, feeling very tense, because when you sing you express joy, and when you express that joy, get up and dance. You see, in spirituality, you don't just dance any way of dancing, because the body language is important. It's not just to sing, but how you express your Love to the Divine is also, very important. When you dance, there is a certain vibration that emanates from your body, which you are not aware of but the certain vibration that emanates from your body depends on how your psyche is reacting to it. It is the same as a *mudra*. You can do just simple exercises with your hand. This creates a certain energy. Lifting of the hand means: Lord, I'm surrendering to you. Here, I'm lifting my hand up to you. Take hold of this hand and pull me out of the ocean of suffering.

REALLY, I WANT HIM!

Darshan, Basel, Switzerland, 16 July 2008

It's lovely to be here with all of you. In spirituality we always talk about the Love of God, and how to attain the lotus feet of Sri Hari or the Lotus Feet of God. I tell you, it's very easy to attain His Lotus Feet. Firstly, you just need to really, sincerely want it. If you sincerely want Him, He will come to you. He will make everything possible so that you gain Him.

As you know, there are four types of people in this world. The first ones, they just live in the material world. They just live in the world, so for them, they are not aware that there is a greater energy. Even if they know about it, they don't bother about it.

The second ones are the ones that they know that God exists, but they can only pray to God when they go to temples or to churches. When they are out, God doesn't exist or God exists only when they have a problem. Then go when they are happy! Again, when they have a problem, they come back to God.

The third type of people, for them they are aware of the Love of God and they will do everything to attain the Grace of God, to attain the Love of God, which will lead them to God-Realisation or back to Godhead.

As for the fourth type, they are ever free. For them, they are born realised. From the beginning itself, God is in their life. There is no question about anything. For them their trust and their surrender to the Divine is so great that there is nothing that can move them. That's what Christ always said "If your faith is built on a stone, on a rock..." That kind of faith they have inside of them, they are born with it. They are ever free within, this fourth type of people.

God is loving. God will always give whatever one asks for. Which type of people do we want to be? We are searching. We want to attain His Grace. We want to attain His Love, but we are so much stuck in our mind. We want to attain Him, yet how many among us will really surrender everything to Him? How many among us will surrender ourselves completely to Him, will say "Lord, here I am. Take me."?

We say yes, we want to do God's will, isn't it? On the spiritual path we always want to do God's Will. Yet in our ego self, we want to do our will also a little bit, but we say "It's the Will of God." As long as it makes us happy, as long as "I am happy" that's it, it's the Will of God, but when it's not turning towards "What makes me happy", it's wrong. What do we do then? We start criticising, we start judging. Does God's will have judgment into it? Whatever the Divine does is *always* for the people. Whatever a Master does is *always* for raising the spirituality in the disciple.

As I said in the beginning, you have to want Him. Then He will come to you. When you say "I want to realise God", it's not just superficial, you know? You have to really mean it. When you say "Really, I want Him," there will be such Love inside of you, such great peace and calmness inside of you, that you will feel Him.

Whatever He gives you, if you surrender into Him, if you are surrendered and you really trust that He, His will be done, then you have to remove your desire. You have to remove what makes you happy, but what makes Him happy, that's the most important thing. That is called complete surrender. Such was the life of Madhava Puri.

Madhava Puri was a 17th century Saint, who lived in Vrindavan. He used to go begging for his food, but it came to a point that the Love for God was so strong inside of him, that he stopped begging.

He said "Whatever God gives me, I will eat." For days and days he would go without food.

On one occasion, he was around Govardhan, the holy mountain, which Krishna lifted with His little finger; he was there for four days. He didn't eat anything, he sat there. One day, after four days of not eating, a boy, a small boy came to him with a pot of milk and gave him this milk and said "Madhava, drink this." He looked at the boy and said "Who are you?" The boy, smiling, looked at him and said "Well, I heard some women talking about you not having eaten, so I brought you this milk. I provide for the one who doesn't beg for anything. I provide for the one who is surrendered to the Lord." Madhava Puri took the milk and he asked again the boy "Who are you?" He said "Don't worry about who I am. You drink the milk. I will come later on to get the pot."

Madhava Puri drank the milk. It was like nectar. It was like milk he had never drunk before in his life. He was wondering who this boy was, and inside of him he said "Milk can't taste like nectar. Milk can't taste so sweet like that." As he was thinking and waiting for the boy to come back to get the pot, he had a dream. In the dream he saw Sri Krishna standing – the same face as the boy. He said "Madhava you didn't recognise me. It was me who came to you. As I told you, I feed the one who doesn't beg and who is surrendered to the Lord." In the dream Krishna said to him "I'm guiding you to a well. Go there, deep inside this well, I am lying for some years. Take me out and do my service."

Early in the morning when he woke up, he was so much in Divine ecstasy. He was feeling so much great joy inside of him, he went around and started calling everybody "Come, let's go to the well and remove Krishna." Just as directed in the dream, he went and really they found the well. They removed the beautiful statue of Krishna out from the well and then he took Him out and made a nice temple for Him.

They started doing lots of prayers and service to the *Vigraha*, to the Deity. One day Krishna came again in his dream and said "Madhava Puri, you know I was so long in this well, my body has so much heat from the sun. I need to get sandalwood paste from Puri (which is about 2,500 km up north from Vrindavan). I need to get this sandalwood paste so that I can cool down."

Without thinking, Madhava Puri rushed, left everything, gave the duty to one of his disciples to look after the Krishna. He rushed quickly on the way to Puri, walking. Without thinking *how* he would go, without asking for the direction, anything. He just let himself be guided.

At that time India was ruled by different kings. Each time you passed a kingdom, you would have to pay something to enter the kingdom, then they would let you in and go on. He didn't even bother about it. His trust in the Lord was so great that he just walked.

On the way, there was a famous temple of Gopinath. As he was passing by, he remembered having heard that in this temple their offering was so great that they would offer twelve pots of buttermilk to Krishna every day, and the buttermilk tastes like, really, like *Amrit*, like nectar. So he sat down there in the temple and he looked how they were doing their service to the Deity, and he said to himself "I will also do the same."

As he was looking how they did the offering to the Deity, he wanted to taste the buttermilk. Inside of him he had this great desire, but he didn't dare to go and ask the priest "Give me some." He was so scared that at night, when the priest had closed the temple, Krishna came in the dream of the priest and said to the priest "My dear priest, there is one of my devotees, one of my disciples, outside in the market. He is singing. I have a credit towards him. You have to take one pot of buttermilk. Go and give it to him. This is his."

The priest did according to what Krishna had told him in the dream. He woke up, took a shower and then took the buttermilk, and as the Lord had said that Madhava Puri was in the market place, he reached there and he saw Madhava Puri singing in ecstasy. He called to Madhava Puri "The Lord has sent this buttermilk for you. Here, take it."

When he heard that this was sent from the temple, from Sri Krishna Himself, he just drank it all. He was so happy that he started to eat even the pot afterwards. When he could not eat more of the pot, because the pot was made of earth, he kept some. He said later on he would eat it.

Of course news don't stay in one place. They start spreading. So before the news spread, he left the place going towards Puri. As he reached Puri, of course, the news had already reached there. Nobody knew who the person was. The moment he entered the temple of Jagannath, the moment he was in front of the Deity, the Jagannath, he started dancing in Divine ecstasy. So much was his Love for God that there was no consciousness of the outside. The people knew it was Madhava Puri about whom they had heard the story. Of course, news travels faster than one walks, you know.

> When you say "Really, I want Him," there will be such Love inside of you, such great peace and calmness inside of you, that you will feel Him.

For four months he stayed in Puri, and the devotees, the people there, enjoyed his presence very much. After four months, Krishna said to him in a dream "You forgot about me. I sent you to Puri to get me sandalwood paste. Bring it to me. I am still waiting for you." So after four months he went, he got his sandalwood. Big, big, lots of sandalwood he took on his back.

He started walking back. Again, he passed by the temple of

Gopinath. He stayed there for a few days and at night the Lord appeared in his dream and said to him "My sweet Madhava Puri, you have fulfilled everything that I have asked you without even thinking. You have shown the greatest Love, the devotion you have inside of you. I am so pleased with it. You don't need to bring the sandalwood to Vrindavan. Give it in the temple of Gopinath. I am, myself, there. Tell the priest to make it into powder and apply it on me."

This story shows how much one can surrender, if one wants to. Especially when we say we want to do God's Will, we have really to do *His* Will, not *our* will. To know how the Will of God is, this will be the question, you know? When you pray there is always a feeling that awakens. If you are praying sincerely, and you are sincerely chanting the Name of God, there is this great longing and the great peace and calm that awakens.

When this awakens inside of you, there is also the inner voice that will start awakening. When you hear this inner voice, it is even greater than what you have in the mind, because even if you want to do what your mind wants you to do, this one will be greater. You will know that. Your heart will pull you towards that voice.

When you chant the Name of God, it's not just mere chanting when you recite the sweet Name. It's not just chanting it like that, but what it creates inside of you, what it awakens inside of you, because you see, it is said that the Name of God, and God, are one. There is no difference between the Name of God and God. So when you chant the Name, He is next to you.

It is said that when you chant, first your Guru has to be in your mind. From the Master, the Lord will show Himself. So always, when you chant, always place the Master first. In that way, it will be like what Sri Krishna said in the *Gita*, "If you want to attain me, surrender yourself to your Guru and you will attain me." To sing the name of the Guru is so easy.

There are so many names. Everybody feels close with certain names, but in this age, as it is said, the sweet name of Sri Hari is the most important one. Chant always, and as you chant, let your mind be focused on the Divine. Don't just do it mechanically, but do it and feel that the Lord is with you, and is standing next to you. It's like when you call somebody, let's say I call Swami Vishwapaarthananda, so if I call him, he will come, no? Only if he is here will he come, whereas with the Divine Name; He is always there.

Once Rama and Lakshamana were passing by a lake, and as they passed by the lake, they noticed a crow. This crow would always fly to the lake to try to drink water, but the moment he came near the lake, he would look at the water and then fly away again. So Lakshmana asked Rama "Tell me my Lord, why does this bird always fly to the lake to try to drink water, but he doesn't drink any?" Rama said to Lakshmana "This crow is a great devotee. He doesn't drink any water. He is scared of losing one moment of reciting the Name of God."

Even though his throat was very dry, he was thirsty, but he would not let go of the Name of God. Such was his surrender. So if a bird can do that, humans can do better also, no?

NEW YEAR, NEW YOU?

Darshan, Steffenshof, Germany, 11 January 2008

Firstly, I wish Happy New Year to all of you! Since it's the beginning of the New Year – it's already the eleventh of January – I'm sure that for the new year everybody decided, willingly or unwillingly, to change something in their life, isn't it so? You say "It's a new year; I have to do something new! I have to change or get rid of some habit of mine!"

It's good to initiate change, but the best change that you can initiate is to trust, to trust in the change, to trust in yourself firstly, to trust in the Higher Consciousness which is called God and to know that He is always there for you. No matter what you do, He is there – whether you ask him or not, whether you are positive or negative – He's there all the time. Inside of you, know that whatever you do, He loves you. He is always next to you like a mother is near her child. The child only needs to call to the mother and the mother rushes to the child. When the child is crying, does the child run to the mother or the mother run to the child? Wherever the mother is, when she

> The best change that you can initiate is to trust, to trust in the change, to trust in yourself firstly, to trust in the Higher Consciousness which is called God and to know that He is always there for you.

hears that the child is crying, she will run. It doesn't matter what is in the way, the mother will run to the child.

Here we are talking about the Divine – the Divine, which is even a thousand times greater than a mother – imagine how close He is. We have just to learn to trust that He is always present. Through this trust you will have the awareness of Him and you will know that nothing in this world is wrong – well, apart from the mind of Man – but whatever nature does is right.

Learn to trust and move with this trust. This is one of the things to change if you really want to change. If either you have changed or you want to change, to do something new, learn to trust.

LONGING FOR THE DIVINE

Darshan, Vienna, Austria, 10 October 2009

It's nice to be here with all of you. We all know we are searching for something. Whether we are in the world outside or we are spiritual, we are always on the search, but what are we searching for? Happiness? Joy? Freedom? Where are we searching for it? Outside? The search is here, inside ourselves, to rediscover who we are.

We all search for something. We all long for something and when we get what we want, we long for something else. When we get this new thing, again we long for something else. The longing on the outside never finishes. The longing of the heart is the most important thing, but it's not possible to understand the longing of the heart with the mind. When we talk of Love, we all have an idea of how Love has to be. We say "Love has to be this way, this way and this way," but if you really know how Love is, you don't talk about it.

Once, there was a well-known king who had two sons. He decided to send them to a *guru* in an *ashram* to learn the knowledge of the Self, *Atma Brahma Vijnana*. So the two sons went to the *guru* and they learnt for three years. When they came back to their home, the father wanted to test them and said "My sons, you have both learned so much now. You went to the most famous *guru* in the whole of India and you have learnt the knowledge of the Self."

Then he asked his first son "My dear son, tell me, how is God?" The first son started to chant different verses and different *mantras* to express how great the Divine is. Then the father thought "OK, he has learnt something." Then he asked his younger son "My son, what about you?" The second son just looked down without uttering one word, a few drops of tears flowed from his eyes, but he didn't mention anything about how great God is. Then the father said "My son, *you* have got a little bit of understanding of the Divine." Can the mind really understand the Divine? No, it can't. Love can't be understood by the mind. That's why God has given human beings a heart, for them to understand with the heart.

We have many spiritual practices, different meditations, different *mantras* and for what – to attain who we are, to clear this mind. The more you advance towards the Divine, the more the Divine will show Himself to you and the more different aspects of the Divine will come to you, until at the end, you will perceive the Divine everywhere. It's a longing, a longing for the Divine.

> Do you know about it – that intense desire for the Divine, the intense Love for Him, no matter what happens? If you have that, the Divine will show Himself to you.

Do you know about it – that intense desire for the Divine, the intense Love for Him, no matter what happens? If you have that, the Divine will show Himself to you. First He will come in different aspects, different forms. Some will have the Divine Mother with ten arms. The more it deepens, this intense Love, the form will turn to Krishna with two arms. Until at the end, you see that He or She is just sitting here inside of your heart and that everything all around you is just an emanation of Her Love.

Probably you have heard about Sri Ramakrishna, who was a great devotee of Ma Kali, a staunch devotee of the Divine Mother. He would long for the Divine Mother; he would cry for the Divine

Mother. He would sit every day in front of the statue of the Divine Mother and say "Mother, are You just that, just a statue? I call for You. Why don't You come to me? Why can't You see the longing, the paining of my heart?" Every day he would go mad. He would roll on the ground, crying for the Divine Mother, to just have a glimpse of Her. Such was the intensity of this *bhakta*, this devotee, that after so much longing, the Divine Mother came to him and that's how all the great souls really long.

When Ramakrishna was doing prayers to the Divine Mother, he was not doing it just to the Divine Mother. He would throw the offerings all around; he would throw them on the utensils, he would throw the flowers on himself, saying "Mother, You are everywhere. You are these utensils. You are these flowers. You are everything that I see around." It was the same thing with St. Francis who could perceive the Divine everywhere. That's why he called everybody brother or sister.

If you have such intensity in your longing for the Divine, you will have Him. But if you just say "Well, I long for the Divine, but it has to be my way." Of course the Divine will come in your way, but you will encounter certain limitations. Even though I am talking so much about the unlimited Divinity, these are just words. Know that words have limitations, but when you turn your gaze from the outside, deep to the inside through meditation, *yoga* or *mantra japam* and awaken this longing, you will see no matter what, that the Divine will be present. When the Divine comes, there will be no doubt at all.

There was once a man who went to a palace and said "I want to meet the King." As he was passing the first room, he saw a very elegant gentleman sitting there talking to all the people. The man thought "Is he the King? No, he is not the King." Then he went to the second room. Another person was sitting there dressed, also very elegantly. The man wondered again "Is he the King?" But then he said "No, he is not the King." So on he continued to the third room, fourth room, fifth room and sixth room. Finally, he reached the seventh hall. As he entered there, he saw the majestic look of that place and he saw somebody sitting on a high throne, very elegantly dressed, even more elegantly than the others. Without any question he knew that *this* was the King, so there was no point in asking "Is this the King or not?"

Try to get what is behind this story. In one life we go through many levels –the seven gates that we have inside ourselves. In each gate, we encounter certain aspects of the Divine, yet the mind is still present; the mind is still wondering "Am I there already or not?" The more you advance, the more you see that there is more and more to do. Until finally, when you are face-to-face with *the King*, there is no question. There is no doubt. There is just absolute peace and even more than that, there is this absolute Love. If your aim is to attain that, no matter what comes on the way, trust. Never lose hope and you will reach there.

The Divine is ever present around you. He comes in many forms to help you. With the eyes of your heart you shall see and feel Him, so practice. Don't practice the opening of the mind; practice the opening of the heart, so that you can Love unconditionally, so you can love and feel the Divine Love inside of you and not only inside of you, but everywhere. The easiest way to do that is to try to be calm and to be in silence.

BE DETERMINED TO BE STRONG

Darshan on Divali, Shree Peetha Nilaya, Germany, 17 October 2010

First of all, happy *Divali* to all of you! I explained already before about *Divali*, the Festival of Lights, especially about finding the inner light and letting it shine through. Let it shine from deep within your heart to everybody. Often people say "But Swamiji, we would always love to have this Divine Light shining through, but it's so difficult. Am I right? No?

You see if you want it to be easy, you will do everything and anything possible to make it easy. It doesn't matter how hard it is, you will do it. But if you make yourself weak by saying "difficult", this word, which is so very easily used – it is a barrier and we create this barrier – we make it difficult and then we say "Oops, it's difficult."

It's the same when you say something is easy. What happens inside of you? You build up this confidence. You put this self-confidence on yourself when you generate this energy inside you of "Yes, I can do it" and you receive the blessing of the Divine to do it also. On the other hand if you already make yourself weak, then God will say "What's the use of me giving the grace to this person if he can't handle it? He's already weak. It's of no use giving the blessing or the grace to that person." Actually, we ourselves stop

When you pursue God-Realisation or Self-Realisation – no matter what comes, you have to be strong.

the grace then. How do you think the light will shine?
I was telling you the story of Rama. You see, his life was not that easy. He was sent into the forest and of course He encountered many challenges, but his challenges, He faced them. He didn't make Himself weak. He didn't run away or go crying. He didn't say "I renounce my mission. I'm finished with it." It's the same thing when you pursue God-Realisation or Self-Realisation – no matter what comes, you have to be strong. Through this determination of being strong, the Divine will give you the energy, but this part is not God who has to do it, but you who have to do it.

A guided meditation

Let's do a little meditation now. I always do this mediation with the people. It's about the light meditation.
First of all, I will ask all of you to take a few deep breaths in and out. When you do the exhalation, release your shoulders. Release all the tension from your shoulders.

- Inhale deeply. Inhale and exhale. Exhale to your maximum. Again breathe in. Exhale. Inhale and exhale.
- Now try to empty your mind completely. Bring your focus on your third eye and on that point of the *bindu,* see the *OM* sign.
- When you see the *OM* sign, focus all your attention on this *OM.*
- Slowly, let the *OM* beam this Light. Let the sign of *OM* grow bigger and bigger, covering your face completely.
- Let this *OM* grow even bigger now, covering the upper part of your body.

- Even bigger now, covering the lower part of your body.
- And say to yourself you are that Light; you are *OM*.
- Now, let this *OM* radiate even beyond the boundaries of your body.
- Imagine your neighbours or the people who are close to you. See that they are, also, in this light of the cosmic sound *OM*.
- Now, expand this light to everybody who you know: friends, colleagues, your boss.
- Furthermore, extend it in your town where you stay. Then to the city where you stay. Extend it to the country you are in.
- See it extending now to the whole world. See Mother Earth full of light.
- From deep within your heart chant the *mantra: Lokah Samastah Sukhino Bhavantu. Lokah Samastah Sukhino Bhavantu. Lokah Samastah Sukhino Bhavantu.*
- *OM*, now, with these three *Shantis* bring all your focus to your heart.
- *Shanti, Shanti, Shanti.*
- Concentrate on your heart and let peace reside there. Let that Love reside there and let it be given to all freely.

THE GREAT POWER OF A POSITIVE MIND

Bhudevi Yagna Weekend at Shree Peetha Nilaya,
Germany, 1 May 2010

The past two days we've been celebrating Bhudevi. Tomorrow is the last day and you well know how precious our world is. Several times I have said "Our Mother Earth is the most beautiful planet in the whole universe, not only in our solar system, but everywhere else." What is so special about her within the whole universe – the universes – is that all the other planets and all the other spheres, they are governed by only one or two elements. As you all know, we have five elements, Earth has all the five elements in Her. That's what makes Her special. All that is coming out of Her, which is everything that we can see, is made up of these five elements. Even our body, which we took from this earth plane, is made up of these five elements, so we are part of this creation. We are part of Her.

It's sad to see nowadays, how people behave, how people think. This creates a great impact on her, our thinking. It's so easy to become negative, but very difficult to become positive. I have met many people who ask how to change that. You see, if we analyse how quickly we can change ourselves, that means that inside us we have a very great power. We have a great energy that can change from minute to minute, from second to second, from positive to negative from negative to positive. Why does one get stuck in the space of negativity? Do you think this brings positivity to you? No, it doesn't. When it doesn't bring positivity to you, it also affects nature. When nature gets affected, it affects this world, the surroundings that we are in. One person can change a lot. You have seen it in the past what the negativity of one person could do, here in Germany itself. One person in India – take the example of Ghandi – just one person's positivity can change a lot also. So imagine, if inside of yourself you can change so quickly and change also not only you, but you can influence the outside and change the outside, then imagine if you become positive, how much it will contribute to Mother Earth, how much it will contribute to Prakriti, to Mother Nature – a lot!

For that positivity – if you look at it both ways – I have given you two examples. I don't want to mention the names, but in these two examples, one which is negative and one which is positive, what has made them really able to change the world? It's amazing! Both of them are amazing. This is because of the full trust they had in what they wanted. In both ways, each one thought they were doing good, but the intensity of how much they believed in what they were doing, that is what brought the changes.

This intensity is present in each one of us, but in place of making us more positive and more trusting in ourselves or making us stronger in our own will, what do we do? We make ourselves weak. Of course, when one becomes weak, one can't expect what's around them to be different.

> Imagine if you become positive, how much it will contribute to Mother Earth, how much it will contribute to Prakriti, to Mother Nature – a lot! Your positivity can influence everything.

It's like with one's body – if the hand gets hurt, doesn't it affect all the body? It does! You feel the pain everywhere. It becomes a handicap that you can't use the hand because it hurts. Just the same way, when one becomes positive, one influences the wholeness. One influences firstly oneself – one influences the mind, the body, the spirit. From that, one influences one's surroundings and the surroundings will also influence nature and nature will balance itself. It's simple!

Well, I can say it's simple. That's what many will say "Well, it's easy for you to say it is simple!" Like I said, it takes everybody together. We want peace in this world, we want peace in ourselves, we want to be happy, we want to make the world happy, so then we have to change. Nobody can change us, only we can change ourselves. It's not what I am saying that will change you. No, only when you say to yourself "I want to change" with intensity, with full belief in yourself, then you will change. When you change, it will affect your surroundings. It will affect you; it will change you.

A few days ago I was talking with somebody who a few months ago found out that she had cancer. Of course, normally when people hear that, how do they become? Depressed and sad; it's like the world is finished for them. Well, that person was very positive from the beginning. This positivity has changed her. She is getting better and better. That's wonderful!

You see, your positivity can influence everything. You influence yourself, for example, tomorrow morning, when you wake up, if your first thought is, "Oh, my goodness, another day, I don't know how it will be" – do you think the day will be positive? It will not! If you wake up and feel happy, you will see how happy the day will be. Then of course everything around you will rotate into happiness, and at the end of the day, what you will say is "Today was a lovely day! Today was a beautiful day!" But this day, what made it beautiful? It is you who made it beautiful, because from the beginning you believed that it would be a beautiful day and that thought made everything beautiful. It's not about the outside, it's about you, nobody else. If you change, the world will change. If you change, peace will be here. You will be happy. Even one person being really happy will make a big difference.

TRY YOUR BEST TO BECOME DIVINE

Darshan at Shree Peetha Nilaya, Germany 22 May 2010

I guess you all have heard that this is the last *darshan* here at the centre, well not really the last one, just the last one for now for us to carry on with the construction. As long as the construction is on, we will not have any programmes here. For this construction to carry on, we'll need everybody's help, so you can help however you feel. Above all, this place is not my place. You all come here for *darshan*, but it's a place for all of you, a place where a lot of people have gotten help.

Above all, Love is the most important thing and *Shree Peetha Nilaya* – the name which the Divine Mother has given – is an abode of the Divine Mother Herself, where Her Love is given to everybody; this Love which we all – every human being – long for; this Love which is the call of your true Self, who you are and who you will always be. The only thing is to attain this unity, to attain this oneness with the Divine. There is only one thing that stops us of realising this unity – the discrimination, the judgment. Of course, all of these qualities emerge from one's mind. The control of the mind over us is what stops this Love.

When we look at a Saint who is in union with God – what is the name of the union with God? We have the Sanskrit name, *samadhi*, don't we? What is *samadhi*? Everybody longs for *samadhi* but the state of *samadhi* is without any discrimination, without any judgment. It is pure Love. As long as you see the judgment in your mind, as long as there is discrimination in your mind, you will still have to work to attain the non-discrimination state and then, only this real Love, this pure Love will awaken. When this pure Love awakens, it embraces you. It is not a feeling that you will say "Yes, I feel happy or I feel sad." It is beyond that. If I could express it with words, it would not be what I'm talking about.

This is the state where you find union with the Divine, where you realise your Self. As long as you are searching, you are just searching for that Love. When you find it, you will only find that Love. So don't lose hope, no matter what, know that the Divine is always with you and wherever you are, whatever you do, it's Him who is doing through you. Try your best from your side, you have always to try your best. The human being is not perfect and I'm sure later on it will not be perfect either, because when one becomes perfect, one has this quality that I just said before.

> Try your best to become Divine. That is what all the great Masters have taught. Christ came and taught that, Krishna has taught that and all of them have taught to realise your own divinity, because only then real happiness will be there.

When one becomes perfect, one becomes Divine, so one is not human anymore. But as long as one has this quality, one stays human. Try your best to become Divine. That is what all the great Masters have taught. Christ came and taught that, Krishna has taught that and all of them have taught to realise your own divinity, because only then real happiness will be there. Then you can say "Yes, I am happy," because that happiness will not go away, it will stay forever. Otherwise you will stay in illusion. You will think and try to make yourself think that you are happy.

As long as you have not attained that, keep trying. You will receive all the help needed as long as you give your hand because if you don't make your effort, you can't expect God to do His effort, do it for you. He is fully realised, but He is here to help you to realise your Self, but you have to give your hand. You have to do your part. Otherwise it will be like somebody who is thirsty sits down and says "I am thirsty, I'm thirsty, I'm thirsty!" Do you think the thirst will go away? No, it would not go away.

The person has to get up, make the effort of opening the tap, take a glass, put it under the tap and bring the water to the mouth and drink it. Then the thirst goes away. It is the same if you just sit around and say "OK, I wait for God-Realisation to come." It will not jump from there on your head. It is only when you prove yourself and that you are making an effort that the Divine will help you. You know the saying that says "Help yourself and God shall help you."

THE UNIQUE LOVE RELATIONSHIP WITH GOD

Darshan at Shree Peetha Nilaya, Germany, 29 August 2010

Often when we are on the spiritual path, we ask ourselves or we ask somebody why it is that we do everything to be happy, but in spite of being on the spiritual path, we are not so happy. We are happy just a little bit, but not that happy, not feeling this enthusiasm. We have it a little bit in the beginning when we first start the spiritual path, but then what happens? It gets less and less. Why? It's the same thing also, in the world outside it's happening. People go to work and they are very happy in the beginning, then after that they go down. Why is it?

It's simple – because human beings on the spiritual path or in the material, in the working field, they become envious. When envy enters the mind of man, man becomes blind and when man becomes blind, he doesn't see the light anymore. Your true Self needs this light to survive, but the way the mind functions drags you into illusion. When this envy enters the mind, one steps away from this light, or the light starts to diminish within oneself. What happens is – it's like you have a mirror, you clean the mirror, it is beautiful, you can look at yourself nicely, but after some time the mirror accumulates dust. What do you do? You clean it!

All the qualities of the mind like envy, jealousy, pride, ego, when these arise, it is very difficult to clean them. It's hard, even when you try your best, they are there. Like when you clean the mirror to look at yourself, you wipe it clean, you don't leave it dirty. Yet, when humans clean the mind, they always leave a certain residue of darkness inside. They don't really want to let go of all of it completely, because this is a sign of insecurity in oneself. You say "If I let go of everything, what is for tomorrow?" Hasn't Christ said "If God is looking after everything, He will look after you, also"? It's the same if you want to change, you have to let go of all this negativity. You have to let go of all this darkness. You can't keep this darkness and say "Yes, I am changed."

> The Love for God is unique, because each one has a personal relationship and this relationship to the Divine is between you and the Lord. There's no other person in between. The uniqueness of this Love dissolves all.

It's the same when envy enters the mind. It blinds you, because then you will always be jealous, you will always be angry about your neighbour. If you see that your neighbour is advancing spiritually or the neighbour, your friend or your colleague is progressing, what will happen inside of you? You will try to be competitive. You will try to compete with your colleague to be the best. Are you concentrating on your spiritual path, or are you concentrating on his progress? You should be happy if somebody is progressing, because when you start to progress on this spiritual path, you develop this Love.

Know that God's Love is the same for everybody. Whether you are a wicked person or whether you are a saintly person it is the same, but its reflection is different. How much you reflect towards Him, He will reflect back towards you the same. That doesn't mean that for a saintly person the Love of God is more or that He doesn't love a wicked person. No, He loves everybody the same. That's why He graced so many people who were wicked to become Saints, so they could reflect this Love.

This Love is unique. The Love for God is unique, because each one has a personal relationship and this relationship to the Divine is between you and the Lord. There's no other person in between. The uniqueness of this Love dissolves all, but if you start comparing like "Oh, this person loves God more and I have to try my best to become like him," it's true it's good, but at the same time you have to be content with yourself. You can do that, you can become the same only by being content, only by looking in yourself, what and how you can change.

It's not about looking at the others, otherwise your thoughts will always be on the outside, focusing on "Oh, my goodness, this person has made so much. What about me?" you know – self-pity. The more you look for self-pity, your chances of growing, your chances of making your life better, are getting less and less. That's why it's said that you have to take your life into consideration and transform yourself, because this quality inside is to be transformed. You can't kill this quality, you are born with it. It's part of you, but it depends on how much you focus on it.

If you focus more on it, it will overrule you. It will start to control you. In reality, you have to control this quality, because you are the master, not this quality. As hard as it can appear to be, you have the Divine inside of you and it is this Light that is giving you energy. If you concentrate more on this energy, this divine light will shine through you, but if you are concentrating on the negativity, this will shine through you more.

Where you put your mind, how you put it, how you control it – there are many ways. Some ways are harder and some ways are less hard. You are wondering why I didn't say easy. I didn't say easy because when you start it is easy, when you are in the middle, it is less easy and then after that, when you meet people after some time, they say "Swamiji, I don't do this because it's hard." That's why I said it is not that easy. If you are determined to do it, if you really wish it, if you really have self-confidence inside of you that you can do it, you will do it.

It's the same thing when you have self-confidence in doing anything else. Let's say when a certain job is given to you by your boss, for example, can you say no, you will not do it? Can you? Why can't you? It's because he is the boss, yes. Well, the Divine has also given certain tasks to you and He is the boss. So don't make yourself weak by focusing on your negativity, but awaken this strength inside of you. Awaken this Love inside of you and let it grow, as hard as it can be on the outside sometimes, because life is not always in a straight line.

There are ups and downs, but how you see it and how you take it contributes a lot to your spiritual growth and to the peace of your mind. When the mind is darkened, you lose this peace and when you lose peace of mind, you lose everything. When you lose peace of mind, even telling you to concentrate or to meditate will not help. Attain this peace and be happy – not a superficial happiness, but an innermost happiness.

THE SOUL IS SHY

Darshan, Shree Peetha Nilaya, Germany, 7 January, 2011

I hope you had a wonderful New Year. For the New Year, for Christmas, actually, we were talking about the urge for the Love of God. Very often we love God, no? Because He is the creator, we love Him, but we love the world also. Right? That's the difference. That's why I said urge, longing. We say superficially to make ourselves be happy, that we love God, but in reality what do we love? Tell me. What is this Love? If you have not yet known what Love is in itself, how can you say you love God? If you have not yet known your Self, you have not yet realised the Love inside of you, how can you say you love God? It's easy to say, because scriptures talk about it. You come here; Swami said, "Yeah, love God" isn't it? But what is this? Man is created, in a way, with three things; firstly the body, secondly, the mind and, thirdly, the soul. Let's put it like that; the mind, body and the intellect, that's what makes Man human. If we look at the combination of these three things, they are three things that dwell towards the outside. The body, which is bound by the senses, enslaves man. The mind is very difficult to control, because the mind always runs in the outside. And the intellect – what is the intellect? Not being too intellectual, but what is the intellect? The intellect is the search for the truth. It's not in the mind, but rather it is in the consciousness. All three of these combined together dwell only in the outside, because these things need an object – the object of the outside.

How will one know how to surrender? We talk about surrender, but the outside makes a lot of pressure. The easy way is to first, before the senses, mind and the intellect enjoy the object, to offer it to the Divine. Like that, in the mind there will be no question what one has to choose, because if it is already offered to the Divine, only what will benefit you will arise inside of you. The lower quality can't access something which is in the higher level. In the same way, when we say we love God, until we discover the Love inside of us, we still have to search. We still have

Just as you long for Him, He longs more for you.

to dig deep inside, not outside. We all start here (pointing to the head). If you can't calm your mind, if you can't calm yourself, it's very difficult. The first step is to try to calm yourself. Then what happens inside is that you will feel a little calmer. You will feel a little joy, but that's not everything.

Many people, they feel this and say "Yes, I have reached there" and then, one month later you ask, "How are you?" and they say "Well, I felt this Love only for two weeks and after two weeks it's gone." Or you come here and you feel it, then after two weeks it's finished. Actually, this Love never finishes. It is there, but the mind covers it. What must happen to keep this love burning inside of you? Interact always with people. Usually when I say interact with people, what you will do? You will sit and gossip. That's what interaction is nowadays, no? Talk about spiritual things, talk about what you feel, talk about God. The more you talk about God, the more this Love inside of you will grow more and more. Not only for two weeks, but it will always be with you. You will always feel it. That's what Christ said: If two or three are gathered in my name, I shall be among them. This 'two or three' is this mutual Love – not in gossiping things, but in awakening the Divine Love within one's Self. When this Love gets awakened, the longing, it's like when you give a nice cake to somebody. You will always want this cake again. It's the same thing once you discover the Love of God in you and around you, you will always long for more and more and this longing crosses over the body, mind and intellect. Then the soul reveals itself. Very often when people talk about the soul, it's just mere words, because the soul in itself is very shy, in the same way that God is very shy. That's why He shows Himself from time to time only. Until Love reaches a certain degree inside of you, the soul doesn't reveal itself. That's why when you do your sadhana, be sincere.

When you do your work – any kind of work – be sincere about it. Do it with Love. You know this proverb I say: Work is worship, no? You know about it? That means, wherever you are, whatever you do, God is present with you. If you do it with the awareness that you are serving the Divine, He will reveal Himself. There is a saint who was a road cleaner who received the darshan of God where Krishna appeared in front of him, even Rama appeared. This is about how much Love you put in what you do. Often Love varies. When you sit in meditation, you are full of Love. When you sit for prayer, you are full of Love and then, when you go out, where is that Love? You left it inside the prayer room or you left it only in meditation. Be aware that, even if you don't feel it, the Divine is always with you. As you long for Him, He longs more for you.

Then the question will arise, but why doesn't He do anything? Well if, for example, you put Man and ask "What do you want?" You have a beautiful valley here, with so many beautiful flowers, the most beautiful things, and on the other side you put God, what do you think Man would do? Tell me! Please, don't be shy. You know your answer. That's why you don't want to say. The temptation of the outside will be too great, because God's way is a bit boring, but actually, there is a lot of excitement, because He always keeps you busy. He never makes your life dull, boring. He will always keep you busy with one thing or the other. Whether it's up or down, He always keeps you busy.

I hope I'm not scaring you, but it's about time to analyse yourself, analysing yourself with truthfulness, not towards anybody else, but towards yourself. Look at you. Look at yourself in the mirror and ask yourself what *you* want. One thing that Man can do, is to be sincere towards himself. If I said for you to be sincere with somebody else, you would not be sincere. Even if you think you are sincere or you appear to be sincere, no, you are not sincere, but towards yourself you will be sincere. Look at yourself and say it. Look at your life and ask yourself is that the life you want or should there be some change.

There was once, in Bombay, a gentleman. He was very high class. His life was just enjoyment – party, friends; just that, nothing else. Every weekend his life was like this. He worked during the week and looked forward for the weekend to have a party. One day, when he was thirty years old, on the day of his birthday, he had some drinks, he went upstairs to his bathroom and as he was looking at himself in the mirror, he looked deep into his eyes. At that moment he looked at his life in retrospect. He looked at his life and saw how many times he was really sincerely happy. Then he realised there were not many times that he was sincerely happy. There were very few times. Then he started looking at his life and said to himself "Is this the life I want to live? How long will I live this life, because this happiness, which I perceive as being happy, is not happiness in reality. I'm just pretending to be happy. I'm pretending to make myself happy, but in reality, I'm not happy." Like that how many people pretend to be happy? A lot do. From that moment he changed his life completely. He opened a school, an engineering school, and he started to help street children and he changed his life completely. He lived very simply, but very happily.

You see, Man doesn't need big things to be happy, because happiness is there. You are the incarnation of that happiness. It's not far away from you, but you have to have the right direction. It's like when you have a radio, if you don't put the right frequency, you will never hear the right music. If you put the right frequency, you will hear the right music. In the same way, the frequency, the button to turn is your heart. If you turn it towards the right way, you will have what you are looking for. This new year that has just started, hopefully, through God's Grace may be good for you all, especially regarding your search, because you see, even if it seems very far away, everything is here.

LOVE IS A GREAT TEACHER

Darshan, Berlin, Germany, 18 March 2011

The search of man, the search to be happy, harmonious, the search of love – that's what mankind is looking for. Sometimes this search is very difficult, in the outside. You agree, yes? How many say it is difficult? The majority. Actually, the search has two qualities. One finds it difficult, because one looks towards the outside. Then it becomes difficult. But when we look inside, it becomes easy because what man is looking for doesn't lie in the outside, but lies in core of one's heart. In the core of the heart, throughout centuries, people from different countries, different places, have put many names to that. They have called him God, Jesus or Jehovah. Even in India they call Him Bhagavan in the north and Parameshwar in the south; it's the same thing.

To make contact from the mind to the heart, is not difficult. It's a process which demands discipline towards yourself. Discipline is not to force you, but with self-discipline, in the smallest things, you find joy. If you are sincere in your search, you will find. Very often, why does it become difficult? It's the sincerity that you put in it. The more sincere you are towards your search, the more sincere you are towards searching for God realisation or Self-realisation, it will be easier. The more insincere you are towards yourself, the more difficult it is – when you want to find excuses for something. Throughout this, the yogi, the saint, has to walk four paths. The first path, is where the student or the seeker searches. What is he searching for? He has searched the world outside, but he has not found peace. So he searches for a mentor. Once he finds a mentor he asks "How do I find peace? How can I be in harmony with myself?" The mentor replied "To be in harmony, you must find your true Self. You must look for God." So he said "How do I find God?" The mentor said "Hunger for him!" then the seeker asked "How can I hunger for him?" "Well," the mentor replied "be among people who hunger for him. Then you will hunger for him also." This is called the Bhakti path. Like I said earlier, there are four paths; who can tell me four paths? There are four kinds of yoga – Bhakti yog, Gyana yog, Karma yog and Raja yog.

Any of these four kinds of yoga, can lead someone towards self-realisation. What is karma yog?, selfless service – some will also say working. But that is just the karma not the yoga. Karma yog is selfless service, selfless help. What is this selfless service? People do a lot of service, but selfless service is very rare. There is this part in the bible, where Christ said "When your right hand gives, your left hand should not know" – it is better you cut your left hand and throw it away. Selfless service means, that when you render service, you have to forget about it, the moment you have rendered this service. Does the mind

> Love is also a great teacher. A teacher is not here just to give you good things, he has to teach you.

forget about it? Very rarely. You see, when one does service, there is always an expectation. Even the expectation of "thank you," or "thanks." When one doesn't get a "thank you" he becomes very upset, thinking "I have helped that person, but yet he didn't even thank me for that!" But selfless service is not like that – when you render service, forget about everything.

Deep inside of you, you are rendering service to the Divine, but you don't expect the pride of knowing that you are rendering service to the Divine, to rise. So erase completely the expectations of the mind – and that is selfless service.

The next yoga is Bhakti yoga, which is considered one of the easiest yog. In bhakti, the first step *you* make but in that form of yog, the first step that you make, the Lord makes ten steps towards you. You know your goal in life. In karma yog, you have to walk towards that goal, you have to climb to the peak of that mountain. In Bhakti yog, you are flying towards that mountain with a helicopter. Then, the third yoga is Raj yog. Raj yog is divided into many forms of yoga. That's where your spiritual exercises come, like Atma Kriya, Hatha yoga; all these yog fall into the Raj yog. In Raj yoga you come to the point where you go into Samadhi. If you do your sadhana sincerely, when you do your spirtual practice sincerely, you come to the point of the samadhi state. What is the state of Samadhi? I said there is a mountain; in the first one you have to walk up there, in the second one you fly there and the third one, you don't even need to carry your body. By will, you are there. Many great saints or sages have reached that point, where they could be in many places at once with this will. Like Christ – a man wanted Him to heal his servants and he said "Lord come to me, to my house, You shall heal my servant." Christ said "Go home, your servant is healed."

This is the state, where you have touched the cosmic consciousness; you realise the infinite of your true Self. The last yoga is Gyana yog. I will ask you; what is Gyana yog? – tell me please – *(someone: knowledge, knowing who you are)*. Yes, knowledge. The knowledge of the Self. But real Gyana yog; very often people think that Gyana yog can be found in books, or one may find it or by practising, but real Gyana yog is to have the wisdom, not just to know it, but to have the wisdom, that what you are looking for is that the beginning is the end, and the end is the beginning. With these four forms of yoga, anyone can attain self-realisation or God-realisation. Each one is free to follow whichever path of yoga one wants to. The main aim is to awaken this Divine Love, because without Love, you will not do anything. The key of all of these four kinds of yoga, is just the Love, the core of the heart. A love which consumes everything, a Love which will liberate you. When we talk about Love, you know about love, no? They say when somebody is in love, they are in the seventh heaven, yes? Good. You are in seventh heaven, but what happens after two months? It decreases. Well, you see, real Love always keeps, there is no decrease in it. Once you have touched the love of the Cosmic Consciousness or the Higher Consciousness, there is no decrease, even if several lives – I am not talking about months! – You will carry it always with you, and it will grow more and more. Through that kind of Love, there is peace and harmony. It is the freedom that one is looking for. It's not outside somewhere, it's here inside of you. If you sincerely long for it, it will come out. You have to be patient, because remember that Love is also a great teacher. A teacher is not here just to give you good things, he has to teach you. The more he teaches you, the stronger you will become. If you are real seeker of that truth, nothing will stop you, not even the teaching of the teacher. So be a true seeker, or at least try.

JUST LOVE 2

Sadhana&Service

Meditation / Puja / Japa / Effort / Discipline

We make a living by what we get,
but we make a life by what we give.

Winston Churchill

THROUGH WATER AND FIRE

Retreat, Steffenshof, Germany, 28 July 2007

I see that everybody has their own *kund*. It's beautiful. We'll start the prayer by doing the *Kalash Puja*. The *Kalash Puja*, actually, is where we invoke the Deity – whichever Deity you're praying to. We welcome Him along with all His associates and offer Him a place to sit. You wash the feet and offer water to rinse the mouth. It's the same thing that somebody will do when a guest comes to his house. Normally, when you go to a *Brahmin's* house, the *Brahmin* has to do it. The moment a guest comes, normally, you have to offer water to the guest. They don't do it nowadays, but they do it to the *Guru*, to the Master. You offer things that they normally would offer when a Master goes to somebody's house and they welcome the Master. The second thing that they do is wash the feet of the Master. Thirdly, they offer water and then they start talking. For the Deities it's similar: we invoke the Deity, we call upon the energy, like yesterday we did for *Nrsinghadev*. We invoke Nrsinghadev, we ask Him "God, Narayana, send the energy of Nrsinghadev here!" Like I explained yesterday about Nrsinghadev, He's the destroyer of pride and ego, the destroyer of anger.

So we invoke Nrsinghadev to participate with us, to come here; and like He stripped all the negativity from Hiranyakashipu, we ask Him to strip all this negativity from each one of us. As I said yesterday, it's only by chanting the Name of God, that it can be removed.

So He will come. Of course, if you have the eyes to see Him, you will see Him, but He will come and strip all the negativity from your mind, from wherever it is. He will free you from all these things, but you have not to hang onto them. If you hang onto them, it will be like a fight. Yesterday I explained about Hiranyakashipu. Even though he knows that the Lord is in front of him, he still fights with Him. Even though he knows that he doesn't have a chance, still he fights with Him.

When we analyse our mind, the same thing is happening. We know God is here, but what does our mind do? It tries always to contradict this; it tries always to think that we are the best; it tries always to think that we know the best and always fights about that. So for now, put away everything. Say "Lord, take possession of me completely. Get rid of all this negativity." All of you want to get rid of all the negativity. It's good that you all want to get rid of the negativity. So don't hang onto it. Offer it to Him happily. Say "Look, Lord, You have come, so take it as a gift!"

We'll start with an invocation. First, we'll start by praying for the world, that there will be peace everywhere, that there will be peace with each one of you, in each one of you, in your mind, in your intellect, in your Self. Then, we'll chant the *mantra* for the peace of the world, because prayer is not only for oneself. When one prays, of course one prays, also for oneself, because one has to advance, one has to get rid of all of one's things. But above all we pray also for everybody – the people we know, the people we don't know, the people we like, those we don't like, the people who are sick, the people who need help. We pray for everybody because when you call upon the energy of God, it's not egoistically, it's not only "for me". When He descends, when He comes on Earth, He comes for everybody equally.

When He comes, when we invoke Him here, we're also invoking Him for the whole world. Even if there are a hundred people here and millions of people living in the world, He's sitting in each one's heart. Whatever they do, there's Him inside of them. So we invoke this Higher Consciousness. When we invoke this Super-Consciousness to come, in each one's heart also, we invoke Him. We invoke Him to awaken peace in the heart of Man.

Among all these millions of people, if only one person is sincere in that, it helps a lot. Like it's said: if one person prays *sincerely*, it's worth more than a hundred people who are not sincerely praying. So this one person, the sincerity of this person can transcend everything, can cleanse everything, can change everybody's heart, can pervade everything. So as you are all so pure and very sincere – I know you're all very sincere – I'm sure this will make a great impact on the world. If you're not sincere, pray to the Lord telling Him "Make me sincere. Open my heart, so that I can love unconditionally."

In that way you will change and when you change, the world will change. Many people talk about peace in the world, but if someone talks about peace and they themselves are not in peace, where are they running for peace? You have to become peaceful first! When you become peaceful you can bring peace in the world. But if you are not peaceful, forget it, because then you bring the same confusion that you have. That's why people always talk about peace. They just talk, talk, talk and they do nothing else. They don't do anything; they just talk. So talking will not help.

When we invoke the Lord, we have also to invoke Him inside our hearts. When He takes complete possession of us, we become Him. When we become Him, there is no difference. The positive energy that He brings will be radiating from us and when it radiates, it destroys all the negativity around.

When you become Him, you let the Lord shine from you. You let Him take possession of your heart; you let Him take possession of your mind; you let Him take possession of your body. Let Him shine from you, completely. Nothing can move you. Like Christ said " Have faith and your faith has to be strong, like a house built not on sand, not on earth, but on stone." Everywhere you will see it. When we are doing the *yagna*, believe in it, trust in it and feel and most of all, open your minds; open your hearts. Feel that He's here, present with you.

We will do the *Kalash Puja* and then the *abishekam*. Like I explained yesterday, I will explain a little bit more about the *Abishek* – what is the significance of all these things – because you see, often in the West people ask "Why is this?" Remember yesterday I said people like to feed the mind.

So you see, in Hinduism, every step in the ritual that we do is not just fancy. Even if it looks fancy with different things, looks very beautiful, colourful and joyful, everything has significance. Similarly, whenever you come to me or to any Master, the first thing you do is say "Jai Gurudev", no? So when you do *Namaskar* what is happening? The significance is that the left hand represents the *Atma*, which is your individual soul, the soul with identity. The right one symbolises the *Paramatma*, which is Divinity, God. So by joining the two together, the *Atma* is joining with the *Paramatma*. When somebody comes to you and you just shake hands, nothing happens, but when you greet somebody in this way, it's like you join the *Atma* and the *Paramatma* together and at the same time, you are saying; you are asking that person indirectly "Do you know the way to *Paramatma*?" and the person will respond back to you "No, I don't know the way. I'm not yet there."

When you go to a Master, a *Guru*, when you do that, what does the Guru do? The Guru will not respond back like this. The Guru will bless you. The Guru will lift his hand – which is called *Abhayahasta* – He will bless you and He will say at the same time "Be patient. I know the way. I will lead you there." And what do you do? You bow down to the Guru. By bowing down to the Guru's feet – of course, by the Feet of the Master is the best place for everybody to be –

you're surrendering to the Master.

What is happening when you're greeting the Master by bowing down to the feet? You're showing the Crown *Chakra* to the Master. At the same time you are saying "Lord, bestow upon me Your blessing, so that I can Realise my Self." What does the *Guru* do? The *Guru* puts his hand over your head and says "Be patient!" You don't like hearing this word, eh?

That's why in Hinduism each ritual has its meaning. Of course, if I would have to tell *every* meaning of *every* step, we would not finish in three days; it would take much longer . One would lead to the other. Actually, in Hinduism each word, each Sanskrit syllable has a meaning and not only one meaning. It has at least thirty-five meanings, so it depends on what context you're using it. You can imagine how many there are. Even in the word *Guru* itself, there are so many, but I will not explain this now.

So, when I'm invoking the Lord now, you also do it inwardly. I will just explain a little bit about it. Then inwardly together, with me, you invoke. We call upon Lord Nrsinghadev to come and be present here.

The *kalash* in itself, as you will see, is a pot filled with water with several things inside and above there is a coconut. The coconut symbolises the heart of Man, which is always pure. The fibres outside symbolise all the negativity of Man. Inside the heart everybody is pure. Somebody can be very bad outside, but inside he is pure as the coconut is white inside. That's why we offer a coconut to God. In Hinduism we always offer coconuts, because we are always offering the heart, even if some people don't know the significance, it is to offer one's heart to the Lord. The *kalash* itself represents the Trinity: Brahma, Vishnu, Maheshwara. Brahma is represented by the lower part, Vishnu by the middle part and the upper part represents *Shiva*. The five leaves that are put around the mouth of the pot symbolise the five elements, which are water, air, fire, ether and earth. This symbolises the five elements; it can also symbolise the five senses, the five main organs and so on. As I said, the coconut is the purity of one's heart. We can call upon the Divine to be seated in the heart of Man. When I call Him to be seated here, actually, I call Him to be seated in my heart and also in each one of your hearts. So, we will invoke *Nrsinghadev* to come now. You invoke Lord *Nrsinghadev* inside of you. You have the *mantra* so you can chant it also.

Now we will do the *Abishekam*. As you noticed, in the ritual we use lots of water all the time. When we chant *OM Gange cha Yamune chaiva, godavari Saraswati...* these are the three main rivers: Ganga, Yamuna and Saraswati. Ganga is considered by the Hindus to be the most sacred river. It is said that Ganga took Her source at the feet of Narayana. Coming from Narayana's feet, She cleans everything. It is said that by taking a dip in the Ganges, one's sins are forgiven. One is purified from all one's past karmic things and one's ancestors are also purified.

Bhagirath, who brought Ganga on Earth, did lots of penance because his ancestors didn't get liberation. When he did lots of penance, he pleased the Lord and the Lord said "OK, so be it. I will send Ganga to Earth!" Ganga left Heaven and came on Earth. As She was coming on Earth, She was a bit arrogant about Herself and She said "Oh, I am a *Devi*, I am a Goddess! What is this world? If I come with full force, it will destroy the world." and She proudly came on Earth. The *Devas* knew that if She came on Earth directly like that, She would split the Earth into two. Imagine a *demi-god* has such power to do that.

Shiva interceded. They called upon Shiva and Shiva said "OK." He looked up and said "This girl is too arrogant. I should teach her a lesson." Shiva went and stood where She was going to come on Earth. As She saw Shiva down on Earth She said "Oh, I will split his head in two!" She didn't know the Consciousness of God. As She was coming down on Shiva's head, thinking that She would break the head of Shiva, with His energy Shiva entangled Her, trapped Her into His locks, His matted hair.

Seeing that, Bhagirath said "Lord, I have done so much penance, I have pleased Lord Narayana and now that She has come down, You have trapped Her. I know She's a bit arrogant but, *please*, I'm sure She has learned Her lesson", because She was trapped and She could not get out. Then She asked forgiveness of Lord Shiva and Shiva released Her. That's why you see on Shiva's head there is always Ganga coming out. Shiva released Her and as She came down, Bhagirath was always in front of Her, so She followed Bhagirath. Bhagirath brought Her to his ancestors, where the ashes of his ancestors were kept and as She passed over the ashes of the ancestors, they all became liberated.

When that was done, because She came down very majestically, with lots of water coming from everywhere, She started flooding everywhere. There was a Saint, *Jahnu Muni*, who saw that Ganga was flooding everywhere. He went and drank, swallowing Her whole. When Bhagirath saw that Ganga had been swallowed, He asked the Saint "Please, let Her out. She will not do any damage."

The Saint looked at him saying "Are you sure? Do you promise me that?" He said "Yes, yes, I promise you!" Then the Saint said, "OK, I will not release Her the same way She was, but I will release Her as rain!" So from his ears, Ganga came out as rain. By that time, Ganga had calmed down so much. After She had purified all the ashes, all the ancestors of Bhagirath and of other saints also, Bhagirath asked Her "As you have come from the Lord, please, stay on Earth, help everybody who will come to you, who will ask for your help. Help them. Purify them. Remind them."

In Hinduism it is said that once in one's lifetime, one should take a dip in the Ganges. But it's also said, that if somebody can't go to the Ganges, one drop of Ganges water can purify him. If somebody goes to the Ganges, the first thing they do is greet the Mother. They greet Her, bow to Her, touch Her with the head. This is a sign of respect for the Mother who gives everything.

Because of the water, the world exists. If the world didn't have water, you know how it would look – completely dry, like a desert everywhere. So water is very important in one's life. The body is made of sixty percent water. The world is made three-quarters of water. So the Mother is very important. The *ashrams* and the main pilgrimage places in India are all by the Ganges, on the banks of the Ganges and on the banks of the Yamuna.

So like that, when somebody comes to have the Lord's *Darshan*, to have the Lord's blessing, they can also purify themselves. Like I said yesterday, to advance towards realisation is good, but you have also to go through certain purification, because in one's life, one accumulates so much negativity. Even only in this life one accumulates so much negativity that needs to be purified. Imagine through so many lives, how much negativity one has accumulated! That's why one doesn't become liberated. So the first step for anything is purification. Mother Ganga, She offers this purification. She offers to purify everybody.

If we look at all the saints, in the East or the West or anywhere, where did they live? All of them have lived by the riverbank. If there was no riverbank, they always made it so that they were near a source or they miraculously created a source by themselves. Water was very important.

In Christianity, when a child is born, what is the first thing they do? They baptise the child. Being baptised has the same significance as taking a dip in the Ganges. It is said that by getting baptised, by putting the water over the head of the person, by chanting "In the Name of the Father, the Son and the Holy Spirit", one is purified from one's sins or faults. It is the same thing when one goes to the Ganges: one is purified not only in this life, but also for many lives before.

That's why you see a similarity when somebody takes a dip in the Ganges. It's always three times – for Brahma, Vishnu, Maheshwara – and this has been done for thousands of years, not only recently, not only for the two thousand years that you know of baptisms. Even before Jesus, they knew about it from John the Baptist, who used to baptise. He got it from the Great One. He took it from Him and brought it here.

Of course, Jesus knew the meaning of it. He knew the significance of getting baptised. He knew how powerful water is – so powerful that it can cleanse somebody. Don't think that the Jordan is just holy because Jesus was there. No, through the prayer they knew the Mother was there, the Mother would take care of the children and the Mother would clean the children. He *knew* the power of water.

For everything that we do, we use water to clean. When you clean something, water is taken to wash the thing and to clean. The water is clean and the water takes away all the dirt. Let's take a plate. I clean it; after I clean it, the plate becomes clean, but where does the dirt go? The dirt goes into the water. The water keeps the dirt, but the water doesn't become dirty. After some time the dirt goes to the bottom of the water and the water becomes clear again.

She knows how to clean. She knows how to purify and that's why in all rituals – we're talking about Christianity, we're talking about Islam, we're talking about Hinduism, Buddhism – in all religions you see that there is water. Christians go to Lourdes, to the Jordan to take a dip in the water to purify themselves. The Muslims go to Mecca and they take the *Zamzam* from there – the Holy Water. They purify themselves with the water and they take the water home and drink the water. Hindus, they go to the Ganges to get the Holy Water and take a dip in the water.

In all traditions water is so important because it cleans us, it purifies us. That's why when you call the three rivers – Ganga, Yamuna, Saraswati – you're invoking all the rivers, you are invoking all the Mothers "Come, Mother Ganga. Purify us, purify our hearts, purify our minds. Cleanse us from the dirt that our minds create." You are invoking Her.

For the *abishekam* you have to understand the significance of the offering. You offer everything that comes from the Lord back to the Lord. Everything that comes from Him will merge back into Him and you will become one with Him eventually. How long it takes depends on each one individually. If

> When we invoke the Lord, we have also to invoke Him inside our hearts. When He takes complete possession of us, we become Him.

you want it to be quicker, it will be. If you want it to be longer, it will be longer. It is each one offering back to the Lord what is from Him. Like I said, the body is made up of the five elements. These are the five elements that we will be using.

Yamuna, which is near Vrindavan; it is said that Yamuna was already sacred, but Yamuna became more sacred when Krishna played in Her, when the Lord took His bath in Her. Imagine how blessed Yamuna is to receive the Lord every day in Her from when He was small. The day He was born, She could touch the feet of the Lord!

As you know, Krishna was born in a prison and His mum and dad were locked inside by the wicked brother of His mother; Kamsa. He killed all the children because when the father and mother of Krishna were married, he heard a voice that said "You fool, Kamsa! The eighth child of your sister and brother-in-law who you're bringing happily to their house will kill you!" This worried him and he got so angry, that he put them in prison. When the husband heard that Kamsa wanted to kill his sister, he said "Don't kill your sister! Look, everybody will say 'This brother has killed his sister!' I myself will bring all the children to you." Then Kamsa said "OK, don't bring all the children, I only need the eighth child."

So he let every child live happily in the palace, but one day Narad Muni – like I explained yesterday, he is the messenger of God who goes around distributing messages – was around there. He went to Kamsa and said to him "Dear King, the Voice has said the eighth child, but which one is the eighth child? You don't know which one is the eighth child. You should kill all of them." He thought for a while and said "Yes, you're right!" Very angrily, he rushed to the house of his brother-in-law and sister and killed all five, breaking their heads on a stone.

But why did Narad do that? He's very clever. If he would not have done that, the Lord would have taken a longer time to come on Earth. To accelerate His coming on Earth, to make it quicker, He said "Do more terrible things!" Like I said yesterday, the Lord comes on Earth to save the world. When the world is at an extreme, of course He will come quickly. As Kamsa accelerated it by killing all the brothers of Krishna, the time for the Lord to incarnate came very quickly.

When Devaki was pregnant with the seventh child, the foetus was transferred, miraculously, to the first wife of Vasudev who had run away to Vrindavan. Overnight she became pregnant, miraculously. This is how Balaram, the seventh brother of Krishna, was born. When Kamsa heard that he was very happy and said "Look, even the unborn child was already scared. He wasn't born."

The eighth child was Krishna. When Krishna was born, they saw Narayana in front of them. They were tied, on one side was the mother; on the other side was the father. So how was Krishna born? He was not born the normal way. There was a ball of light from Vasudev that came to Devaki. This is how the child was conceived. When Krishna was born, there was a bright light and Narayana was standing in front of them. Both of them saw it was Narayana and He said to Vasudev "Take me, bring me to Vrindavan and there you will see that there is a girl that has been born. Bring the girl back here."

Miraculously, the chains from their hands and feet opened up and they were free. Vasudev took the baby in a basket and went out. The gate opened up and all the soldiers had fallen asleep. He walked out. As he was walking, he had to cross the river Yamuna. He went inside the water, but the baby's feet were outside of the basket and Yamuna was overflowing just to touch the feet of Krishna. Every time She would touch the feet of Krishna, She would go down, because She was so much in bliss, so much in ecstasy that She would go down happily.

Vasudev went and changed the babies, brought the girl back to the prison and again, the chains went back on their hands and the door closed up. When Kamsa heard that the baby was born, he rushed to the prison and he saw that it was a girl and said "It doesn't matter whether it is a girl or a boy! I shall kill this child!" So he took the baby and as he threw the baby against the wall, the baby flew up. It was Shakti, Maya Devi, and She said "Kamsa, you fool, why do you want to kill me? You can't kill me. The One who will kill you has already been born! So prepare yourself; get ready!" From that Kamsa became very angry and started killing all the children in the villages around, sending many demons but it was of no use.

Krishna's pastime was always lying near the river Yamuna, and Yamuna was very happy to have Krishna all the time in Her. The *Shilpa Upanishad,* actually, mentions the greatness of Yamuna, how great She was to receive the Lord every time. How great is the Jordan to receive Christ. How great is Padma, who received Lord Chaitanya. These rivers are not just mere rivers, you know. They are there to purify humanity, to purify them so that they can advance on the spiritual path freely without any obstacles in their way, to remove all the dirt that we create every day in this mundane life. Like I said, the body is made up of the five elements and the five things that we use – milk, yoghurt, ghee, honey and sugar – are the five elements. When we chant the *OM Gange cha Yamune chaiva, godavari Saraswati...*, the three rivers are also inside each one of us. Ganga and Yamuna are on the outside. They are present, you can go there but Saraswati is under the Earth. Ganga and Yamuna are the two *Nadis* inside the body and the third *Nadi*, which is the *Sushumna Nadi*, is Saraswati.

By offering honey to the Lord, you're asking the Lord to make you soft, to make *you sweet*. Like the honey is sweet, you ask the Lord also to make you sweet as the honey, so He gives you a sweet voice. Honey is very good for the throat. So when you offer the honey to the Lord and say "God, I am offering this to you", then He'll make your voice very beautiful and you can sing beautifully! The *Panchamrit* is the whole of you, the body. You have offered the five elements separately. You have offered the five senses; now you're offering yourself. So it's like you're lifting your hand and saying "Lord, I am surrendering to You. I'm offering everything back to you."

The Nrsinghadev Yagna

This is one of the most important times, now. Fire is very important. Just the way water is very important, fire is also very important. Fire is also an element of purification. When water purifies, the dirt goes to the bottom of it, whereas when it is purified by fire, everything is burnt. Fire has the capacity of destroying even the molecules. When something is burnt by fire, what is left over is always pure.

Now we'll be offering to the Lord all the negativity – we have already offered our bodies. Nrsinghadev, will remove all negativity from your heart, all negativity from your mind and all the karmic things, He will strip them out, all the negative things that are keeping you here, stopping you from advancing, but from your side, let go of it. When He's pulling it, let go of it. Don't hang onto it. Don't fight with Him. You don't have any chance. Even the *Devas* don't have any chance with Him. So what about humans?

When He's taking something out, let Him take. What He takes out will be replaced by Divine Love. You will feel this Cosmic Love inside of you. You will feel this Great Love of God inside of you, and in this Love you will cry, you will laugh, you will not even understand it with the mind what is happening to you. Let it happen,   don't question it, because you have to let the Love of God completely take possession of you. As long as there is the mind, you will never understand His Love.

Only when you renounce the mind you can understand His Love. You can't analyse, you can't understand Him, because understanding is with the mind and with the mind there is no point in understanding Him. You have to renounce, you have to surrender to Him. When you surrender, you don't question Him. You don't question why it is like that, why it is like this. You just accept it, because you know He's with you.

While you are going through this purification, know that the Lord is near to you in whatever form you call Him. If you like Him in this Nrsinghadev form, He will come in this form. If you like Him in the form of Jesus, he will come in the form of Jesus. You see, God is not limited to one form. He's unlimited. That's why He is God. If God were limited, then He would not be God. Then He would be the fashion of one's mind, but God is not that. Even if you give a form to Him, He's not that. He's beyond our creation. He's beyond our mind's creation.

Like it is said in the Bible "Give what belongs to God back to God." So what belongs to Him is everything. In our mind we think that something belongs to us. Yesterday I said that we came with nothing; we will go with nothing. All that belongs to us is from Him. He creates everything and He will annihilate everything in Him. Everything is born from Him and everything will merge back into Him.

It's of no use to resist Him. You can try your best, you can try life after life, but at the end it's only Him who will win. Only your True Self will win. And you are part of Him. You are the droplet in the ocean, but you are not yet the ocean and you will never become the ocean, because you stay always this drop. When the drop merges into the ocean, there is no identification. Where is the drop and where is the ocean? Until you reach the point of merging into the ocean, Love Him. Serve Him. Enjoy Him. This is in your capacity to do. All that we are doing is to express our Love to Him, to express how much we want Him, how much we want to Realise Him.

Someone asked me "Swamiji, why do you always say God as *Him*?" God is also *Her*, but in the world we always use words which have limits. God is beyond all these things, like Narayana for example. He takes the appearance of Mohini Devi or Shakti when He has to show that He's beyond this duality. He's neither male nor female. He's beyond this concept. He loves everybody equally, but in the mind of Man there is this concept, there is this duality. As long as we think of this duality, we'll have the duality, but if we think of ourselves as being the Spirit, like Christ said, we will become this Spirit.

This is what you have to identify yourself as. The more you identify yourself with the body, the more you limit yourself. The more you identify yourself as the Spirit, as this droplet of the ocean, the more your longing will be to be back in the ocean. I guess that's what all of you want, no? It has to be a "Yes" from within. It's not about how loud it is. You can scream "Yes!!" or whatever, but if you don't mean it, it will not happen. Somebody can be quiet, but when he's meaning it inside, it will help.

In Hinduism, we consider a prayer as unfulfilled, firstly, if the *Guru* is not venerated, and secondly if there is no cow dung, which is for purification. In all the prayers - also when we move into a new house or when we install the *murti* statues – in everything we use cow dung or cow urine, because the cow is one form of the Divine Mother. That's why in Hinduism we don't eat cows unlike here in the West, where people eat everything; we respect the Mother, because in a cow every part is sacred. Each Deity resides in the cow. Every part of Her, everything that comes from Her is sacred also.

We'll start with eleven *OMs*. We will pray to Ganesha to remove all obstacles, so that everything that we do here is sanctified. Then we will pray to the *Guru*. Inwardly, in your heart, bow down to the Guru and ask for the blessing. Afterwards we will do a prayer for the planets; invoking all the Deities and we will light the fire.

THE SEVEN FLOWERS

Darshan, Steffenshof, Germany, 4 April 2007

Often we say to ourselves "How to please God? In which way shall we please God? How can we make God happy?" There are many ways God is happy with, but what is the best way to make Him happy? When do you think God is happy? It is when we are happy. God is happy when we are happy, because our happiness is His happiness, because we are part of Him. We will make ourselves happy through serving, through helping, because the greatest happiness comes from serving. The more you help, the more you make somebody else happy, the more you will see the happiness inside of you grow and grow. The less you help, the more you push yourself backwards. The more you think "No, why should I help", the more you become untrue towards yourself. When you become untrue towards yourself, you don't let the heart open up. The more this happens, the more you become miserable. When you help, like Christ said, it has to be unconditional. When you help, you should forget about it.

When we love, we love and forget. We don't expect anything when we love somebody. Well, there are two different kinds of love. There is a love on the outside, where you only expect something, but there is another kind of love. There is a love where you will do anything for this person. Just to please this person you will do anything. Even that kind of love is divided in two. Whatever is done unconditionally will always make you happy, but whatever is done with a condition will always make you unhappy. To awaken this Love, to make this Love greater and greater is not that difficult. I always say, you just need to want it.

I'll tell you a small story. Once there was a Sage, a great Saint who went to a town. He was so famous that people were very excited when he was coming, so they started preparing four weeks before, busily preparing a lot of things. Then someone said "I heard that this Swami likes to use seven flowers when he performs his prayer." That's a lot of flowers – a big confusion started happening. They wondered "What flower shall we take to give to this Swami?" They didn't know what flower to take. So they ran to the Saint and said "Reverend Sir, we heard that while praying you use seven flowers, but there is such a variety of flowers that we don't know what flowers to use."

> I want that each one of you gives these seven flowers to me. The seven flowers are: truthfulness, Love, service to people, prayer, devotion, loyalty and control of the senses.

The Saint looked at them and started laughing like mad. He said "Yes, I use seven flowers to pray and I want that each one of you gives these seven flowers to me. The seven flowers are: truthfulness, Love, service to people, prayer, devotion, loyalty and control of the senses. These are the seven flowers. He said "If somebody gives these to God, gives them to one's Self, God will be pleased with that. There is no greater thing than that.

This reminds me of Krishna who said in the *Bhagavad Gita* "When somebody offers to me just a small leaf with Love from the heart, I shall accept it." People offer a lot of things to please God – big, big things on the outside, but everything is from Him. It is He who gives; we are just taking what is given by Him and offering it back to Him.

This Love that we have inside is also Him, but it is up to us to develop it or not. It is up to us how we handle it. We can go and do service on the outside like many organisations that just buy a lot of things and give them to the poor countries. Does this mean that this is service? You can always put a hundred euros aside every month, put it into an account of some organisation somewhere and say "That's service". The moment the money is gone you don't even know what is happening with it, but when you yourself go; when you yourself participate in it, it creates another joy. It is this joy that God wants you to develop.

People say "Yes, but I don't have time to go and serve", because in the mind they think that when you talk about that kind of service you have to run to India or to Africa. Your neighbour is dying, your neighbour is hungry by your side and you are thinking of India and of Africa, but God is thinking about them. Service starts near, around you. Stop seeing the difference, clear your mind of differences and see the same Lord everywhere. Offer the flowers that I just mentioned from deep within your heart. Offer them to Him. In this way you don't even need to sit to pray, because He will be always with you. Open up your heart and serve whenever you can. Help whenever you can.

FASTING AND PURIFICATION

Darshan, Shree Peetha Nilaya, Germany, 2 April 2009

Last week in Switzerland, somebody asked me a question "Why do we fast?" As you know very well, it is a fasting time for the Christians. Then the person asked me "Why do we fast, for what reason?" For the Hindus, there are also nine days of fasting for Lord Rama right now. Why is fasting so important? Fasting, we think that we are doing it to please God, you know. I had a talk with some people and they said "You know, now I am fasting for Easter. The first week we'll stop eating this, second week we'll stop eating that, third week we'll stop eating this and fourth week we'll stop eating another thing, and the last day we eat everything." Also in Hinduism, not only in Christianity, when we talk about fasting, we say we will not eat meat, we will not eat eggs; we will not eat for these nine days of fasting, but the last day have a big, big feast.

Why do we fast? Does it please God? Does it please us? Some people fast because they say it's a time where they think of God more and some do it to lose weight, like dieting. In both ways we are wrong, because when we fast, what is happening to us? We say that we are letting go of certain things, but it's not only during the time of fasting that we have to let go of certain things. We really have to let it go, not thinking about it, not thinking or rejoicing what will be after the fasting. Very often people say they are fasting *today*, but the mind is always focusing on tomorrow "What will I eat to break the fast?" That is wrong, that is not a fast and if you fast as a diet, of course you will lose weight.

If you fast for the Self, to elevate it, this is the fasting that is put in front of all during the feast time in all religions. You don't find it only in Hinduism. You find it in Christianity, you find it in the Muslim tradition, you find it everywhere; fasting is very important. What is happening during fasting is that in our head, something gets changed. You will notice that during fasting time people are quieter within themselves. It is not the food that we are eating, it is not what we are drinking, but it's our attitude. It's what we have programmed ourselves with, the intention, the power that we have given to ourselves – that's what is making everything strong.

During fasting time you go through a purification of your mind. Of course, when pure things are put inside the body, the mind gets pure, also. As it is said, the mind also depends on what you are eating, what you are putting inside of yourself. If you put something, which is negative inside your body, do you expect your mind to be positive? It's quite difficult. Yet you expect your life to be positive afterwards. It doesn't happen. This purification helps you to become positive, so that whatever you do, you become more within yourself, discovering who you are in reality. That's why you will see that scriptures say that one – at least once a week – should have a day that one fasts. It's not to please God, you know. It's to please your true Self.

The question will arise "Is my true Self not God-Self?" It's true that your true Self *is* God, yet there *is* a difference. What we call God, the Supreme Consciousness, doesn't have any ego, but we are bound by two forms of ego – the right ego and the un-right ego. The right ego is the ego that perceives our self being the true Self, which means that whatever we say, whatever we do, it's always in the right attitude of serving and going towards God-Realisation or Self-Realisation. The un-right ego is the ego that always wants for oneself "I want a car; I want a house; I want this and I want that," the wants that never finish. These are the two forms of ego with which we identify ourselves. Sometimes it is the ego of the outside which is the un-right one, and sometimes the ego of the inside, which is the right one. Both are good until you know where your goal is and what you really want. If you are anchored into the world, of course the un-right ego will take its position, but if you anchor into spirituality, then slowly you will move from the un-right to the right. That will make you see everything in a completely different way. It's like you say "Yes," during this time of fasting, "I am letting go of everything", but the main thing that you have to let go of is this big "I", that always says "I am this and I am that."

A simple example that I like to give people is this: Can you, for one moment, forget about your mind and your body? Can you? Go on, be truthful for once – yes or no? It is quite difficult, because the identity that we often talk about is mostly the mind or the body. Very rarely do we talk about the Self. It's very rare that we talk about who we are in reality, though this is the most important thing.

We meditate, but the moment we come out of meditation we start to think about the world outside and what we have to try in it. We want to be happy; we want to be always not in the happiness of the outside, but in the inner happiness. We have to try our best, so that whatever we do, wherever we are and whatever is our path, we are happy with ourselves. If we try to find happiness outside, without being happy inside with ourselves, we can forget about it.

It's time to delve deep into the inside and let the beauty of what you have inside, come out. You will see that once you have found what you are looking for, not on the outside, but within you, how easy it is to love. This great word "Love" that I always talk about; I ask myself often this question, "How many people really understand what this real Love is?" For sure in life all of you have felt this true Love and for you to be seated here or to be searching, for sure, this Divine Love has awoken. So when you meditate and when you chant or pray, let your mind and body all pray together, so that what you have inside of you shines.

We will do one simple meditation now. This meditation was actually given to me about four, no, three months ago. I did it once.

Meditation

- I will ask you all to take a few deep breaths, in and out. Inhale strongly and exhale strongly, without any break in between. This way of inhaling helps you to concentrate and to stop the power of the mind.
- Now, take your right hand, place it just at the level of your heart, not on your chest, not on yourself, but in front.
- Feel the energy that is emanating from your hand to your heart, from your heart to your hand. Leave it there. Don't touch yourself.
- Now, without any pressure, put the hand on your heart and feel what is happening, especially with your heart.
- Slowly you can open your eyes.

If you are sensitive enough, you will feel what is happening to the heart. For meditation there are millions of trails the heart goes through. That's why the *rishis* and the *sadhus* are addicted to it. If you are sincere towards yourself, whenever you meditate, you can lose yourself into it. You can awaken the greatest form of Love, the greatest form of devotion. It all depends on you, how sincere you are, because if you are not sincere in what you really want inside, you can try it as much as you want, you will not reach there.

Very often people say "I have been meditating for very long. I have done so many kinds of meditation, but I don't feel anything." It is true that you will never feel; you can go to the ends of the world, from North to South; East to West, if you want; but if you have not known here, if you are not sincere here in your heart, it's of no use. So keep trying, keep trying even harder and know that the One you are looking for is here, knocking at the door of your heart. Open it and let Him out. Let Him take complete possession of you. Then you will see that whatever you do; that your whole life is a meditation. It's not only to sit and forget about your mind and body, but whatever you do is a form of meditation and whatever you do is prayer.

THE MOST IMPORTANT THING
ON THE SPIRITUAL PATH

Darshan, Springen Village, Germany, 1 August 2009

We often ask ourselves "What is the most important thing on the spiritual path?" The most important thing on the spiritual path is self-discipline. It is a word which many people don't like to hear, but it's only through self-discipline that you will be able to do your *sadhana*. Without self-discipline it's very difficult, because you will *always* find excuses not to do something.

What is *sadhana*? What does the word *sadhana* mean? It means something by which we will attain our spiritual goal. In *sadhana* there is perseverance, there is eagerness and there is patience. Without these three you can try as much as possible, but it will be very difficult. Your mind will always make you think "Oh, today I'm a bit tired. I will not go to prayers." or "I will not do this." or "I will not do that." You start to build up this self-un-discipline, because there is a lack of perseverance. You want to achieve your spiritual goal. You want to realise your Self, but do you think it's just like that? No, it's not.

If one thinks that just by sitting around and thinking "OK, I think I will go to the prayers whenever I want. I will do my *sadhana* whenever I want." Then God will also say "I will come to you whenever I want." Well, He *will* come to you whenever He wants, it's true, but you can make it happen faster. You can make Him awaken within you and be consumed,   attaining Him faster, and this can be done only through your discipline. If you want to become self-disciplined and have one-pointed mindfulness on your spiritual path, in your *sadhana*, you must aim for what you want; but what is this single-mindedness?

I will tell you a small story. Once there was a fisherman who was sitting on the riverbank, throwing his bait into the river and waiting for the fish to eat the bait. He was very focused. He was just looking at the floating bait, waiting for it to sink. He knew that there were a lot of fish around. A stranger who was passing by asked the fisherman "Mister, can you tell me where Mr X lives?" The fisherman was so concentrated that he didn´t answer. The stranger repeated his question again – one time, two times, three times – still no answer. He got really angry and walked away. As he was walking away, the fisherman saw the bait going down, so he pulled and caught a fish. Then he called after the man "Hey, you were calling me, asking me something? Tell me what your question was." The stranger said "I repeated my question several times, but it was as if you didn't hear me or see me. Why should I repeat it again?"

That was single-mindedness, one-pointed focus. When you meditate, when you do your *sadhana*, you can achieve this state where nothing can disturb you. No left and right, no hearing, no seeing, because in the deepness of meditation, in the deepness of your practice, you have to be fully focused. If you are not disciplined with yourself, do you think you will have this focus? No, this is where everything gets uncertain. You will do prayer, but you will be really superficial and then not be satisfied with yourself. Self-discipline is something that you have to work for. It's purification of the mind and of the senses.

When the mind gets purified, when the mind becomes positive, you will see how easy it is in your *sadhana* also. It doesn't matter if you don't succeed in one go. I know that people when they start practicing, they would like to have quick results, like in one month.

They want it very fast. Know one thing, if you go *in* fast, you will go *out* fast also.

You see, it's like cooking. If a *Mataji* would like to make syrup, but she just took the fruits and threw them into a pot of water and then removed them quickly, would the sweetness go out from the fruit and into the water? It would not. You have to leave the fruits inside for some time. It is the same with your *sadhana*. If you just go inside and then quickly out of it, being impatient with yourself, it will be the same. It will not be sweet. The sweetness that you have inside of you is waiting to be awakened.

It doesn't matter which path you follow or which *sadhana* you are doing. *How* you are doing it is the most important. When you love to do something, you are not disturbed by anything. When you love to do the work that you are doing – let's say that someone, for example, loves to be a carpenter – you would see how much Love he projects into his work, because he would do it with a full focus.

I love painting. I love to paint, because it brings you to such a focus that nothing will disturb you, not even people around you who are talking. Have you ever painted? How many among you paint? That's nice. So you know what I am talking about. It's not only about painting. Anything that you do, when you love what you are doing, you will come to that focus that nothing will disturb you. There can be lots of people, thousands of people around you, but you will always be in that focus. That's what sadhana is – to discipline yourself with such an intensity. It's not that you become narrow-minded – this has nothing to do with it – but it's to find what you are looking for. Even if you don't find it in one month, it doesn't matter, or in one year, still it doesn't matter. There are yogis who have been meditating hundreds of years. I will not say that they have not found it, but they are in this deepness with themselves, with the Lord inside of them.

The Kingdom of God, Christ always talked about it, didn't He?

How many times He talked about it when He was here. He said "The Kingdom of God is near." Yet people are waiting for the palace, the Kingdom to appear, but it is here, inside of you, this inner kingdom. You will achieve it only when your mind is clear, when *you* are clear with yourself, when the mind becomes pure and clear. *Sadhana* helps you to control your mind. There are many forms of sadhana. Each person has their own way, their own practice that they feel close with.

If I like something, I don't expect you to like it also. Let's say I love mangos. I know that a lot of Europeans don't like mangos at all and I can't force you to love them, just because it is pleasant for me. It is the same way with *sadhana*. Not everybody has to have the same *sadhana*. If you follow your path, you have your own *sadhana*. Enjoy it and love it! That's what will bring you closer and closer to your real Self. That is what will awaken this deep longing for the Divine, because once you have tasted this sweetness of the Divine, you will want more and more. This is the drug that the Divine gives you and it's the sweetness of His drug that you will always want. It's like when you taste something sweet. Take a baby – when it is born, you don't give him other things right away. For some months the mother will give the baby only milk, for once the baby has tasted something else, he will not be satisfied only with milk anymore.

> If one thinks that just by sitting around and thinking "OK, I think I will go to the prayers whenever I want. I will do my sadhana whenever I want." Then God will also say "I will come to you whenever I want."

That's how it is for you as well. You have tasted the world. You have seen the world – not only through one life, but through many lives, and yet, for you to be here, to have the urge of wanting spirituality; of wanting to realise your Self, it's not completely from now only. It's not that when you were born you just thought "Yes, I'm spiritual." It's for many lives that you have wanted it. It's there. Wherever you finished in your past lives, this urge did not finish. It's still there. It just needs you to tap into it and through your sadhana you will really achieve this. There's no question. Be disciplined with yourself in your *sadhana* and pray.

If you have not yet achieved the calmness of the mind, pray. If you can't meditate, do *nama japam*; recite the names of God. Whichever deity you feel close with, recite the Divine names, because they carry the vibration to calm the mind. If you really want to calm your mind and really succeed on your spiritual path, the best time to do your *sadhana* is in the morning. The earlier it is, the better your *sadhana* will be.

Why is it like that? Some people like to meditate after work. I will not say that this is not right; it is right. You can meditate any time you want. You can do your spiritual practice any time you want, but when you practice at night, what is happening? The pressure of the day is fully on you, so when you try to meditate, or you try to do your spiritual practices, what happens? Often you fall asleep. Then you say "Swamiji, but why do I fall asleep when I try to meditate?" The best time is early in the morning, when your mind is calm, because your mind is calm after sleeping. You are in a very fresh state. That's the best time. Even for prayers, it's the best time.

IN SILENCE IS EVERYTHING

Darshan, Shree Peetha Nilaya, Germany, 18 September 2009

On the spiritual path, the utmost thing that we have to do is to control our mind. We say to watch our thoughts. What is a thought? A thought is an image. A thought is a creation. Why is it said that we have to watch our thoughts; because most of the time our thoughts make us negative. We have to watch them and have them under control – very often it's quite difficult. Our thoughts make us who we are, because we always run behind them.

A few days ago there was a reading in the chapel where there was a saying from St. Silouan of Mount Athos that said "Let your thoughts be in hell, but *you* rejoice in the Divine." I will comment a little bit on that. Nowadays, the moment you see your thoughts running to hell, you are all running with the thoughts to hell. Your thoughts are jumping, jumping and jumping and then *boom* – there they go. You are also jumping behind them and doing the same, throwing yourself after them.

When we watch ourselves, we see that very often we like to speak out what we have in our minds. We like to tell everybody how great we are. We like to publicise ourselves and say "Oh, I have seen that light, I have seen this and I have seen that. I have felt this and I have felt that." Why? It is to feed that thought, so that the thought can become bigger.

It's like when you analyse a reptile. A reptile can be very soft, very easy, going its way, but the moment it falls in a pit, it will try it's best to come out. The moment the reptile comes out of that pit, it will be more aggressive than ever. This is how our thoughts are also. The moment we let it out, it's inflamed with this vigorous power, saying "Yes, I am out." Like Christ said "It's not what goes inside the person that makes them polluted, but what comes out of the person." In the *Gita* it says "A controlled mind is your best friend, but an uncontrolled mind is your worst enemy." Like I said, the way we think is the way we are.

There was once a great *sadhu* in a great ecstasy, in Divine ecstasy. He fell down in the middle of the road; he was in *samadhi*. A few hours later, a thief was passing by. He saw the *sadhu* on the road and he thought "This must be a thief who has been stealing last night. Now he is tired; he is just resting. The policeman will come and get him." Then he went away. Next came a drunkard. He saw the *sadhu* lying down and said "Oh, you have fallen down. You have drunk too much. Look at me; I am still standing." Then he went his way. The third person who came was another *sadhu*. When he saw the other *sadhu* lying on the street, he knew that he was in *samadhi*. He sat down near him and started to massage his legs.

This shows how our mind functions. We will always see what we have inside of ourselves. Christ has said: Don't judge your brothers. Don't try to find fault in your brother when you have the same in yourself. Don't try to remove the splinter in the eye of your brother, when you have a big pole in your eye.

Firstly, we have to control our thoughts. Prayer and continuous remembering of the Divine help us to control our mind. They help us to bring our mind, which is always running, into calm, into silence. Through silence, the thoughts will disappear. If your thought is negative and you let it out, all around you everything becomes negative. There will be nothing positive. But if you keep this thought inside, through prayer and through inner silence, it will dissolve. But no, we like so much to express ourselves, to express our thoughts. You can; I won't say "No, don't do it", but first, master it, then you can express it.

If you silence yourself completely, if you silence your mind, you will receive everything. You will not even need to ask. You will receive, because God is merciful. He is the all-knowing, so do you think you really have to ask Him? How many of you think that we have to ask Him? Most people think that we do have to always ask, ask and ask. We never finish our asking. Our asking is endless, but what are we asking for? We are always asking for something "Give us this, give us that; give us this *and* that." Very often our asking is so limited that it's never finished. You are right that we have to ask, but we have to really know what to ask. Some people will ask for love, but it's already there! What do you think we can ask from God? If He said what He wants from you, would you be able to give it? Actually, let's ask Him one thing – to purify our thoughts, help us to go beyond the thoughts and help us to go beyond the mind. That's it. When you have gone beyond it, it will be very easy. To go beyond it is the most difficult part where everybody gets stuck, because the mind is very active. We see it every day in whatever we do, our thoughts are always in front of us. At the beginning, when you were always with the Divine, how was your thought? It was always focused on God. There was not a second when it was diverted to limited things, like a Mercedes, but nowadays, how many people's thoughts and minds are on God – only a few. If you consider the amount of people living on Earth, how many people do you suppose are thinking of God – very few, a handful. The rest are thinking how they will get a Mercedes, how they will get this and how they will get that. They will even pray "God, get me this." As the *Mataji* said, God also says "Yes? What can

> If you silence your mind completely, you will receive everything. You will not even need to ask.

I do for you?" We must be prepared to make only the appropriate request. It is through prayer, through *japam*, through meditation, that we learn to control our thoughts, but the best of all is through silence. Pray, chant your *mantra* and silence yourself. Feel the *mantra* inside of you. When you chant the name of God, don't just *say*, Narayana or Durga or Babaji. It's not just the name. They are not simple names, you know? These names create a vibration and even when you are not aware, it's still vibrating. The main thing is you have to be aware of that vibration inside of you. You have to feel that each part of your body is vibrating these Divine Names. You can really feel it and really know it only when you are in silence. Silence doesn't mean that you have to stop your work and say "I sit in silence and that's it – finished!" No, silence means that whatever you are doing, you stay calm and you control the tongue. The body is made of 206 bones and they say that wherever there are bones, we can control them, but the tongue is not made of bones, so we have to *learn* to control it. If this tongue can chant the Divine Names all the time, you will be able to control it. When you have controlled the tongue, you will be able to control your mind.

When you express your thought, if it is Divine you will see the positivity, you will see the result of it. If it is negative, you will also see the result. Then you will ask yourself "Why am I not advancing? Why am I not seeing and feeling the Divine?" - though He is here with you. Ask yourself "Am I calm? Am I quiet? Am I in silence?" or "Am I in pride and wanting to express it?"

Watch your thoughts, always, and be in silence. This is the first basis of spirituality. You can go anywhere and all the religions will tell you the same thing. All will give you a *mantra*, whether it is the name of Allah, the name of Jesus Christ or the name of Rama, and they will say "Go, chant and make yourself calm." If you want a better meditation, if you want to advance, control your thoughts and be in silence as much as possible.

RISING ABOVE LIMITATIONS

Darshan, Shree Peetha Nilaya, Germany, 26 December 2009

First off, I would like to wish a Merry Christmas to you all. To all who were not here, I hope you have had a wonderful Christmas time and that you were filled with a lot of joy and happiness. Like I was saying a few days ago, it is a time of change. It is a time that we have to change ourselves, a time that we have to start taking responsibility. As long as we don't take responsibility, we weaken ourselves.

Often we will see that we let ourselves be dominated by our mind. You will say "Swamiji, we try our best, but we don't succeed." Why? We know very well, why we are here. We know very well what we are searching for. It is all inside of ourselves, but why is this mind always troubling us? Why is it so difficult to let it go? Why? It is simple. The answer to that is that we like our limitation. It is simply that.

We like to limit ourselves and we like to dance in this limitation. That's how, when we analyse ourselves, we see our own limitation. Deep inside ourselves, there is another voice that says "Hey you have to wake up! There is something greater than that", but the limitation of the mind shows that that's it. We are in our own game and we don't want to jump out.

It is like we are caging ourselves like an animal, and we run from one side to the other. Then we are back again to the same place. Like that, we let our mind darken our true Self, but from time to time, through the Grace of God, through the Grace of Divine Mother,

143

there are some rays of light and the gate is opened and you go out. Then, out of fear, you run in again. Where does that lead you? Krishna has said to Arjun "Dear Arjun, be free; be like *a yogi*. Raise your weapon and fight." When He said that to Arjun, He did not say that to Arjun only. He said that to all of us. We are all *yogis*, but we have to be free. What is a *yogi*? He is somebody who is free. When we see our limitations, we see that we are not free. Whenever fear arises, whenever a thought of "Oh, I should have done this, I have not done that", we run around always in circles.

We don't free ourselves, because we are scared. We are scared to look at that limitation. What if this limitation is everything? No, what you have to do is to face it. You know very well that this limitation is not you. It is not for that purpose you are here. Face it. Look deep into the eyes of this limitation and let it go. As long as you don't look deep into the eyes and face it by yourself, you will always be into this game.

Unless you like it! I don't know. You have the free will of choice about that. Like a great Sufi said "You have the choice of life to take this way or that way. It is your choice. You are free in that choice." You will come to a point where the yogi which is inside of you, the greatness which is inside of you, will have to make the choice, also. Your true Self will have to make the choice. This true choice which is inside of you will overtake the

We don't free ourselves, because we are scared. We are scared to look at that limitation.

limitation of what you think it is. Cross over this limitation; face it; don't have fear! Start, firstly, with little things. You know yourself. You know that God will always provide for you. Even an animal knows that and we abound with more qualities than an animal, so we can realise who we are.

We are all one family that we call humanity. Everybody talks about humanity, but very few really behave humanly. If we call ourselves human, we are part of this society, we are part of humanity and so we have not to behave like animals. Even animals behave better in society, because they know who they are and they know where they are going. They trust in the Higher Consciousness that God will always provide.

Us poor human beings who have more than just an animal, we like to degrade ourselves. We like to make ourselves worse. It is time to cross over this limitation. It is time that you really let what you have inside of you awake. How many among you, out of fear of what people think, are not doing something? Many. Then you are limiting yourselves. Be free! That is what your inside is calling you to do – to be free, to learn and to move on.

Life is the most beautiful thing that God has given you. Don't waste it, because at the end, when life is departing this body, you will look back and you will say "Oh, my God, I have missed so many choices, so many chances God has sent to me, but my mind has been ruled by so many *matrikas;* I blinded myself." Why do I say "I blind myself"? The choice to be blind or to see is up to you. How to do that? You do your *sadhana* every day, no? You see, the spiritual *sadhana* helps you to free the mind, helps you not to get entangled into this limitation.

Once a student went to his *Guru* and said "Master, I am troubled." The master stood right in front of him and came very near to his face, like this microphone and said "Why do you hang onto the illusion? You know that whatever is in this mind is an illusion. Why do you hang onto that? You know very well that deep inside of you only God resides. Why don't you find joy inside of this?" Then the Master said "My dear child, recite for 24 hours non-stop your *Guru mantra* and meditate intensely for 4 hours and you will conquer the mind."

Of course, the Grace of the *Guru* was there, but it's the same thing – the Grace of God is with you. Chant the Name of God, if you can, 24 hours. You will say "What if I sleep?" How can we chant when we are sleeping? That is the secret of *mantra japa*. The more you train yourself chanting the Name of God throughout the day, the more you train yourself in reciting continuously, in every action to remember the Divine, the more it will become automatic. Even when you sleep, you will carry on chanting and will carry on singing the Divine names.

Practice your spiritual practice, because your spiritual practice is like a shield, like armour, that has been given to you to protect you. When you are protected, you don't need to fear anything, but if you have been given armour, you put it in a wardrobe and here you have many enemies attacking you, how will you protect yourself? Tell me, would you be protected? No. So why put the armour inside a wardrobe? Wear it and be disciplined about it, self-disciplined.

Happy New Year, also! Hopefully, next year we have many great *yogis* amongst you all. Well, it's good to hope for something. We have to keep hoping!

THE ART OF CONTROLLING THE MIND

South Africa, January 2010

It was nice to see the difference when all of you were quiet and then all of you were singing. You see, very often we look with our eyes at what our neighbour is thinking. Even though we don't see the thinking, still we think we know what they are thinking. Like that we are never free, we always bother about what people think, what others think of us. How can we sing the Name of God? How will we build our strength inside of us, if we always wonder what our neighbour is thinking? It will not help us.

Tell me, how does it help you when somebody thinks something about you? Does it help you? Then why do you worry about it? When you eat, your neighbour's stomach does not get full. The same thing is true for the opposite. So why are you looking at others? Look at yourself. The Divine is inside of you and the Divine wants to come out, wants to vibrate through you. Stop wondering about other people, because the more you wonder about what other people are thinking, what other people are saying, then you will never be free. When you are singing, when your eyes are open, you are tense.

There are different kinds of meditation. There's one thing that you learn before you start meditating. It is about concentration. To strengthen your power of meditation, to become better in your meditation, you have to learn, firstly, how to control the mind. One way of controlling the mind is through concentration. Just before, I was saying that your mind always wonders about other things. Even while you are sitting, your mind is always jumping around.

When you close your eyes, focus it and concentrate on the Divine, so that you won't allow the mind to jump, you tie it, but this is not going to happen in one day or two.

Firstly, what is concentration? What does the word concentration mean? It means to focus. Concentration, the word concentration, means to fix one's mind on something for an amount of time without being disturbed by any emotions or anything. This means you sit down and you focus without wondering "What is this object, why is this object, for what use is the object?" Just sit and focus. Just concentrate on the object only for five minutes a day. At that moment, you should not think of anything. You choose the object and just look at the object and how it is. This will help you to bring your mind into a controlled state where, later on, you can utilise the power of this realisation.

A part of this realisation is one's greater power. We develop our inner strength. We are not just this human aspect that you see on the outside, but we also have a Divine Self. In that Divine Self there are many qualities. The qualities of the Divine Self are still only the qualities of the Divine, not the Divine itself. This gift comes when you can handle it, when you can control it. After that, you can meditate.

Whenever you talk about meditation to people, first they sit and close their eyes. That's what you will do when you talk about meditation. You make yourself straight and then close your eyes. When you close your eyes, what do you see? You see thoughts. How are these thoughts at that moment? They are jumping around! We have one word about the mind, which is *manasa puja*. When you do everything in a visualised form within yourself, this increases the power of concentration and this is considered one of the most powerful ways to control the mind, to control yourself and to attain the Divine. *Manasa puja*, have you heard about it?

I will tell you a story. Once there was a great king. He wanted to build big temples for Shiva. At the same time there was a poor man sitting in front of the place where the king wanted to build the temple. Inside of him he was also building the temple for Shiva, but even bigger. When the temple of the king was finished, he sent an invitation to Shiva, which said "Shiva, my Lord, I have built up your temple and I request you, please, come for the inauguration of the temple". Shiva sent a message back saying "My dear king, I would be very happy to come for the temple opening, but I have to go on the same day to another man. He has built a bigger temple than yours and he lives in your kingdom. His temple is much bigger than yours and I have to go, because he is opening it also and it's at the same time as yours." The king was wondering about this. He didn't know that in his kingdom somebody else had been building a bigger temple, so he inquired. He found out that it was this man who had been sitting there, who Shiva had said He had to go to, because he also had been building a temple.

The king went to him and said "You have built the biggest temple for Shiva in my kingdom. I thought I had been building the biggest one ." The man was shocked and said "What are you talking about? I am a poor man, I can't build anything for Shiva." The king replied, "Shiva said to me that you have built the biggest temple." Then the man realised that in his mind, when they were building the temple outside, he was building a temple three times bigger than the one they were building. His concentration was so intense when he was inwardly opening the temple that Shiva was really present there. You see, the power of concentration is very powerful.

Like it is said, man can use only five percent of the human brain and ninety-five percent is sleeping. As the mind is sleeping we also like to sleep and let it always sleep. After so many lives we attain a human body. A human is very special. A human is gifted with the grace of attaining and merging with the Divine and becoming One with the Lord, of realising the Lord within himself. Why do we always limit ourselves? Why do we always like this limitation? Why are we not free?

It is there. It has been given to you, but you forget about it. Work to concentrate, to focus your mind, to make your mind positive. Work through increasing the power and the strength inside of you. When you know that the Divine is with you, you really know He is with you. Whenever you chant the Divine Names, don't think that the Divine is far away. The Divine *is* present, is nearer than your heartbeat. So close is the Lord, you know, but yet we see Him as if He is so far away. When we talk about attaining the Lord, it seems like some distance but, actually, it's not that far.

When you have learned to control your mind, when you have learned to concentrate and focus it, you will see that He is ever sitting in each part of your body, because the human body is not just made of flesh and bones like we say. It is indeed, but when we look at the mystical form of the human body, there are all the Deities present inside. A certain Deity is responsible for each part of your body. This is beautiful. If you can look beyond the physical body and see the Divine, which is seated in each part of you, you will learn to respect this body. You will learn to love it.

What about the word 'Love', which we always talk about? One time in Germany I was asking the question "I always talk about Love, but I was wondering how many of you really understand what I am saying about Love? " We know many forms of love, many kinds of love. In all kinds of love, there is Love, but when we are on the spiritual path, we talk about *unconditional* Love. It's another degree of Love. It's a Love that transcends the mind itself; that transcends what we understand with the mind. It's a Love that even transcends the heart itself.

How many hearts do we have? Well, we have one physical heart and one spiritual heart, but we have only one brain. I have never heard of a spiritual brain. Since you have two hearts and one brain, why does this mind seem so much bigger? Isn't it said that two are stronger than one? This is the illusion that the mind always creates, to show that it is more powerful, to show that it is stronger, that it can control everything. In reality, it can't control anything and it knows that. That's why the mind creates fear, and when you hang with this fear you are never free. That's why on the spiritual path we say "Think with your heart and feel with your heart. Stay in your heart always."

Our physical heart is always hanging out in the realm of thoughts, but our spiritual heart is much stronger. That's what we have to discover. To attain this spiritual heart, the journey is from the physical heart to the spiritual heart, from the spiritual heart to the higher Consciousness. That's the journey for each one of us; if it is not in this lifetime, it will be in the next life, or in the next, next, next life. But if you can do it in this lifetime, don't waste time! Don't lose hope, because we are all part of the Divine, whether we want it or not. Whoever we are, we are This and we will attain Him. It doesn't matter how many lifetimes one takes on Earth. He is the source. He is the beginning and He is the end.

> Even if you don't see any changes that you expect, change is happening inside and you are changing. The moment you chant the name of the Divine, It has the power to cleanse, to liberate you.

Very often people talk about themselves as if they know themselves. You know only one part of yourself, only this self that you think of as yourself now in this life. In this physical body, in this present moment, you think you know yourself. You don't know anything about yourself. If you want to know about yourself, you have to start working. The more you work on yourself, the more the veil of ignorance will be removed, and the more clearly you will see, because you will not see with these two eyes; you will see with the eyes of the spiritual heart. This is where the *sadhana*, your spiritual practice, comes in.

When you started, you wanted to have a quick result, you know, everybody does that. When you stop practising after one month you say "Yes, I am very holy." It's not like that. It takes time, you know. When you look at the Himalayas, there are so many great souls sitting and meditating for years and years and years. Many can't even spend one month's time to sit and meditate daily. One has not to lose one's resolve. Keep practicing, even if you don't *see* the results. When you want to see the result, just know that the change is happening.

There was once a disciple who went to his *Guru* and said "Guruji, please give me advice about how to change." The Guru said "Read the *Srimad Bhagavatam*." So he read it one time and it didn't make any sense to him. He went to the Guru and said "It didn't make any sense to me." The Guru said "Read it again." He read it again and still it made no sense. He went back to the Guru again and he received the same answer. He read it again and again and again and again, until he had read it about, probably, ten times. He was fed up completely and he went back to the Guru and said "Guruji, there should be something else. Please give me more advice." What did the Guru say? "OK, fine." So, the Guru got a very dirty bucket with lots of holes in it. He said to him "Go to the river, fill it with water and bring it to me." You know the word of the Guru is everything. When the Guru says something, even if your stupid mind is jumping around trying to figure it out, you have just to listen, not to think "Oh, this is stupid." You can't do that because through the Guru everything can change.

This reminds me – once in the battlefield, Krishna and Arjuna were on the chariot. Krishna looked up, saw a group of birds flying and said "Oh, look at those beautiful red birds!" Arjuna said "Yes, my Lord, they are beautiful red birds." Krishna said "Well, they are not red, they are blue." "Yes my Lord, they are blue", replied Arjuna. Then, Krishna said "Oh, no, but they are not blue, they are green." Arjuna said "Yes, my Lord, they are green." Krishna said to Arjuna "But why, when it's the same bunch of birds, you are just saying 'yes' to me?" Then Arjuna said "You are my Lord. I know that you can change anything. This is nothing. So if you say it's blue, it is blue. Even if my eyes see it as a different colour, my eyes can be wrong." Coming back to our little story, the disciple went to the river, got the water and as he was coming up, all the water dripped out completely. So he went to the Guru and said "The water has come out" and the Guru said "Go back, again, and get water!" Again and again he went – ten times going and coming. He was tired and in the same way he was reading the *Srimad Bhagavitam* ten times, getting nothing, he could not see any difference in the bucket. He said "Guruji, nothing!" and the Guru replied "My dear child, look properly. Each time you were going down and coming up, the bucket was cleaner and cleaner." It was shining, but in his mind he was expecting something else, so he could not see that the change was happening!

It's the same thing with your spiritual practice. Even if you don't see any changes that you expect, change is happening inside and you *are* changing. The moment you chant the name of the Divine, It has the power to cleanse, to liberate you. You do *Japa* hundreds of thousands of times every day, no? How many times does the name of the Divine come out from your heart? You don't know about it, but the Lord knows about it. You chant it many times and maybe, out of these thousands of times, just one fraction of that *mantra* really comes out from your heart.

You chant it a thousand times just to get this fraction. This fraction of *mantra* chanted from your heart is even more powerful than any millions of *mantras* that you can chant, because this one comes from deep within your heart and it's full of Love – this goes directly to Him, but the rest cannot even touch His shadow. Imagine when people say "OK, I did this 108 times." 108 times your mind was there or not?

Keep chanting the Divine names until you really perceive this great Love inside of you, until you feel this great Love inside of you and don't stop it. Until you feel it, don't stop it. Know that each time you are chanting the Divine Names changes are happening, whether you see it or not. Remember, always, this story that I have just told you. There are always changes. When you look at the world around, you see that each second, things are changing and you are changing, also. You are becoming better, I hope!

WHAT IS SHIVA MEDITATING UPON?

Darshan at Shree Peetha Nilaya, Springen, Germany, 5 February 2010

Right now we are in the time of preparing for *Shivaratri,* which is the great night of Lord Shiva, one of the main Deities in the Hindu tradition whom we venerate as the One who is with form and without form. When we look at the image of Lord Shiva, we see that He's always sitting in deep meditation. Why? What does He teach us here? He's *Pashupati,* He's the Lord of all creation, yet He is meditating.

What is Shiva meditating upon? He is a realised soul. He is fully One with the Divine, but He is always in deep meditation. It's to remind us that we will realise our true Self only when we will be in that deep state of meditation. We have not yet realised the purpose of our incarnation on Earth, we have not yet realised how great it is to have a human body, but we can reach that state. We have to really want it, but not superficially.

Very often people go on a spiritual path in a very superficial way, saying "Let me try it. Let me see what it is about", but these people will not reach anywhere. If you have one foot in and one foot out, one day you will drop in the middle. It's like it is said – you can't enter two boats at the same time, because when the boats start to move, what will happen? You will fall in the middle; you will fall in the ocean. In the same way, if the boat is sinking, you have to run quickly and find the boatman, so that he can help you to cross this ocean of life.

By being in deep meditation, Shiva is inspiring you all to look inside, to turn your gaze not to the outside, but inside. You all know how to meditate, no? You sit down and close your eyes. Is this meditation? Most of the time, when you tell people to meditate, they sit down, close their eyes and meditate, but they don't even know *why* they are meditating! They are meditating because you told them to meditate, because you asked them to sit and meditate like this, but what is the purpose of meditation?

There are many purposes. Now I ask you to give me some reasons why you meditate. Like I have said before, this question will have hundreds of answers, because each person is trying to find something that is corresponding to what they want, what they need. Like she just said, meditation is to find one's Self, but the question is how? It's not just by sitting and closing the eyes that one will find one's Self.

Let's analyse how the human body is. The *Shastras* say that the human body is made of the five elements, the *Pancha Tattva*. If you look at these five elements, they are constantly at war with each other. They can't be in peace with each other. Can water be in peace with fire? No, it can't be! That's why in the human body there is so much imbalance. Even if you see somebody appearing perfect on the outside, there's no such thing as perfection like that. There is always something going wrong in the body. Imagine if all the five elements would start fighting with each other, what would happen? It would be terrible, catastrophic. This is within you, not outside! That is what is happening in people

> Actually, the human being, in the ladder of creation, is at the top. It's true, because only by attaining a human body, a human life, you can really attain the Creator and become One with the Creator.

nowadays.

When you analyse the people, when you look at people walking around, you see them walking, yet they are not present in their body. The elements are so much at war inside of them that they are somewhere else. What keeps these elements in balance in us is the Holy Spirit, the Spirit of God within one's Self. How would you energise this Spirit? If the Spirit leaves you, you fall dead. You lose everything. Here, when you are alive, you say "This is mine, that is mine; it's my possession."

Imagine if the Spirit leaves you; what will happen? What is yours? What is mine? Nothing stays. The *Gita* says " You come with nothing and you will leave with nothing." All that you take, you will leave here. We have incarnated for a reason. We have a human body for a reason, but we will not find this reason until we turn this body into pure Love and devotion. This is where your *sadhana* comes in. When you develop this pure Love and devotion, then you will really know the meaning of this human body; then you will really enjoy being in this body; then you will know the purpose of being here. Otherwise, you will go left-right, left-right, left-right, left-right and when the boat sinks, having no boatman, you will sink. Then you have to wait for another life. So don't waste time, because the time you waste is gone and once it's gone, don't think you will have it again. You are living in the right time, the best time of all.

It is said that to realise the Divine, to realise the Divinity, it's so easy in *this Yuga*, in this moment, but – there is always a 'but' – what makes it difficult is us. Look, whenever something good happens to you how easy it is for you to forget about it. Good things are always happening, but when something not good happens to you, you treasure it. You treasure it with your mind. Your mind has to dwell on the Divine, not on your problems.

While I was coming here, I met one *Mataji* outside and I asked her "How are you?" She said "Too many problems!" I said "Well *Mataji*, by drinking, problems will not be solved." Like that, there are so many people who think they can solve their problems by an outside means. No, you will not solve your problems by any outside means. You will solve your problems by the means which God has given to you within yourself – by faith and devotion. If you develop these qualities, if you make use of these qualities that God has given you, it will be the best medicine to cure everything.

Like I explained a few months back, when somebody goes to a Saint and says "Oh, Mr. Saint, please, heal me" and the Saint says "OK, just take this medicine and you will get well", what makes it happen? It's the faith that the Saint has that the person will get healed. So this faith makes everything happen, makes the healing happen, resolves all of your problems – not the drinking, not the smoking. These are just excuses that humans always try to find and they get peace just for a short while and then after that, more trouble. Even the *Devas*, even the angels, even the Gods and Goddesses envy this human body. They all envy human beings. One will say, but why? Why do the Demigods and Goddesses envy human beings? Actually, the human being, in the ladder of creation, is at the top. It's true, because only by attaining a human body, a human life, you can really attain the Creator and become One with the Creator. They can't do it. They can't do it because they have their duty.

The *Devas* have their duty and they have to fulfil their duty, so they can't say "I let go of my duty and merge with the Divine." It's impossible for them to do that, because they have to do their duty! Indra has to do His duty; Varun has to do His duty. What if Varun said "OK, today I will leave my job. I quit!" We can go to a job and say "OK, I will leave this job; I am finished with it." But imagine if Varun were to say "I am leaving my job and I am finished with it!" What will happen to the whole of Creation? There will be an imbalance, because Varun is the God of Water. If there's no water, it finishes! They are bound by their duty. The same thing with angels and *Devas* – they are all bound by their duty.

They can't leave their duty and become One with the Creator, whereas we can leave everything and become One with the Creator, but we have to want Him. To want Him means to devote oneself sincerely, to develop this pure Love that is already there, just to let it out and let it spread around. With this devotion and pure Love, one will realise that the Divine is not outside, but it is inside, in this microcosmic form of the Universe that He has implanted in us. When a *yogi* looks inside of himself, he doesn't see in the same way that human beings see things, because human beings want to see many things. How many human beings want to see the Ultimate within them? If you haven't found the Ultimate inside of you, how would you find the Ultimate outside? How would you find it in all His Creation? We say God pervades everything but how many people achieve this state? Very few! Like in the *Gita*, it said "Out of a million, only few will attain Him."

Through the Divine Names, which have been given, go inside. Utilise the Cosmic Names of God and attain Him. That's what Shiva teaches us. That's what all the Deities, if you analyse them properly, teach us: to realise this oneness with the Creator. We have to take time and be patient. Not in one month of spiritual practice will you attain the Divine, not even in one year! If you read the *Vedas*, if you read the *Upanishads*, you will see that it took *yogis* hundreds of years to attain the Divine, but it was that age. So it's a lucky age now, because just by chanting the Divine Names you can attain Him. It's so simple, no?

You know there is a thing called dying while you are still alive, which means *samadhi*. We will do a meditation and, if you do it properly, you can go into *Samadhi*. It doesn't mean that you will die. No, you will come back again. If you think you will not be coming back, please write a note, OK? It's very simple. If you don't have a *mantra*, just chant, *Om Namo Bhagavate Vasudevaya Namaha.*

A guided meditation

- Close your eyes.
- Take few deep breaths. Inhale and exhale. Remove all your tension. Remove all the thoughts from your mind. As you are breathing out, let all the thoughts from the mind be released.
- Inhale and exhale, without any break in between. Inhale, directly exhale and when you have exhaled completely, directly inhale.
- Now focus your attention in between your eyebrows. Whatever thought is in your mind, which is passing by, don't try to stop it, let it pass, let it go! Don't hang onto it, because if you hang onto it, it will hang onto you.
- Focus your attention on the centre point in between your eyebrows and chant the *mantra* at that point. Don't chant the *mantra* in the heart, but chant it in between your eyebrows.
- Chant it slowly and feel each word of the *mantra* that you are chanting.
- Now, come back to yourself and open your eyes.

Maybe you have not reached the *samadhi* state, but like I said, you will not reach it in one go. This is how you can energise the Divine Names inside of you, how you can energise the Spirit with the Divine Name. So practice it; do it for 15 minutes every day. It's not much.

You see, when you sing *bhajans*, I noticed many people had their eyes wide open, but if you close your eyes, you will meet Ram inside of your heart. The mind gets distracted very easily on the outside.

By looking with these eyes, you get distracted. You say "Oh that is beautiful." You think it is beautiful, but it's not beautiful. The beauty lies inside of you. Even if you are looking at the beauty on the outside, what you have on the inside is much more beautiful, because what you see in the outside will fade, but what you see in the inside will never fade. So when you chant the name of the Lord, look inside and you will find Him. If you open your eyes and look in the outside, you will just see *Maya. Maya, Maya, Maya.* You will be in *Mayajaal*, nothing else! You will be in the play of *Maya.*

That's why, when you look at somebody who is really enjoying the *bhajans*, when someone is *really* enjoying the singing, what do they do? Their eyes are always closed. When somebody knows a song by heart their eyes are always closed. Why? It's because their concentration is deep inside. It's the same thing when you sing for the Lord: try to close your eyes and find Him inside of you. Don't let yourself be distracted by the outside, because it will all disappear and so will you. Find the real One!

AWAKEN THE SPIRIT OF HELPING

Darshan Shree Peetha Nilaya, Springen, Germany, 13 March 2010

As most of you know, I just returned from Kenya. Actually, I will not talk a lot today, but I would like to share something with you, something which, every time I go to Kenya, we always do with the *seva* group there. Since I started this *seva* group five or six years ago, they have been carrying on this *seva* to the handicapped and blind children. I will share this with you, because we have to be grateful to God, to Divine Mother, that we are full, that we can use our hands, we can use each part of our body. There's no point in complaining, but yet many people, in spite of having everything working properly, like complaining.

As I say very often, what you see, sometimes, in the eyes of people who don't have much, you don't see in the eyes of people who have a lot, because often people who have a lot are never satisfied with life. They are never satisfied with what they have. You know that very well. The more one is in the material world and the more one has, the more one wants. The mind is always running to the outside, forgetting that we are not here to run to the outside. We are here to run to the inside.

I went to Kenya again after three and half years, and this trip of five days there was amazing. The day we arrived, in the afternoon, we went directly to the home to see the handicapped children there. The next day there was the *Darshan*, so I was very, very busy. Almost every day we went to bed at 2 or 3 o'clock in the morning, but it was worthwhile. The *seva* group there, the people who have carried on this work, are amazing.

I will just share a little bit, just a few pictures where you can see the project there. After seeing these pictures, take a look at yourself. Look at how your life is and thank God for whatever He has given you and be grateful about life. Awaken the spirit of helping inside of you.

We are all running after the Love of God, but what is the Love of God? The Love of God is the Love that you can express. You express Love towards the Divine, of course, but it doesn't have to be only to God, but to anyone who needs help. As it is said, if you want to experience the Love of God, help, do charity. This will open the heart, because when you do charity, you don't think of yourself, you think of serving. That's what Christ said " The least you do to my brothers, you are doing it unto me." The little you do to someone who really is in need, you are doing it to the Lord. In return, He is giving you much more. In return He is filling your heart with lots of Love.

> **If you want to experience the Love of God, help, do charity. This will open the heart, because when you do charity, you don't think of yourself, you think of serving.**

It reminds me of a Saint; once a man went to Him and said "Dear Saint, tell me, how can I love the same way you love?" This man was a doctor. The Saint closed His eyes and thought for a while, saying "My dear doctor, I know you treat a lot of people, but for all that you do, for all the people you treat, you always take money. So do one thing: once a week, treat for free! Whoever comes to you, give your treatment for free."

The doctor listened to the Saint and he practiced it. After a few months, the Saint approached him again and said "How are you?"

He saw that the doctor was radiating so much joy and happiness. He said to the doctor, "You seem very happy nowadays." The doctor said to the Saint "Yes, my dear Saint, I have taken what you have said to me and I have practiced it. Once a week, I give free treatments to everybody who comes and truly this has opened my heart and this has made me really feel a great happiness inside of me."
You see, when you start to think of others, God will give you the most important thing. Some people will say "Yeah, but many people help." Yes, there are many people who help, but the help doesn't come from the heart. Help doesn't mean that you have to go to a house like this or help these kinds of people. Help means anything and everything! You can go into nature and do something simple, help planting a tree where it is needed or if you see some trash on the way you pick it up. Something like this is also help, a help to nature. The next project that the *Vishwananda Seva Group* in Kenya will be doing is taking care of abandoned animals – dogs, cats, even other wild animals whose mothers have died when giving birth.

Some comments of Swami about the pictures that were projected on the Darshan evening:

1. This is the home for children. I will tell you something – when you look at their eyes, there's so much joy in them. When they smile, it's truly from the heart. It's not just for the sake of smiling, but really from deep within them that their smile comes and you really feel it.
2. These are some wheelchairs that we gave.
3. Look in their eyes! Even if they are disabled, there is Love.
4. This picture is amazing. These are three children from three confessions. One is Muslim, the middle one is Christian, and the third one, I think, his mum or dad is Hindu and the other parent is

local, but they are all blind. When they prayed, they were all sitting on the same table, but each one was doing his own prayer in his own language, in his own faith.

5. Some of these children don't even have spines.

6. What they are doing there is teaching the children to be self-sufficient so they don't have to be dependent on anyone.

7. They cook the food there.

8. You see he's eating with his feet. I will tell you something amazing: I was sitting with him and it reminded me of an uncle my mum had. He was a brother of my grandma. He was also handicapped of the hands, but he could eat with the feet. He could draw the most amazing pictures and this boy is the same. He can write better than my own handwriting.

9. These are children with brains that get big hydrocephalus and the parents can't even help them, they can't do anything. Some of them are just thrown away, just like that, in the bin. You see in this culture there it's like this; when a child is born handicapped, most of them always think it is from the devil. They think it's a curse. So because of fear of society, they throw their children away; they throw them in the bin. Sometimes they leave them right in front of the home. They just leave them.

10. That's Rakesh who is standing there. He's in charge of the *seva* group. It's him who is pushing the group there into this *seva* direction.

11. They are handicapped, but they help each other. Sometimes people have their feet, everything is perfect, but they never help someone else.

12. You see here this girl – the one who is taking the biscuit right now – she was so sweet. It was nice, because next to her there was another boy and before she would eat, she would feed him first.

I guess that's it. Just a little bit. I didn't want to shock you or anything, but to show you so that you can open your hearts more.

There are a lot of people who need help! Of course, we all need help, but there are people who need help more than us. So think about that.

THE JOY OF SERVING

Darshan, Holy Saturday,
Shree Peetha Nilaya, Springen, Germany, 3 April 2010

Today as I was sitting with the Czech group, somebody asked me a question about eternal Love, about God's Love. Actually, the infusion of the Divine Love is present everywhere. There is not a moment when this Love is not present. That's what gives us the power to act, that's what gives us the power to do everything. The question is, why don't we feel this Divine Love all the time? Why do we feel it only sometimes and then sometimes it is just dormant? The thing is, the Divine Love always flows through us, but we are not always with the Divine Love. That's why very often we don't feel this Divine connection, but if we are always in connection with this Divine Love, if we are always in connection with this Divine consciousness, we will always feel it. This comes to the point we always want and want. Are we ready to also let go of certain things? We are celebrating Easter now. Christ showed us a great example. By taking the Cross, He resurrected to show us that until we let go of everything, even our pride and ego, we will never be free. Until we let go of certain things, of how our mind thinks, we will not find God, because we darken Him. We darken the light which is inside of us. We put our own shadow around this light and we blind ourselves and then we say "We are blind."

We don't want to see. Even when we say "Yes, we want to see", yet there is a thick shadow around us, so how will we see? A blind man wants to see, but there is a veil over the eyes. Until this veil is removed, we will stay blind. This veil is our ignorance. This veil is our pride. Are we ready to renounce it? How many are ready to humble themselves? Because this light, which is inside of us, has left God to incarnate, it is a great form of humility itself. Once this light has incarnated here, it builds up the shield. The mind builds up a shield that darkens this light.

An easy way one will feel this Love is through service – *Karma Yoga*. There are three kinds of *yoga*: *Jnana Yoga, Karma Yoga* and *Bhakti Yoga*. Of course, all these three *yoga* systems go together hand in hand. They can't exist one without the other. One can't be ignorant if one is on the spiritual path, be ignorant of the Divine, so all three go together and one of the easiest – what the *Vedas* always say – is *bhakti*.

One simple form is through Karma Yoga, through the joy of serving. If you want to feel the Divine Love, try to make somebody else happy.

For some, *bhakti* is very difficult. Even if it is the simpler one, in *bhakti* one needs lots of dedication, but nowadays people are not so dedicated. Very often they will find more excuses for not doing their *sadhana* than finding excuses to do their *sadhana*. I have heard many excuses like that.

One simple form is through *Karma Yoga*, through the joy of serving. If you want to feel the Divine Love, try to make somebody else happy. If you can make somebody who is not happy, happy, you will be able to remove some of the shields, some of the layers, which are around this Divine Love and Divine light.

In the word *Karma Yoga*, the first part is *karma* – service – and the second part is *yog*. *Yog* is union. Through doing *Karma Yoga*, through doing service, you bring the union that you have inside of you, inside somebody else. Through that union, lots of karmic negativity that you have created from previous lives is being burnt. That's why the more service you do and the more help you give, the better it is.

Some people will say "Yes, but sometimes there are people who do service just like that", but even that creates certain joy. Even if it is just a little bit of joy inside of you that you can perceive with your mind, this little bit of joy, when it is all amassed together, becomes a big joy. One of the easiest ways is through service, through helping. Some time ago I was talking with somebody and he asked "But Swamiji, how will we know who to help?" You know, this is also another question, because nobody wants to depart from what they have. Look, Christ has given a beautiful example by saying if your right hand gives, your left hand should not know. This is beautiful, isn't it?

Why is it beautiful? Because it doesn't matter to you if you are giving and you are helping; it doesn't matter whom you are helping. If you think the person needs help, even if the person doesn't need help, if you are doing it with the right intention, it is always good for you. To do things with the right intention, that's the best.

I was laughing one time with Pritala. He was telling me, that his father always used to give when some people who drink would ask for money. The father would give them some money and say "Drink in my name." You see, it brings joy to that person. It's not to encourage them to drink, but from your side, if you are giving, it doesn't matter what the person does with it. It is not yours anymore: it's theirs. So feel the joy inside of you and forget about it. Don't hang onto it, because if you hang onto it, you will never be free. You will never feel this Love, because you will have expectation. You will expect, but know that every expectation will bring pain.

That's the easiest way and once you have felt it, then you can find the inner Love, you can look for the Divine Love within you. You will see that when you render service outside, you will be freer and when you are freer, you will feel more. When you sit down for your meditation, you will see the Divine Light inside of you, you will feel it more inside of you, because there will be nothing stopping you. Your mind will rejoice because you are free, whereas when your mind is so filled with so many things, how can you be free? You will never be free.

Last time I gave an example. In the life of Sri Ramakrishna there was a doctor in a certain village. Whenever Ramakrishna would see the doctor, the doctor was always with a heavy face, sad. Ramakrishna said to him "Why are you sad, doctor?" He said "I don't know. I come to you. Give me a solution to be happy. Give me a way that I can feel the Love of God and be happy." Ramakrishna said "Look, doctor, I know every day you have hundreds of people, you charge them lots of money, but even that doesn't make you happy. So do one thing: one day a week, give service for free."

After some time, the doctor came to Dakshineshwar again and Ramakrishna saw him; he was very joyful and very happy, radiating so much joy and happiness. Ramakrishna said "Doctor, you look different today. What is the secret of it?" Then he said to him "Well, I took your advice and I started to give one day a week, free of charge, service to everybody. The more I do it, the more I feel to do it more and more, because this brings me great joy inside and this great joy doesn't finish."

Like that, there are many examples that can be given about how service brings the union of the mind, the heart and the spirit and makes you whole. Don't be scared to serve, in whatever way you can, however you can, whenever you can, because you don't know when God can come to you and in what form He can come to you. Feel blessed and feel the Love of God!

WITH EVERY STEP YOU TAKE...

Darshan, Steffenshof, Germany, 9 April 2005

Isn't it beautiful to sing the name of Narayana? Let yourself be drawn into it? Such is the greatness of the name of God, that whoever is singing it with an open heart, whoever is singing it with faith, will be pulled more inside. And the more you go into it, the more you lose yourself in this Divine name, the identity of being human disappears. What stays is only the Divine; that which you all are. Removing the body, who are you? The soul, isn't it? What is the soul? The soul is with a stain on it. The stain is in the mind of man. By singing the name of God, any aspect, Krishna, Jesus, Allah – it has to be sung with devotion and Love. It is nice when you join together and sing the name of God, it creates this vibration, it creates this urge of merging in God.

That's why it is very important, wherever you are, find a few people and sing. If you don't know how to sing, just recite Divine names. When you recite the names, picture the form of the Divine in your mind. Keep concentrating on the form and let yourself flow, let yourself just slide in this Divine energy. And enjoy it! Remove all the darkness from the mind, remove all the barriers and just jump into it. *Bhakti*! There are different ways of attaining God, but one way is bhakti – devotion! You can have devotion to the *Guru*, complete surrender to the Guru's feet. Devotion has no limit. When you open up your heart, Love flows – do you think Love has a limit? This Love doesn't have any limit, but the love here *(points towards the head)* has a lot of limits. As long as we limit this Love, as

171

long as we say love has to be like this or like that, do you think we will attain this Divine Love?

We can't. I can talk about Love, I know about Love. All of you know about Love, but for you to really know it, you have to experience it. And to experience it, you have to let go of the egoism, let go of the "I" that keeps you from realising yourself. Remove the "I", let you and God merge together. Like sugar, when merged with water, they become one. In the same way, let yourself merge together and disappear in the Love of God. There will be no sugar; there will be no egoism that separates man from being Divine, because only the Divine exists. Only the universal consciousness of man exists. Being separate, we see the duality of things. We experience the love, hate, jealousy and all of these things.

Being the consciousness, being completely Divine, all this disappears – you become as you were before. And that is for everybody, it's not only for me. It's not only for a few people who are around me; it's for all of you, even people who are not here. It's accessible to everybody. If people really take time, just drop inside – everything is there. But how many people really take this time? They meditate for little bit, that's it. "Too long, let's stop it!" You see, the mind of man expects quick results – lack of patience! Everything, when done without patience doesn't last long! It's the same with prayer. A new job, if you aren't really patient in this job, what happens? You get fed up, you get tired of it and you try to look for another one. How long you will continue like that? One time, two times, three times, four times...? One day you have to say "Enough is enough!" So don't waste time, say "Enough is enough!" now!

You have to look inside. When the ears are turned inward, the Lord will reveal Himself to you, your Self will reveal itself to you. But you have to be sincere with yourself for that. You really have to take your time, and really enjoy it. So many times people told me "Oh you know, half an hour of meditation is already long, and one hour is too long!" You should not force yourself, if you can't meditate for half an hour, you should not do it. If you can do it for one minute, do a perfect one! Now there is one minute between you and God, between you and your Self – enjoy it! It's better than meditating for a whole day and not attaining anything!

So keep practicing. I always said and keep saying it all the time, on this way, you also have to make your effort. The moment you make an effort, the Lord will run to you. There is a saying "Make one step towards God, and he will make a hundred towards you," it's true. The moment you are sincere with yourself and you make this one step, you'll receive it. The door will be wide open, and you will see the Lord running to you! You know how beautiful it is to experience that? How joyful it is? Words can't express it. I can

> **Don't be scared to open up your heart; don't be scared of getting hurt. Just love for the sake of loving. Just love because you are Love. Just love because you have this fountain inside of you.**

just say "joyful", I can just say "very happy," but it is beyond that. It is beyond the word "love" itself! In the mind we can imagine it, how it is to be continuously, constantly in love. It's marvellous.

This Love is unconditional, it's without expecting anything. It's just flowing and flowing. Be this instrument, all of you! Don't be scared to open up your heart; don't be scared of getting hurt. Just love for the sake of loving. Just love because you are Love. Just love because you have this fountain inside of you. The more this Love is open, the more this tap of the heart is open, the greater will be the flow of Love.

As long as you expect something in return, you invite sadness and grief to come. You will never be happy, because you have expectations, and expectations bring sadness. Even when you sit down for meditation, or when you are singing the name of God, don't expect that God will appear in front of you! Many people think that there will be "poof", a big light, and you will see Jesus saying "Hi, my child!" Remove this from your mind. Just do it because you love to do it.

SPIRITUALITY STARTS WITH THE MIND

Darshan, Munich, Germany, 4 June 2005

What I would like to talk about with you today is meditation and thought. Lots of people meditate. Meditation is very good. Once you start the spiritual way, the first thing they tell you is to sit down and meditate. But you can`t meditate for twenty-four hours, it's quite difficult, isn't it? For some yogis it is possible – but even them, after some time they do take a rest. Some yogis can stay in samadhi for days. For years! But after that they have to take a rest. I have met a yogi in India who is about two hundred years old. Even more than that – there are more. Of course among all the yogis, the Raj yogi Mahavatar Babaji is more than five thousand years old. Raj Yogi means the king of all yogis, but even Him, He walks around with people. So, we can't meditate always – especially here in the West. But there is a substitute to it – the thought. The mind that God has placed in humans is very powerful.

You can create or you can destroy. It's upon each one of you how to control it. The first thing in spirituality, the best thing you can do is to control the thought. The more the thoughts are negative, it reflects outside. Very often these negative thoughts are about one's own self – thinking "How bad I am, how negative I am." You know you are negative but you enjoy it. But why enjoy it? First we have to change the thoughts about ourselves. Then we can change the thoughts towards other people. As long as we self-judge, we only look at the negative parts of our own self. Thoughts are very easy to control. You don't need to sit down to control them. When the thought is passing through your mind, you know about the thought. You know whether it is positive or negative. So if it is positive it will be constructive – feed it, then let it grow! But when it is negative, try not to feed it. Then you say to yourself – "This is not me!" And let go of it. When you let go of the thought you will see how beautiful your own life is. How great it truly is, this life that God has given you. In your meditation you will be more easy-going. The powerful thought is the positivity in human being. Through this thought, whatever you wish, whatever you think about for your own self, you will receive it.

The thought is the willpower of man. It's the way that you use to realise the Divine. All spirituality starts here – in the mind. Then it reaches the heart. You use thought to open the heart. And this thought of the heart – you may want to call it the voice of God – you will learn to listen to it, without any doubt. Whenever you will sit in meditation, you will then feel that deep bliss and the consciousness that you are Divine, will be always with you. Whatever you are doing, wherever you are – you will have the consciousness that the Divine is with you. There are different ways of controlling the thought. I told you to stop it the moment you know it

The mind that God has placed in humans is very powerful. You can create or you can destroy. It's upon each one of you how to control it.

is negative. The next is to sing the name of God, to keep reciting. God has taken many forms and in each form there is energy to transcend man, from mere human to Divine. As long you have not mastered controlling of the mind, you use *namasmarana*. Sing the name of God, wherever you are. And when you sing don't close your eyes, leave them open. You see, when you close your eyes, you start thinking. And then you say "Oh I'm singing the name of God" but the thinking is still there. The mind is still jumping like a monkey. Leave them open. If you don't want to focus on a form, concentrate on something formless; a white wall. Focus on it!

There are also different asanas to control the thought. One which is well used is the tree asana, where you stand on one leg. The other one is lifted up completely, to the maximum, with your hand upright and focusing also on a picture, or on the white wall. This helps a lot to control the mind. You will see that by doing this, you will experience how unbalanced human beings are sometimes. When the thoughts are pure you will also reflect this purity. Wherever you are, this Love will always flow and people will see you reflect divinity. Not the egoistic way, but with the Love, there will be no misery if you reflect the light of God. All the misery that you see outside, the responsible is one's own mind. If the mind, the thoughts you have, will be pure, there will not be such misery. In this world, humans think that they are only humans, and they enjoy this humanhood. Very often they forget that behind this humanhood there is also divinity. To reach this, they should not have fear, as it is your true nature, what you really are. You just need to want it sincerely. Want it sincerely to your own self! Then from inside to the outside it'll reflect.

HABITS CHANGE

Darshan, Shree Peetha Nilaya Springen, Germany, 26 February 2011

A few days ago, somebody asked me "Swamiji you always say to pray to God, always, but I'm working on the outside. How will I attain the Divine?" I think many of you ask this question. The answer is simple. There is one sentence in the Gita about doing one's duty. One can't neglect one's duty. In the Gita it said that the *dharma*, one has to do. No matter what, *dharma* is very important, but how one has to do it, that is the most important thing.
There is one form of doing one's duty, which is *nishkama karma,* which means to do one's duty without expecting anything, to do one's duty in rendering service to others without even thinking of the result. That is what the Gita said "Whatever one does, if one is attached to the fruit of the action, one will suffer." It's true, because when we expect certain things, when we do certain things, there is always certain expectation and when the expectation is not met, what happens? You get sad, no? You feel upset. Where does this come from? *You* created it. You make yourself sad.
So when one does one's duty without even expecting something that means that the mind is already surrendering to the Divine. In another way, the mind, when it has the *sattvic* quality, the mind doesn't have any power into it. This is where whatever one does is a complete surrender to the Divine, but whereas when one gets a little mixture of *rajasic* quality with *sattvic* quality, then one, always, says "I will do good to the world." In that state we'll see that the *I* is very big. Whenever the mind pictures the *I*, it doesn't mean

the *I* of the Self; it means, always, the *I* of the ego "I can do this; I can do that." As long as you have not Realised your Self, the *I* of the ego is always big. That's why it is said in the Scripture: Remove this I. Put Him, you know, the Lord, because as long as one has not realised anything, one has to remind oneself continuously that All is Him.

Even what you perceive that you are doing yourself, actually, it is Him which is acting through you. That's why the great Sages, when they have realised themselves, they always praise the Lord by saying "Lord, I am the vehicle, but you are the one who is driving it. I am the chariot, but you are the charioteer. I am the wick of the lamp, but you are the light. I am the house, but you are the dweller of that house." So in that state one has fully transcended the human nature seeing only the Divine working in everything. In that state, one sees the world in a different angle, not the same as with the egoistic mind point of view. Often people come, they say "Oh, Swamiji, I have seen this vision and that vision." No, no, because people always want to think that they are special in whatever they do. Very often, without judgment, you see them very proudly "Oh, I have seen that. I have seen this.", but what is that if it is not just pride? Because when one comes face to face with the Divine and really experiences something from the Divine, one doesn't talk about it. One treasures it as the most precious treasure inside one's heart. In that state, the mere mention of the Divine Name will make one cry out of joy knowing that this experience that one has received from the Divine, is real. And this is all due to the *nishkama karma*.

> Wherever your dharma is, wherever God has put you, no matter what kind of work he has lead you to, there's a reason for that.

Whenever you do your duty, it doesn't matter where you are, it doesn't matter what you do if you do it with a mind surrendered to the Divine, if you do it with your heart completely full of Love, even there God will come to you. I always give an example. There was once somebody who cleans the road. People always consider this job as a very low job. They will always say "What will somebody like this be?" There was once a great Saint. He would always clean the road and one day when he was sweeping, Krishna Himself came to him and said to him "Bless you, because though you clean the road for me to pass every day, you never ask for anything. You never even ask me for my blessing. You just do it out of Love knowing that this road leads to the temple. That's why, today, I came to you." Like that, there are so many Saints, you know – in the lives of Saints that I can give you – who were in the outside world doing very simple things, but yet, deep inside of them they are fully connected with the Divine. That shows that wherever your *dharma* is, wherever God has put you, no matter what kind of work he has lead you to, there's a reason for that and if you do it with Love and real happiness, real joy inside of you, even there you can Realise God. For sure nowadays we can't ask everybody continuously to think of God, which will be quite difficult, but from time to time if one has a little bit of time, in place of gossiping, in place of doing unnecessary things, if one takes the time and communicates with the Divine within one's Self, that will help.

So in this communication, when you are alone with the Divine, you have also to learn to listen. And how would you listen? If the mind is busy, it's very difficult, you know. So that's why it is said to first chant the Divine Name to calm your mind. When you chant the Divine Name, don't just chant it mechanically and do some other rubbish things like many do, you know. They think that yes, by doing that in place of thinking of other things, God will come to them. No, it will not happen. Then it's just purely mechanical.

But when you chant the Divine Name, you have to fully have the vision inside of you. You have to have the Divine Image inside of your mind. Then you are chanting the Divine Name. Then He will manifest Himself. If you are chanting doing something else, you know, "I'm doing this whatever, yet I am chanting the Divine Name", it doesn't help. So even if you can't do it, just try.

It doesn't mean much to try, no? It's easy to try something, no? It's true that old habits catch up from time to time but old habits do change with time. There are always new habits. So you see, even with the old habits, whenever there is something to change, one will always change. It's like when you drive, you always go to work on the same road, no? But when there is a diversion, what do you do? Do you carry on going through the same road? You go for the diversion, no? So in the same way, old habits change.

So to try something, it is easy actually, but you have to say to yourself "I want to change certain things." This is the first step. If you don't take the first step, well, it will not come to you. And this first step, you must take and when you take it, take it with a strong determination that no matter what, you will achieve it through God's Grace, knowing that He is with you. If you are doing something to please Him, He will help you. And I'm telling you, the Divine Mother is such a good help for that. Don't miss a chance and even if you can't, just ask Him for help or ask Her. She will come to help you because this is Her joy to see Her children awake, you know. Even in the simple things you do, She will come and help you. So just try. It's the same as *bhajans*. You can try to sing also, and if you can't, just clap your hands. It's easy, no?

THE ONLY TRUTH,
THE ONLY REALITY IS... HIM

Darshan, Bremen, Germany, 10 April 2011

SRI RAM JAYA RAM.. JAI JAI RAMA SRI RAM JAYA RAM
JAI JAI RAMA ...
Jai Gurudev. It is so easy – Sri Ram Jaya Ram Jai Jai Rama so please,
sing. I hope you slept well last night. You are full of energy this
morning, no? It doesn't matter if your voice is not nice. Don't judge
yourself. If you are singing for God, as long as it's coming from your
heart, don't think what your neighbour is thinking. Yesterday I was
explaining to them, this mantra, the name of Rama. The name of
Rama is so short. Three syllables R-A-M. In three syllables is the
whole *Trimurthi* inside of it. The combination of Bramha, Vishnu
and Shiva. This combination of these three makes the name of
Rama very powerful. In Sanskrit, you write Rama, Ra and Am. Ra
which means Narayana, and Am is Shiva. The combination of these
two together makes Rama. It's a very powerful mantra; it is said
that just by chanting the mantra name of Rama, one attains mukti.
That's why in India older ladies always chant Sita Ram, Sita Ram,
you will always see them in the corner, chanting.
It's good! At least one is thinking for the future. Because if you
don't train yourself to take the name of God, as it is said, while
passing away, while you are dying, if you take the Divine name, any
of God's names, the Divine names liberate you. They can grant you
liberation, or can release you from certain bondage of karma, so
that in the future life, you have a better life, a better way so that

you can attain the Divine.

Don't think it's so easy. If you don't practice, it's very difficult. That's why in spirituality, when you start your spiritual way, it doesn't matter which religion you belong to, the first thing is it tell you to do, is to chant, recite the Divine names, God's name – take your rosary, take your mala – chant! Only by chanting, this mind can calm itself. Last week someone said "Swamiji, I was chanting so many times, but yet my mind is still busy." When you chant, let's say you are chanting the name of Rama or Christ – when you chant, you should not do it mechanically just like that. When you are chanting you have also to have the vision of the Lord inside of you. As long as you don't visualise Him inside of your head, your mind will not calm down. How will the un-manifested Brahman, the un-manifested truth, reveal itself to you? With the mind? No, it will not. The only truth, the only reality, is only Him. The Upanishad says "Brahma, Sathyam Jagath Nethram" which means "Everything is an illusion, except the Lord." You also have the words La Illah Illa Allah. There is only God nothing else. Like that, the scriptures reveal that God, the Ultimate truth, is everywhere. But it manifests itself in two qualities of Purusha and Prakriti. What is Purusha? The un-manifested force. And what is Prakriti? The opposite; Prakriti is the manifestation. Whatever is manifested in this universe is the Prakriti Shakti, which is the will of the Purusha, the will of God. That's why in the Bible, when you read, the first thing it says; God willed, and everything is manifested. But into the will, the Purusha also infused Himself, because the Purusha and Prakriti, these two energies the Yin and Yang, or the male and female energy, can't be separate from eachother. The Purusha, you will call it the spirit, and the Prakriti, the manifestation, you will call it whatever you see outside. So the Purusha dwells, from the un-manifested, dwelling into the Prakriti Shakti, and does everything through the Prakriti, through the manifestation. When one enjoys

J U S T   L O V E   2

the world, one is bound by the manifestation. Of course at that time, the spirit is hidden deep inside. In our physical body when we look at it, there are two circles of energy which are turning. The spiritual circle of energy, which only when you are aware, when you go on the spiritual path, when you do your sadhana, is turning vertically, from up to down, down to up. Then you have another circle which is turning from left to right, right to left – this is the desire, whatever man is longing for in the manifested. This outer circle this is where one dwells always, and when one's desire is fulfilled, what happens? This one desire becomes two desires more, and the two fulfilled desires become four desires. This is only when one is turning the outside circle. This way the outside circle will become bigger and bigger. When the spirit, which is hidden, sees that the desires are becoming too strong in the outside, automatically it takes charge of it. Take charge of yourself, to remind you "Hey, you are not here just for that!" That's why somebody who dwells in the outside, can very rarely be *really* happy, because the happiness outside depends always on wanting something, one thing to other. But they can't be happy with themselves. When you are happy with yourself, it's the spirit inside of you, which makes the awareness rise. By chanting the name of Rama, or any Divine names, you learn to control the mind and bring it to a calm state. What is happening in this calm state? Yes, you are calm but it's not just calmness that gets awakened. All the Divine qualities which the name possesses, they also get awakened inside of you, because these Divine qualities lie deep inside of you. From deep inside it comes outside. But is that only this? The spiritual path? To awaken this Divine quality? What is the Divine quality? In the mind of man, man always

> **As long as you don't visualise Him inside of your head, your mind will not calm down.**

thinks that the Divine quality is always the *good* quality. It's true, the good qualities make you more aware of this energy inside of you, and also make you more aware of this energy outside of you. That's what makes you open up to Love, to help, to be joyful, to be happy. But to attain the un-manifested One, to attain the Ultimate of everything, you have to rise beyond that. There is something beyond that. When we talk of energy, can we touch it? No we can't touch it. We can just feel it. Blessed and lucky are some who can really see it. You rise into this extension of yourself, where you see only the un-manifested manifestation in everything. Duality disappears.

It is the state where only awareness of the Love of God, which prevails everything, is. As the Gita says "Out of a million, there will be only one, in which this desire and longing for the Ultimate will really arise." When it arises, it is not just "Ok, it's arising, I love God." Everybody loves God. But it's a consuming energy which, as long as you don't get it, you are not free. Like a small child, when it sees a toy. As long as he doesn't get the toy, he will start screaming and crying, until the father will say "Here, take it." just to keep the child quiet. But this is such a strong – it's not a desire – such will inside, that one should have, so that the heavenly Father says "Ok. This one, take it!" He Himself gives Himself to you. You can try your best only to a certain extent. The rest only comes through His Grace. To attain this Grace, to attain this mercy, you have to train yourself. You have to make yourself ready. Not only the mind but also your physical body has to be ready. Because the mind; if you give him a toy to play, the mind will be busy with it. Start chanting the Divine name; then you chant God's name to calm the mind, the mind will get calm! In one month, one year, two years it will get calm. But also your physical body has to attune itself to that higher energy. So you will chant with me now? Yes, or no? I can't hear! (*singing*.)

JUST LOVE 2

Awakening & Transformation

Inner Voice / Inner Journey / Realisation / Change / Spirituality / Light / Freedom

The bamboo that bends is stronger
than the oak that resists.

Japanese Proverb

YOU COME WITH NOTHING
AND YOU LEAVE WITH NOTHING

Darshan, Brugge, Belgium, 2 April 2011

It is lovely to be here with all of you. It's a beautiful place and a beautiful day today. As you all are on the spiritual path you all find the necessity to turn the mind within. Nowadays, if you look at the world and what is happening outside, does it make you happy? Does it make us happy? No. Why? Why are you not happy? Please talk! (One devotee: Too much suffering?) Too much suffering? I wouldn't say that because the result of suffering makes you grow also. When you look at it, we are not happy because we want some changes in this world but will those changes happen? Yes. So when will it happen? (Devotee: When we change?) A very good question and a very good answer. Peace and harmony will exist in this world only when each one decides for themselves to *change*. If you just say "I want peace, I want joy, I want harmony" and you don't do anything with yourself, you are not in harmony. How will it be outside? You know very well that the outside is the reflection of what you have inside of yourself. It's the inner reflection.

Once, somebody asked a Saint "How do you see the world?" The Saint answered "Well, each person creates their own reality in this world." What we see outside is a combination of a mass reality. With this mass reality, of course one person can change and make a difference, albeit a small one. It's better when one person changes, introverts oneself, opening the heart to Love, because Love is the greatest thing in this world and Love is the only way through it.

It's only through Love that people will change and it's only through that, that there can be peace and for that you have to open up. That's what I was saying in the beginning, that it is a time to introvert oneself. Our mind is always running to the outside, so we always see the cruelty, the negativity. Whenever you read the newspaper, whenever you put on the TV, what you see is always negativity. This gets imprinted in you to make your own mind become negative. You believe what you see is very bad, so then what happens? You start to judge and the mind becomes very judgemental. This is like that or this is like this. But are you changing? No, you are not changing. That is the same thing everybody is doing around the world, there is no difference. Does it contribute to bringing peace and harmony to the world? No it doesn't. When you introvert yourself you go into the peace which you have inside of you. You sit quietly and when you sit calmly, of course the mind will begin to rebel. After some time you don't want to get up,

When you learn to accept yourself and learn to be in peace with yourself the way you are, you will see that there is nothing wrong with the world.

for some people they can't get up, it's painful, or they go to sleep. But when you go into the calmness of the depths of your heart, in total surrender through your heartfelt sadhana, you enter the chamber of peace - the true inner peace. Through that inner peace which you will project to the outside, you will bring changes. For example, let's say when you go to somebody you know who is nervous and very agitated, what do you do? Do you try to calm the person down and advise the person to be positive, or do you also sit and cry with the person? It's the same when you go to the doctor. The doctor will ask you what kind of problem you have. It is the first question and then you say "Doctor, if I knew what I have, I would not have come to you." Well, when you go to the doctor, you go because you don't feel well and you open up and tell the doctor what you don't feel well about. Does the doctor sit with you and cry? No, the doctor won't do that. It's the same with psychiatrists. They advise you to move away from the way you're thinking and the way you see things. Moving away from this, changes certain things inside of you. It changes the way you are always looking at it. We were just saying that we see the world and project it as being cruel. The media wants us to see all the cruelty. But there are always also good things and it just depends on how you see it. Very often, one will see one's own projection of what one has inside of oneself. When one suppresses certain things inside of oneself, of course by suppressing energy deep inside, what will happen? Whenever something happens outside, the suppression will project itself. When that happens there will be complete judgement only.

When you learn to accept yourself and learn to be in peace with yourself the way you are, you will see that there is nothing wrong with the world. Things can change and it simply depends on each one. But we can't say "You change and I don't change." No, instead you have to say "I have changed and now the rest will change." If there are certain things inside of yourself that you do not accept, be positive about them. You have a choice, the choice is how you look at things. Either you place a judgement saying 'this is bad' or you can say 'this is not for me' in a positive way. This is the way you look at it differently, in a metaphysical way. The first thing is to open the heart, open the mind, let peace rise inside of you, each part of you. Whenever you have peace inside of you there is no

If we learn to accept the outside, we will change it and we ourselves are going to change as a result of that.

place for anything else. Whenever there is Love inside of you, there won't be any place for anything else either. You will become an instrument of that peace and Love wherever you are and whatever you are doing. Love is not found in reading books but by living it. By making an example in your daily life and by awakening it inside of you, you can really say you are truly 'in Love'. You read books that talk about Love, thousands of books, especially spiritual ones. But if you don't make the first step to open up your heart, if you don't make the first step to open the mind and let the Love awaken, it will remain always a theory. What you are looking for is not out there, it's here, inside of you. Stop digging outside, dig inside! There are enough holes outside, but inside, deep inside of you, you will open up a hole, which will consume you. You know we say this about Love, Love is something that consumes, not only burning. When you burn something, there is a residue that stays, but when Love consumes, nothing stays. For example, when you take the life of any great Saint, who is burning with this Love for God; they don't see anything, they just see the Divine. I always take the example of Meerabai – have you heard about Meerabai? No? She is a 15th century saint of India. She was a model of bhakti; she was a model of devotion and surrender. Like her there are many, but she was a princess who loved Krishna with all her heart. There is not even a single cell in her that was not in Love with Krishna. One day she was sitting in the temple and was singing for Krishna; whenever she would sing for Krishna, people would see Krishna, standing next to her. The King disguised himself. He was a Muslim king, Akbar, so he disguised himself and he was so touched by the devotion of Meerabai, that he gave his pearl necklace to the temple. Of course Meerabai didn't take anything. Because of that, her father-in-law got very angry. As she was a princess, the father-in-Law was a king; so he said "Because you have sung in the temple and the enemy has come, we accuse you of treachery."

Meera said "Well, in the temple everybody is equal, I don't know any bad one or good one, the fight is between you, not between God. Whether the person is Muslim, Christian, Hindu; everybody is allowed in the temple. The Lord is for everybody." For that they said "We command you to drink poison." She said "OK, if you have condemned me for that, I accept it." So they brought the cup with the poison for her. As she was drinking it, she thought of Krishna, she thought that Krishna is giving her Divine nectar – *amrit* – to drink. She drank this poison, and she walked to the nearby temple of Krishna. Everybody followed her. She entered the temple and as she had the effect of the amrit, she became one with her Lord. She disappeared physically into the deity in the temple. Even the poison didn't stop her. How did she view the poison? She accepted it.

The same way is with how we see the outside; if we learn to accept the outside, we will change it and we ourselves are going to change as a result of that. Don't be scared, because very often people say "No, I will not open up, because I will have to change this and that, this and that." Actually, it's not how much you are letting go, but how much you are getting in return. What you are getting in return is much more than what you are letting go. You have come to this world with nothing, what you take in this world belongs to this world only. When you leave, you will leave everything here.

Once, a great king visited Guru Nanak. He was very stingy; he was always thinking only of himself. He would take all the people's possessions and he always used a tactic to take all the belongings of the poor people. When he met Guru Nanak, Guru Nanak gave him a very small needle and said to him "My dear king, when you go to heaven, keep this with you. When you go to heaven, you return this to me." Very happy, he returned to his castle and told the queen "Queen, I will go to heaven." Then the queen said "How will you go to heaven? The king replied "Guru Nanak told me that

I should return this needle when I'm in heaven." So the queen said "You know that when you die you leave everything here. Tomorrow you go to him and ask how you will return it." The next day, early morning, he arrived at the door of the Saint, of Guru Nanak "Guru Nanakji, yesterday you gave me this beautiful small needle, and you told me to return it to you in heaven. How will I return it?" Then Guru Nanak tapped him on the back and said "My king, you have not realised, all the wealth you have amassed, all the things that you have taken; here I am giving you the smallest one, which is the needle. I am asking you to return this to me in heaven; you won't be able to bring this, so how will you bring all of these things that you have bought? The only thing that you can take with you is the good that you have done here. How much help have you given to people? With how much Love have you opened up your heart? Those are the only things that you will bring with you." Saying that the King changed and he realised that. The Gita says: You come with empty hands and you will go with empty hands. Only the good *sadhana* is what you will bring with you. So work for that. It is not about me telling you, it's about you trying your best. You opening your heart and trying to love, sincerely. Try to love with a pure mind. Then this Love gradually, but surely will one day become unconditional.

I will sing one bhajan; please, it would be lovely if you clap your hands. You see the mind is like a tree; with lot of birds. When you go under the tree where there are a lot of birds and you clap your hands what will happen? The birds fly away. The same thing, here the head, the mind, the brain, is the tree, with lot of birds of thoughts inside. When you start clapping your hands, you also let go, they will fly away.

THE SEVEN GIFTS

Pentecost, Flüeli Ranft, Switzerland, 25 May 2007

As you all are well aware, today is a special day: Pentecost. All churches are packed full, praising the Holy Spirit, praising the glory of God, because one week before the Ascension, Christ promised "When I go up, I will send the Spirit over all of you." He promised to send the Spirit of God, to send this realisation over the Disciples. It's similar when you advance on your spiritual path, you discover that the more you advance towards God-Realisation, the more you develop certain qualities, certain gifts. That's what it says in the Bible: When the Spirit of God came upon the Apostles, they were gifted with seven gifts. These seven gifts are the seven stages when you rise up in yourself, when you move from the lower *chakra* to the crown *chakra*. These are the stages through which one rises and receives the Spirit of God. You can see in the lives of saints that some saints are gifted and they are born with the whole of the qualities from their past lives, but some other saints advance stage by stage. This is receiving the Spirit of God. When one starts to advance, the Grace of knowing one's spiritual path is this gift. Very often we forget what we are here for. We get attached so much in the material world that our true Self gets covered. The light that we have inside of us stops shining. You see it very often on peoples' faces that they are so closed up. Everybody is here to look for real happiness, even those who are committing suicide. Why are they doing it? It is because they are running towards happiness, towards something that they don't yet know about. They do things out of ignorance. They are running away from some things that they don't want to face, but this is not the way. You have to run, but you have to run from the mind to the heart, not to the outside. Often we run to the outside, trying to find real happiness, we will find happiness, yes, but temporarily, not permanently. You will have happiness just for some time.

It's the same thing when you want something badly and you pray to God all day and night, saying "God, give me this, give me this, give me this!" When you get this thing, you will enjoy it for some time, but what happens then? It will fade. The same level of happiness you had, you don't get it back. The real happiness is when you can enjoy the Love of God completely, because His Love never fades. The more you love Him, the more you will want to love Him. Such Love one really has to cultivate, you have to love Him and want Him. Bug Him, call Him and as long as He doesn't give Himself to you, keep harassing Him. Then He will get fed up and just say "Let me give it to him."

If we look at the world as it is nowadays, we can see that even if God came on Earth in front of somebody and said "Hey, I am here", the person would say "Go away!" A story of Jesus just popped into my mind right now. After thousands of years, Jesus was sitting in Heaven and thinking "Maybe the world has changed. Let me go on Earth and see. Two thousand years ago I was there, but because I said 'I am the Son of God', they put me on the Cross and crucified me but, there were no churches at that time. So let me go and see, maybe they will recognise me and welcome me. They will know that I am here for their own good."

Jesus came to Bethlehem where He was born, He saw a church and He was walking towards the church when, at the same time, the mass was finished. People started to come out from the church and they saw a man coming, who was dressed like Jesus. They all started to make fun of Him "Oh, look at this mad man who is dressed like

Jesus. What do you think he is?" Jesus was shocked and said "Oh my goodness, I thought that after thousands of years that they have been praying and calling to me they would recognise me, but here I am and they don't even recognise me."

Jesus went to them and said "Listen, don't you recognise me?" The people said "Oh, you are just a mad man who is dressed like Jesus." Jesus answered "Oh, no, no, no, I *am* Jesus; you were just praying to me in the church!" but they said "No, he is mad." Jesus said "My goodness, how come they don't even know me now?" The people finally told Him "You better go away before the clergyman comes." At the same time the clergyman, the priest was coming and Jesus went to him and said "Hey, I am Jesus!" The

You discover that the more you advance towards God-Realisation, the more you develop certain qualities, certain gifts. That's what it says in the Bible: When the Spirit of God came upon the Apostles, they were gifted with seven gifts.

clergyman said "You mad man, keep quiet!" He took Jesus by force, brought Him inside and locked him in the Sacristy.

Poor Jesus was locked in the Sacristy and He could not understand what was happening. He thought that after two thousand years with many churches around, people praying and Christianity flourishing, they would know Him. But no, poor Him, He was locked inside, so He sat there and waited. At night He saw a light; the clergyman was coming with a lantern and opened the door. When he opened the door, he fell at the feet of Christ and said to Him "Please, Master, forgive me." Jesus asked "Why?" and he said "You know, I *did* recognise You when I saw You for the first time in the morning, but You see, the people are not ready to accept You. I locked You in here because You would start talking the Truth and it would be inconvenient for You to speak the Truth. People will never believe You, because they believe in the clergymen now."

So you see, even if God came, but you hadn't prepared yourself to recognise Him, you would not recognise Him. Know that God will never come in His real aspect, like I just said, He came as Jesus. He will *always* come in disguise. Like that, I can tell you thousands of stories in the lives of some saints where Christ or the Divine Mother came in different forms to the people.

There was once a devotee of Kali who lived around Dakshineshwar. It was not Ramakrishna. It was a priest, and his Love for the Divine Mother was *so* great that he would praise the Mother wherever he was. In his house there was no food, so he went and begged, but people refused to give him food. The Divine Mother disguised Herself as a fruit seller and went to his house where She gave some vegetables to the wife and said "Cook them. Your husband sent me here." When the husband came back to their home, the wife said to him, "Oh, thank you for sending this lovely lady who brought some vegetables and some rice, but now, I don't see her anymore and she went without saying 'Bye'". Later, when they opened the door of the temple, they saw that the clothes that the Lady had been wearing were now on the statue of Kali.

Once this same man wanted to build a fence, but he needed some help. He called first his daughter, but she was far away. Suddenly he saw her coming and she was saying "Father, sing some songs for me" and in divine ecstasy he sang for the Divine Mother. As he was singing, he was in deep meditation with the Mother and he forgot about the fence, but the Divine Mother with Her *shakti*, with Her power, made everything right and disappeared. Later the daughter came and said "Father, you were calling me, what can I do for you?" The father said "But you were just here, right now. Before, you were just here, helping me!" Then he realised that it was not his daughter who had been there – it was the Divine Mother.

Like that story, there are many stories in each of the saint's lives. If each one of you became a saint, you would also have nice stories to tell. This is your aim to be, pray to God, tell Him "Yes, I want to become a saint" and ask for help. Ask the Divine Mother, ask God, ask Christ for help. They will help you. They are here all the time to help people to advance, to help all their children, all the brothers and sisters to reawaken the Divine qualities. That's what they want that you all become, again, saintly.

Say "Yes, I want to become a saint" and you will become! As long as you see sainthood far away, if you see that God is far away, you keep God away, but if you feel Him near to you and say to your mind "Yes mind, listen, God is near me and I will listen only to what I feel inside my heart. I will listen only to what God wants from me," and clear this mind by chanting the name of God. Clear it by thinking positively, firstly about yourself and also about others around you. Like that, you will see that your heart will open up and this unconditional Love will also grow more and more. It's like a river when it comes out from the source: it's always small, but the more it advances towards the sea, what happens to it? It becomes larger and larger because on the way many rivers have joined together. On your spiritual path more and more streams of grace will join coming towards you and you will grow and grow. This is what you have to do – advance. Stop limiting yourself. Start saying "No" to your mind and make it positive.

THE STUBBORN CHAKRA

Darshan, Amsterdam, Holland, 2 April 2011

It's lovely to be here with all of you. Looking at this church, there is so much Love. Christ talked about Love; many Masters have talked about Love, taught Love and experienced Love. But what is Love? It is a word which has thousands of names because everything is Love. If you perceive Love everywhere, the thing you perceive to be Love turns into Love. Two persons when they meet each other they have a different kind of love. We recognise each other and we feel that there is something, then that love grows. In the same way there is motherly love for her child. For the child, there is love between friends, yet the fullness of Love stays always hidden. How many friends have you made in your life? How many people have you met in your life? Hundreds, maybe thousands. You meet them and feel a connection and then it disappears. Friends also come and after some time they go. When you are at school or college we have certain friends with the same goals, which is to study. You have certain friends and then they disappear and give place to other friends. That's all included in the love that one emanates from oneself. The same on the spiritual path, on the path of searching, there is another kind of Love which awakens inside of you and in this Love it is not about letting go because this Love is always growing. So the question arises can we really love in this time that kind of Love? Well yes, it is possible because that kind of Love is unconditional Love which everybody carries through life from small, 'til you reach your destination. You always carry this universal Love inside of you and whether you love in a different kind of love or the universal Love is determined by how you let it vibrate within you. So the question is, like I said, if it's possible to love? Yes, it is possible to love this kind of Love. To be able to let it grow and awaken inside of you, you should learn first to accept. But accept what? There are so many things to accept. When you look around, everywhere is telling you to accept. Accept this because everybody says this is right or that is right, but it is not about accepting this or that; it's about accepting yourself. Only by accepting yourself you develop this trust inside of you. When you have this trust inside of yourself, this Love will grow more and more. Of course I don't say that doubt will not arise, but this is where you will learn to control doubt by controlling the pride. There is one thing which can be an obstacle in one's path and that is spiritual pride. When you live in the world outside, you don't bother about anybody. You do your things and people do their things. But on the spiritual path very often there is competition. Each one competing with each other thinking which one is the best. It's like if this one is like that then I have to be like that, too.

Whenever there is pride, the Great Teacher knows how to break it.

No; you are individual and your aim, your dharma is different from everybody. Often people say "Swamiji I am on the spiritual path but I am working on this and that, I am so busy. I can't be there!" Well, God has put you there so you have to do your duty there and if He chooses to come to you in that way, He will come to you. He will awaken the cosmic Love inside of you wherever you are the moment you start to accept. Have acceptance of yourself and then control this pride because this pride will always stop somebody.

I will tell you a story. You know Ganesha? No? Yes? How many of you know? Ganesha is the elephant God, the God of wisdom and remover of obstacles on one's way. As He has an elephant head, of course you know there is always judgement around Him. So one day *Kuber*, the Lord of wealth; you know in Hinduism there are three hundred million deities, each deity is responsible for one thing. They are not outside though; each deity is present within oneself. Even science says there are around three hundred billion cells in the body, so the deities are present inside. One day Kuber, who is the accountant of Goddess Lakshmi, came to visit Shiva and pay his respects to Him. Despite having all the wealth with him, He only brought 2 bananas for Shiva. Seeing that, Ganesha said "Well you are the Lord of wealth but you are very stingy. You only brought two bananas!" Of course this offended Kuber very much. He said to Shiva "I came to invite you. Tomorrow I am making a great feast. Could you please come?" Of course Shiva knew what was in his mind. Because he felt offended inside, He wanted to prove Himself to be the best by making a big feast so that everybody would be talking about it. So the next day Shiva with the whole family came to Kuber. Kuber of course didn't do it out of real Love, but instead he did it out of pride. What did Ganesha do? Ganesha stepped into the mud and walked with his feet on the beautiful carpet. Of course Kuber was not happy; he looked at Ganesha in a very weird way pushing him aside. What was the next thing Ganesha did? He went to the kitchen and saw all the beautiful dishes that had been cooked, a massive amount that had been prepared, and He said "I am a guest here and I am hungry right now.

An open mind leads to an open heart. Please, before the great feast starts, let me eat something." Everybody brought the food that they had cooked and He started eating one after the other. After some time, after all the cooked food was finished, He said "Well I am still hungry!" So they got Him all the fruits and uncooked vegetables, gave them to Him and He ate everything that was there to be eaten. Looking for more things to eat, Ganesha asked the cooks to bring all the dishes and utensils from the kitchen and He ate them all. After all that, the cook ran to Kuber and said "Your invited guest has eaten everything and there is nothing left to offer!" Then Ganesha said "Well you invite us but all what you had here fills only half of my stomach! What about the other half?" Kuber said "Bring more things!" but there was nothing to bring as everything what was there had been eaten. In that moment the pride of Kuber was shattered and He realised His mistake. He had invited Shiva not out of Love or joy, but out of pride.

Whenever there is pride, the Great Teacher knows how to break it. Then he realised his mistake and asked for forgiveness, and he changed deep inside of himself. Seeing that, Ganesha said "Kuber, it's not the greatest feast that will fill my stomach. Just one banana itself, given with Love, will fill me up." But Love has to be from the heart. You see when we are first in love, when you meet somebody you are very much in love and this is a trace of the real Love. You forget about yourself and you are always thinking about that love in whatever you do, wherever you are. Constantly in the mind, that person is wondering what the other person is doing and where that person is. You will do everything to have that connection with the person. That is the trace of pure Love inside man. However when it becomes

If you choose to be sad or unhappy, then you will be exactly that, because you will invite this energy to come and make you unhappy.

routine, you forget about that Love. That's why it's important to open the windows of the mind and let some fresh air in. In a house with all the windows closed, you get stuffy, no? The thing is, when there are too many old thoughts in the mind, particularly narrow minded ones, after some time, it starts to get stuffy. This is why sometimes you say you can't breathe anymore and so what you must do is open up. Open your mind, let it have fresh air inside and you will see that the Love that you felt has never gone away. This Love is always there inside you, inside your heart. It's just that the mind, with all the business of the world, forgets about it. It is very easy to love. There is no technique to learn how to love. You know sometimes people ask me "Swamiji, is there any technique to open the heart?" Well there are techniques to open the mind, they are positive thinking and chanting the Divine Names. An open mind leads to an open heart. The heart is an instrument God has created which has a mind of its own. It has its own will. You can't open it or close it. Sometimes people say you have a closed heart but even if you try to close it, it won't close. It's a stubborn chakra! It will do whatever it wants to do. The stubbornness of the heart makes the Love inside you ever present. Just open the heart; you just open the real eyes which God has given you. You will see that it was and is always there. That's what you are in reality and what you will always be, until you dissolve completely into the light. So realise that. How long do humans stay on earth? Maybe one hundred years maximum? Well not everybody reaches that, some reach 80, some reach 60; but know that death is certain. Nobody can escape it. Even Him, He manifests Himself but He has accepted that. The difference between Him and humans is that He transcends humanity into divinity. That's what He has talked about. To love each other. He always told people about this mutual Love. All that He has ever talked about is just Love. In Love you have everything. Everything that you are looking for is inside of you, not outside. Outside things come and go. Look, I talked about

> In Love you have everything. Everything that you are looking for is inside of you, not outside.

friends, love in relationships, yet death takes everything away. But consciousness, your higher Self, moves on one life to the next until you attain the Supreme. If you realise the Supreme, actually I won't say attain the Supreme because it is who you are, you see that the essence of the soul is Him. Try to do everything in a positive way and try to see your life in a joyful way. A way which you really want it to be and then it will be so. If you choose to be sad or unhappy, then you will be exactly that because you will invite this energy to come and make you unhappy. I will sing one bhajan now and if it's difficult for you, which I am sure it is, just clap your hands. It's very good! All the clapping stimulates energy points in the hands and it makes you happy. You clap your hands when you are happy, no? When people are sad they don't clap their hands. Have you seen people when they are clapping their hands? They are happy! When you clap your hands they stimulate all the memories you have that make you happy outside and that make you happy also inside yourself. All the organs which are present inside of your hands are getting energised, so it's very good.

THE TRUE MEANING OF SPIRITUALITY

Darshan, Basel, Switzerland, 1 April 2007

It makes me very happy to give the first official *darshan* here in Basel. We are all aware that we are all on a spiritual path. We all consider ourselves spiritual, or something like that, but what is spirituality actually?

We all talk about spirituality, this way, that way. It is true that in spirituality there are many ways. It's like rivers in the world, we have many rivers and they have different names, but they all flow to the same ocean. All the spiritual paths that one takes lead to the same way, to the same goal. So why when we look at the world, especially when we look at spiritual people, do we see lots of critics, lots of judgements and lots of pride? Spirituality is humility, is respect and is Love. Above all, we all love. All religions, all paths and all Masters say to love and that is spirituality. It is so simple. These simple things that you do, that's spirituality.

As long as we criticise and say "Only my way is the best, only my Master is the best or only this one is the right way", is this spiritual, when all lead to the same path, when all lead only to God? Why do we not see the Divine in everybody? Why do we not love everybody? Behind this body, all of you are Love, all of you are the same Light of God. Why do we forget about it? We call ourselves spiritual, yes, but we forget about our path, about our way. We often forget why we are here, that we are here to spread this Love of God. We are here to give an example. We become spiritual to give an example to others, but if we ourselves see that we are doing something wrong, that we are doing something that is not according to this spiritual path, why do we continue doing it?

This is one thing that we, who are on the spiritual path, have to start analysing – how we think, because the mind is always doubting. The mind creates lots of things, but the mind is also a very good instrument if we learn to control it, to think positively. If we learn to say to the mind "All is God. Everything is part of God", we will see that whatever lesson we have in our life is from Him and that we are here to learn from Him. If we accept it in that way and look at it in a positive way, we will see how our life will change, how we will start to grow and blossom on our spiritual way. Spirituality is born within each one's heart, but it is born in each one's mind, because you have to want it firstly. You want God, you want to achieve this realisation of who you are, but it is not achieved just by saying it. Say to yourself "I want to change my life. I really want to realise my Self, to realise who I am. I really want to do what I have come here to do." There are many paths, there are many ways and they all are good. There is no judgement of any way. Develop *Bhakti*; develop devotion. The first step that you have to make is to develop devotion. Don't try to take a big jump. When I meet people, often I see that they want a big thing all at once. It´s fine, God will happily give you everything that you want, but the point is whether you will be able to handle it or not. Often, although you can only hold so much in your hand, when you look at things, you want to hold too much. It's difficult. When you train yourself, with patience and with Love, you will grow little by little and you will be able to handle what God gives you.

> Spirituality is humility, is respect and is Love. Above all, we all love. All religions, all paths and all Masters say to love and that is spirituality. It is so simple.

Keep reminding yourself of the Love of God and that whatever
you do, wherever you are, He is with you all the time. There is no
moment that He is not with you. Often we say God is not with
us, but we forget that we are not with God, we don't think about
God all the time. Then we say He is not with us. It is easy to put
the blame on Him, but anyway, like Christ said "I will bear your
weight." He is happy to carry it also, but we should not always put
it on His shoulders.

At the beginning of the year 2007, through His grace, Mahavatar
Babaji instructed me to give *Atma Kriya Yoga*. *Atma Kriya* is similar
to *Kriya Yoga*, which is considered one of the easiest ways to reach
realisation, but still there is a difference, because *Atma Kriya* deals
with devotion; it deals with the Love that you are. People who have
practiced it will know what I am talking about. *Atma Kriya* is for
everybody, it's not necessary that you be in *Bhakti Marga* to do
Atma Kriya. Whoever wants to do *Atma Kriya* is most welcome. It
will be good for all of you and it will be good for the people around
you, but you have to want it. Like in all the paths, you have to want
it; you have to really say "God, I want this; I want you!"

A guided meditation

I'd like to do a little meditation with you. I ask you to please sit
straight, if possible.

- Firstly, take a few deep breaths. Inhale and exhale. When you
  exhale, please drop your shoulders, because when you inhale
  your shoulders go up and you put pressure on yourself. When
  you exhale, breathe out all the carbon dioxide, breathe out
  all the air that you have in your stomach. Let your stomach
  go in. Drop your shoulders. Do this five to six times.
- Now we will give a game to the mind to play – use the mind

- Listen to your breath. Listen to how you are breathing, how you are inhaling and how you are exhaling. Listen to how beautiful the sound is.

- Now use your mind, focus your mind on your third eye. Create an *OM* sign there or any sign you like. Each time you inhale, see the Light, the *OM* sign becoming brighter and brighter. Imagine it. Create it. You are children of God, You are part of God. As He is the Creator, you all are the Creator also. So you create.

- Now let the *OM* expand and let the Light become brighter. There will come a point where you will not even see the *OM*. It will just be Light.

- Bring this Light from your forehead to your right eye, then to your left eye. Say to this Light "Purify my eyes and heal them."

- Now bring the Light to the right nostril of your nose, then to the left. Tell the Light "Purify my nose and my sense of smell."

- Bring the Light to your right ear, then to the left one. Say to the Light "Purify my ears, so that I can hear Your name, always."

- Bring the Light to your head. Say to the Light "Purify my mind, so that I can always think positively about myself and others."

- Bring the Light to your mouth. Say to the Light "Purify my mouth, so that whatever I speak is out of Love and that I may control my tongue."

- Bring the Light to your right arm and hand and then to the left ones. Say to the Light "Purify my hands, so that I am always ready to help."

- Bring the Light to your legs and feet – first to the right one and then the left one. Say to the Light "Purify my feet, so that I always walk on the right path."
- Bring the Light to your heart. Say to the light "Make it so that I love unconditionally."
- Feel the Light in your heart. Go deeper inside your heart.
- Stay focused on your heart. Slowly, open your eyes.
- Chant *OM* with me eleven times. So you inhale and when you chant OM, let it vibrate on this part of your chest. (Swami points to His heart chakra)

FLOATING IN THE HAND OF GOD

Darshan, Steffenshof, Germany, 9 March 2007

In this *kirtan* that we just sang, the meaning of the first two lines: *Chori Chori Makhan Kha Gayo Re* is: *very stealthily Krishna is stealing butter and eating it.* The second line, *Sabke Man Ko Loobha Gayo Re,* means: *in the same way He steals the butter, the same way God steals the heart of Man.* God steals the hearts of men, the same way, little by little, He steals the heart.

This is actually the Love. This is what one has to go through to let one's heart be stolen by God. The more you resist, the more it becomes difficult. The more you say "Yes, take it. Steal it. It is yours already," the more you will see how you float in your spiritual path, how you float in the hand of God, but the more you use the mind and try to stop it, the more you will see that there will be lots of pain that will come. The pain gets transformed into Divine Love, merges into Divine Love and becomes Divine Love, because even pain, even problems, all is from Him. The one small step that one has to take is to realise that it is from Him.

We know it and we say "Yes, everything is from God," but when a problem comes we forget about God. We don't say that it is from God. Actually, there is His Hand in it also, we just need to be aware of that. In the calmness of your mind, in the depth of your heart, you know that everything is His game. All of you who are sitting here know it's His game. As long as we like this drama, as long as we want to play this game, we will be in the game. That's what Krishna did as His *Lila* when he was small, and that's the same *Lila* that we are all playing.

We think that spirituality is far away. No, spirituality is very near; it's just here in one's heart. In all the techniques that we will be talking about very soon – through the grace of Mahavatar Babaji we'll be doing the *Atma Kriya* – He is there already. He is already sitting there. All techniques lead you to this path. With all these techniques that we do, including meditation, we are saying to God "Here, I am surrendering myself. Reveal Yourself to me. Let me taste the little sweetness of the *Amrita* that You are, that is deep within me." Like I said, through the grace of Mahavatar Babaji, soon we'll do the *Atma Kriya* and you will see how easy it is to be in the different mood of the Divine, anytime.

Often people think "Why do we have to be spiritual? Why do we have to be ready for God?" Why not just sit down and say "God will give whenever He wants to give?" It's true if you don't make any effort, you will not know how to handle what God wants to give you. It's only when you start making your effort and say "Yes God, I'm working on myself to be ready for You. I'm working on myself to be ready for this realisation and I'm trying to be ready also to help others", then God will give it to you. Even if He has to give it on a silver plate or even on a diamond plate, He will do it, but the effort, you have to do it.

> The heart is not complicated. When you look at the heart, what the heart says is very simple.

That reminds me of a small story. I like to tell stories all the time, but I don't even know from where they come. For sure up there there's a big store of stories.

Once there was a prince. He went to the Queen – the Queen's name was Madalassa – and said to the Queen "Mother, you have sent all my brothers away to become ascetics in the forest. Why?" The mother thought for a while and said "My son, of course they could have realised the Divine here also, but they went to work on this in the forest."

It's like this, if there are two boats – one boat, which is decorated very beautifully with a lot of beautiful lights and very shiny, but in this boat there is a hole and there is another boat, which is simple, very simple, but without a hole – which one would you take – the beautiful one or the simple one? You would take the simple one. This is the same thing the Queen was saying to her son.

Spirituality is often like this boat that is decorated very beautifully; whoever goes into it sinks in the middle of the water, whereas the one who takes the simplest form of life and leads a life in spirituality, lives in an ascetic way, he reaches his goal. In simplicity you will find it, in the simplicity of your heart. You see, the heart is not complicated. When you look at the heart, what the heart says is very simple. It's like the boat, which is very simple. Whereas, when you look at the mind, it's decorated with so many beautiful things that it traps people into it. To become spiritual is to divert this beauty of the mind to the heart, and go in the boat of the heart to reach the final destination, to reach the Oneness of God within you.

All that you are practicing is good; whatever path you take is good. Know that the main thing is that you have to reach

> The more you say "Yes, take it. Steal it. It is yours already", the more you will see how you float in your spiritual path, how you float in the hand of God. But the more you use the mind and try to stop it, the more you will see that there will be lots of pain that will come.

the goal, no matter which path you take.

YOUR EYES CAN MAKE YOU
SEE ONLY LOVE

Darshan, Springen Town Hall, Germany, 4 July 2009

I was talking with my sister-in-law in the car while coming here. I was wondering what we could talk about. She told me to tell why spirituality is difficult. This is a theme, which we can probably laugh about, but how many of you agree with that? Be truthful.

Why do you think for the people who say it's difficult, it is difficult and for the people who say it's easy, it is easy? Actually, why we humans see difficulties is because we are selfish. It's our own selfishness that makes it difficult, and then we say "It's very difficult." Some will say "It's very easy." It all depends on how close you are to the Divine. We see difficulties because we are far away from the Divine. Even if we think we are spiritual or we are religious, when difficulties arise, we tend to forget about it. We forget why we are here. When a difficulty arises, for some this is a time when they will turn to God, but then when the difficulty is gone, they forget about Him. It's normal.

It's in human nature to balance between these two ways, but if you are spiritual it doesn't matter. Krishna said in the Gita "If you want to achieve me, you have to rise above good and bad. You have to rise above everything to attain me." Do you think it is only with the good that you can attain the Divine? That's a misunderstanding that people think about. People like to dress the Divine according to what they want, but the Divine is beyond all this. Do you want to achieve the Ultimate or do you want to achieve something that has a limit?

Your mind has limits. That's why you need a form to achieve more. You need a Deity, and this Deity becomes everything for you. The Master becomes everything for you, but this is only temporary, it's not for you to stay there. This is one part only; you have to rise beyond that. How would you know the cosmic form of the Divine? If you see God as just the Deity that you are praying to – the statue of Jesus or the statue of Mother Mary or Krishna – you will never see the cosmic Krishna. You will never see the cosmic Christ, or if you think God is only the good – but then the mind is wrong. The closer you go to the Divine, the more the difficulty will change; that which you perceive as difficult now will not remain.

I'll tell a story to you. There was once a *rabbi* who was giving a discourse. He was giving his lecture to his students and there was a line which said "The one who is closest to the Divine, to Yahweh, is the one who smiles in the midst of difficulties." Then his students stopped him and said "Rabbi, can you please explain to us how it is possible to smile in the time of difficulties?" The Rabbi said "Well, it's a very difficult question to answer, because when there are difficulties, I myself forget where the smile has gone. I forget how to smile." It's true, our mind is so engrossed into this negativity that we forget the reality.

Having said so he continued "It's very difficult for me to tell you how to smile in time of difficulties or in time of great tests, but I know one person in the village who has gone through *so* many trials in his life. When he was just one week old, he lost his parents. Then later on in life, in everything that he did, he didn't succeed, but he was always very joyful and smiling."

The students went to this person and knocked at his door. They heard the voice asking from inside "Who is it?" The students said "Oh, we are students of the Rabbi and we came to ask you certain questions." The man said "Tell me, what question you have?" They replied "We came across this line in the Torah that says 'The one who is closest to God smiles in the midst of difficulties.' Hearing this the man said "Well, you have come to the wrong address, because I am 78 years old, but I don't know what difficulty is, so I can't tell you how to smile in it."

Know, the closer you are to the Divine, if your mind is focused on the Divine, on your true Self, any difficulty will transcend itself. Everybody wants to attain this true Self, no? But everybody wants to attain the true Self only by being good. You don't need to be good. You don't need to pretend to be good; you just need to be yourself! Even if people think that you are bad, you have to know yourself how you are. How many among you are always truthful with yourselves?

We always try to please other people. We think "If I am not like that, my parents or this person will not like me. I always have to be how the others want me to be." Be yourself! People will learn to appreciate you as yourself and by being yourself you will develop self-confidence. It is only by developing this self-confidence that you can attain the Divine, but if you always try to be what others want you to be, it will be difficult, because then you are untruthful towards yourself.

That is spirituality; that is religion also. Religion is not just to sit and do *Aarti* to the divine from morning until night without knowing who you are. It's good if you have the time to do it and if you think that this will make you more spiritual. Actually, just by being yourself you can really feel God, because God has created you as individuals with certain qualities, with certain beauty, but you have to see it. Don't think "Oh, my neighbour is like that, I have to be like that also." Just be yourself!

I remember a story that my mum used to tell me when I was small. It's a funny story. There were two neighbours who were always quarrelling with each other. One day one of them thought "I will pray to God, I will meditate on Him and when I see Him, I will ask Him for a blessing." He meditated and prayed and God appeared to him and said "My dear fellow, what do you want?" He answered "God, I want one blessing from You. I want to have the blessing that whatever I ask from You, I will get it." God said "OK, but I will give you this blessing with one condition: whatever you ask from me, your neighbour will get double." He thought for a while and said "OK, fine."

He asked God for one tonne of gold, and his neighbour got two tonnes of gold. He asked for a house; his neighbour got two houses. Then, one car for him and his neighbour got two cars. Of course, he was jealous inside, he was thinking "I prayed so much, but how come my neighbour is profiting more?" Do you know what he thought then? He said "OK God, I want a big and very deep hole in front of my house." Well, God had to keep his promise; the neighbour got two holes in front of his house. The next thing he asked from God was "God, I want you take one of my eyes out." You know what happened...

> Be yourself! People will learn to appreciate you as yourself and by being yourself you will develop self-confidence. It is only by developing this self-confidence that you can attain the Divine.

This story sounds really funny, but this is how humans are. We can't be happy for somebody else. You can say "Yes, I am happy for that person," but when you look deep inside, there is something eating at you. Probably you don't think about it, but at night when you go to bed it eats you a little bit, no? You think "How come that person is like that and I am not like that? How come that person is realised, but I am not?"

One very nice question which people ask me often is "Swamiji, how come I don't see things?" God has given you two eyes. You see so many things every day. Yet, they are still asking "Why don't I see the things that my neighbour sees?" Start by taking time and looking at what you feel, what you see, what you want and only then can you really see Him. It's not only about seeing some light or somebody walking around. It's more than that – to see that what you have inside of you is really equal inside everybody. You all know about it, but it's time to realise it, to really feel it.

That's really what love can show, and when this love really awakens completely inside of you – for yourself, firstly – when you become completely consumed with the Divine Love, this Cosmic Love, you can just see Love, nothing else, because all the things that are separating you from Him will have dissolved into Love. What stays is that your eyes can make you see only Love. It's *not a light*, you know? It's beyond that.

LIGHTING THE INNER LAMP

Divali, Shree Peetha Nilaya, Germany, 17 October 2009

Divali also symbolises the reminder of our inner Light. That's why *Divali*, although if it is only a Hindu word, is also celebrated by the Christians. In Mauritius the Christian and the Catholic Churches celebrate *Divali*, because it's not considered only Hindu tradition, but it reminds us that we are that Light. When we light outside the little oil lamp this symbolises our inner light that has to be lit the same way.

Out of darkness the light shall shine. Out of the darkness that our mind creates, out of darkness that willingly or unwillingly we create, we ask the Divine to shine forth that light from deep within to the outside, this light which often we forget about, because when we are so much in our daily routine, we forget why we are here. We forget our true purpose and we forget about the Love that we all carry.

Then we say "OK, just like that or like that only", but then we are limited. What about this inside that we feel? What about this Love that we always long for? We forget about it. *Divali* reminds us that we are that Light, and that Light we shall ever be. Whether we have a lot of *karma* or not, whether we realise it or not, whether we are Hindu or not, it doesn't matter.

Beyond this limitation of our bodies that we have put on ourselves, we are this Light, nothing else. We are this Love. So when we light the lamp, we remind ourselves of being. It's not the lamp outside that has to be lit, but the Light which is within you that has to be lit; realising that this Light is not only inside of you, but it's everywhere. The Divine is not limited; He's everywhere.

Some people will say "But Swamiji, I don't see that Light. Well, sometimes I have seen it, but sometimes I don't see it." You know about that? Well, at night when we look up at the sky, we see a lot of stars. Then what do we say "Oh, how beautiful it is. How great it is, to see all these shining stars," but during the day when you look up, you don't see the stars. Do you think the stars are not there? Or that they only come at night? The stars are always there.

In the same way, the inner Light is always there. When you do your *sadhana*, when you really pray for that Love, when you really ask the Divine "Let that light shine forth", then you become an instrument of this Light. Then it will shine through you. *Divali* reminds us of this inner Light, which is present in each person, in each creation of the Divine – not only in us, because we are sitting here celebrating *Divali* and we are thinking of ourselves as being more special than anybody else. No, it's not like that.

We are not special, you know. When we think of ourselves being closer to the Divine than anyone else – this is wrong. This is our ignorance that makes us think that we are special, for God loves everybody the same way. The same light shines through you, through me, through everybody. One just needs some time to look at it. When your mind is calm, when your heart is fully open, you will see, you will feel that Light. You will feel that Love. This is the real meaning of *Divali*.

There is another symbolic meaning of *Divali*, which is related to the return of Rama to Ayodhya. You know the story of Rama, when He killed the demon Ravana? He took Sita from Ravana, who kept her for a long time, because Ravana stole Sita by force. When Rama killed Ravana, He crowned Vibhishan King of Lanka. It was time for Him to return back to His palace, because it had been fourteen years.

His father had three wives. One of the wives was very jealous, because she wanted that her son, Bharat, become king, but Rama was the oldest son. The mother, while saving the father from the battlefield, had asked a promise from her husband "When one day I ask you for something, you should never refuse me." The king had said "Yes". Dasharatha had said "I will never refuse you." So she took the opportunity to make her son the King of Ayodhya.

Rama was just married. He was sixteen years old. She asked that Rama be banished to the forest for fourteen years. When the father heard that, he was shocked, but he was bound by his promise. He couldn't say "No" to that promise, so he accepted, and Rama and Sita went to the forest for fourteen years. When Ravana was killed after some time, the fourteen years were also over.

Then Rama took Sita back to Ayodhya. As they were flying... because you see now we have aeroplanes, but in the *Vedas* or in the *Ramayana*, they have already talked about a flying object, a flying machine. It is not flying by mechanical means, but by the power of thought. This is actually where the plane was also inspired. So Rama took Sita and they went on the flying thing and flew.

> It's not the lamp outside that has to be lit, but the Light which is within you that has to be lit; realising that this Light is not only inside of you, but it's everywhere.

To celebrate the event of Rama returning to Ayodhya, people also light this little clay lamp. A clay lamp is very symbolic, actually. With the symbol of a clay lamp we say "God, you are the Light, but we are the *batti* – the thread." This is the connection that we have with the Divine.

The clay lamp is our body and symbolises that this body is just dust and dust it shall be. One day we will leave this body. We see it in ourselves, in little ones. Everybody says when we are small "Oh, how beautiful you are, little, little child. How cute he is." Then the child becomes sixteen, the Mother comes and says "Oh, my God, the child is like this and like this and like this." The child grows up and then they say "Oh, my God, my child falls in love" and all those stories and it carries on like that.

You see, our body doesn't stay the same. It changes, it evolves until at the end we leave it. The clay lamp that is burning symbolises this body that is like this clay holder and inside is the burning lamp, is the light burning, is the Love burning inside of you.

So rise, make your intellect be illuminated by the Grace of God, by the Grace of the Divine Mother, so that in this life, you can take the opportunity and realise your Self. Realise where you come from, realise who you are in reality, realise your work, your mission and realise where you are going, what your real duty in life is. Let this light shine through you. Become a messenger of this Love, become a messenger of the Divine – not just limiting yourselves, being what your mind perceives you to be. That's also why we light this lamp.

Rama, who is one incarnation of Maha Vishnu, reminds us of the *dharma* – our duty. He was very *dharmic*. Each person has their own duty and the duty for each person is not the same. Very often spiritual people feel and think that all of the spiritual peoples' duty has to be one thing. Then you would all be the same, no? It can't be. We have one *goal*, it's true, but we have different duties and ways to attain that goal. For some people it's to serve, for some people it's to meditate, for some people it's serving in their family life itself. In Rama's story, you will see such a variety of examples where He has shown that even though it was written ten thousand years ago, it is still applicable in daily life. It reminds us of being compassionate and also of being accepting of life.

We have now completed the prayer to Lakshmi Kubera; like I said before we started, Maha Lakshmi is the Goddess of wealth. Wealth

– when we talk about wealth, what do we think about? The bank, eh? It's true, when we talk about Maha Lakshmi, we think about the bank and money, but is money everything? No, it's not. We need it of course, without money we can't do anything, but She also symbolises spiritual wealth. This wealth is what Christ talks about, saying "The wise ones put their money not in the bank in the world, because somebody can come and take it away, but in the bank, which is up or deep within."

She symbolises this spiritual wealth – that the more we surrender towards our path of knowing ourselves, the more we will be free. We'll be full of spiritual knowledge. We'll be full of the Grace of the Divine. Otherwise, we are never free. One day we want this, tomorrow we want that; then another day we want another thing. It's endless. Can we ever be free from that? No, we never can.

> We are not special, you know. When we think of ourselves being closer to the Divine than anyone else – this is wrong.

Maha Lakshmi helps to fulfil all your wishes, so that you can be ready to fulfil the wish of your soul also. We ask Maha Lakshmi to bestow Her Grace not only on all of us, but on everybody who needs Her help in whatever way. To bestow the wealth of health on people who are sick, to shine forth Her Light, so that our intellect becomes pure, and to help everybody who needs help.

THE CROSS OF CHRIST
AND THE TRANSFORMATION OF LIFE

Israel Tour Talk, October 2009

We have been visiting many places. There's not really much to talk about, because it has been explained already. We've been to the Garden of Gethsemane and you know what happened there. You've been to the Tomb of Mother Mary. You've been to the birthplace of John the Baptist and you've been to the Holy Sepulchre. You've seen a few of the Via Dolorosa stations, where Jesus passed and stopped. Of course, you've been to the main Church where Christ was crucified and where He was buried, where they put His body down.

We already spoke of all of this when we went to the Holy Sepulchre Church. I explained to you also about the Holy Light of Jerusalem, so all of you know about it. I guess, today you've been to the place where Jesus ascended, where there the Footprint of Christ is.

You see, all these places; of course, some people will say "How can you know for sure if it is really there or not?" This question, for sure, has arisen in your mind. Most of the places are how it has been. Only a few things that I can say regarding the stations that were not how they were, but otherwise most of the places where it is said that there has been something, that is how it was.

The Church of the Holy Crucifixion is very interesting. You all have been under the table and you all have put your hand inside. This hole – this is the place where the Cross was. When you put your hand inside and you go around, you see it's not just round, what you have up, but it's also, very large inside. What you can notice is that it's not a square. You see, it's a tree, what they used to crucify the people on and what Christ was crucified upon was a tree.

It was not polished and made nicely for Him to be crucified, like nowadays we have a beautiful cross, carved and polished, varnished even. People think Christ was crucified on a cross like this, which is completely wrong. It was just two pieces of wood that He was crucified on – He was crucified on normal rough wood – that was nailed together. That's why, when you look at the hole, it's like a tree trunk.

Of course, when you look left and right you will see other holes also. Then you will ask how the Church can say "Yes, it was this one." These places were discovered by Saint Helena, the mother of Constantine

He took the karmic things from everybody, so that He could transform the karma. He took it upon Himself. He took the suffering of the world on Him.

the Great, who was the one who legalised Christianity. Before that, Christianity was just a heresy. Helena was very pious, she prayed a lot, she knew about Christ and she had visions. Christ Himself guided her to these places and of course, when she went there, there was always the continuation.

That's why yesterday we were talking of the Apostolic Blessing, which is the continuation. It has been written, yes, but this place is known through the oral way. People have always been talking about this place, that something had happened

at this place and they have kept this place how it was. Of course, now there is also a beautiful church and so on.

For the first Christians it was like it used to be. Following the writing of the Gospels they could figure it out, because in the original Bible they explained everything in detail – how it was, where it was. So they could really figure it out – the exact place where it is.

You have seen where the Crucifixion was. You have seen where they brought the Body. After the Crucifixion they put the Body down on the slate, they prepared Him, they wrapped Him in linen and then brought Him inside the cave.

After they had finished crucifying Him, the Romans removed the Cross and just dumped the Cross – all three of them. From up they threw the Cross down. It was just thrown like nothing and through the years, the earth had covered it and it was underground.

Like I told you, Helena had visions, so she followed her vision. She was guided to the Cross. The place of the Cross is where the St. Helena Church is now. Imagine from high up – it was in a valley – so they threw the Cross down and it stayed there. For 390 years it was there. For 390 years earth had covered over it. Nobody knew about it; nobody had heard of the Holy Cross or anything. They knew about the Cross, yes, but they never used to have the Cross sign. They had the fish sign. They had the fish or they had the writing like we saw in the Church of the Nativity.

So Helena followed her vision and went there. They dug and they found three crosses. Then they had the dilemma of how to know which one is the real Cross, because all three looked the same. So they took a dead body and they put it on the first one – nothing happened. They put it on the second one – nothing happened, but when they put it on the third one, the moment the dead body touched the Cross it became alive again! That's why the cross is called The Life-Giving Cross.

Some people said "Why do you want to venerate the Cross when Christ died on the Cross?" You have to understand why He died on the Cross. Firstly, the tradition says that He took the karmic things from everybody, so that He could transform the karma. He took it upon Himself. He took the suffering of the world on Him. Such a great Master can do that – not everybody can. He had the power to do that. He did it.

At the same time, He showed us that through the Crucifixion there is life, which means that He didn't really die, but He transformed. He took all of these karmic things and transformed them. What we can say about it is that we can transform life itself. The Crucifixion is like what we live in our daily lives here, but that's why we are called to transform – to be our true Selves.

> ## He showed us that through the Crucifixion there is life, which means that He didn't really die, but He transformed.

It's really nice you see all this that you have read about in this brochure. All of you, since you were small, all of you have been reading about the life of Christ and here you are experiencing it, what you have read before. It's there, it's not just a fiction or a story, but reality.

It was the same thing when we went to Vrindavan. We went to this place and that place, and this place and that place. Of course, we have read all this in the *Srimad Bhagavatam*, but when you go there, you experience it, you are going into that energy – it's different. Remember the first day we said "Don't expect much", because when it was written it was two thousand years ago. Of course, in thousands of years, things change. In ten days things change, so in thousands of years how many changes would have happened already?

It's not about the changes, but about feeling it, because here, even when you walk around, just when you walk early in the marketplace, you know – at that time it was not a marketplace. I saw a picture of the year one thousand-eight hundred-something. There was nothing then, not even near Jaffa Gate. Now there are so many buildings. If you go around, there are some pictures where you see there was nothing. Can you imagine two thousand years ago there was a temple and a few shops, but there was not much here. Probably it was green like the forest where we have been today.

THE GOOD SHEPHERD

Darshan, Springen, 1 November 2009

I will talk about my trip to Israel, from where I just returned yesterday and which was very beautiful. You see, when you talk about Israel, everybody has a different *view* of it. Unless you experience it, it's completely different from what you read about. Let's say when you read the Bible, and when you are there, it's completely different.

It was a trip where we experienced a lot of things that we had been only reading or that we knew about. We have heard about it since childhood, for sure, but to be there is amazing. It's the same when we read the life of Krishna and when we are in Vrindavan – it's completely different. We have to adapt ourselves. It's the same with Jerusalem, Bethlehem and around the Sea of Galilee. These places are very special places. They are special because once Christ walked in these places and they have been kept alive through the faith of people. They are special because there is a connection that one feels, which is completely different from other places.

Of course, how I experience it and how others experience it is different and the funny thing is that during the trip I didn't talk about how *I* felt. I let everybody talk and it was very beautiful to see how each person felt and how each person's point of view was. We are all talking about the same Christ, but everybody looks from a different angle. Some will see from the right angle, some will see from the left angle, but it's beautiful to see that experience.

The most amazing is if we can feel with our heart, not what we see on the outside, but what we can see with the eyes of the heart.

When we look at it with the eyes of the heart, we will realise that
all these places are there. They are all present inside of us. We go to
pilgrimage places to remind ourselves of what we have inside.
Sometimes we have to look *outside* to make us realise what is inside
and that's how we humans are functioning. Very often we forget
about what we hold inside of ourselves until we are reminded of it.
That's why in the world there are so many pilgrimage places. The
pilgrimage place is not about the place itself, it's about reminding
oneself of what Christ talked about, whatever He taught about,
and He didn't teach about any dogmas. All that He taught about
was about Love. That's the simplest thing, but we forget about it.
Instead, we get hung up on; we can't do this, we can't do that, we
can't do so many things that we forget about what we have to do.
I remember once, when I was studying theology, I said to the Bishop
"All that you have talked about is about dogma, but there was not
one single time when you talked about the Love of Christ, not a
single time you talked about how He really lived." We read about
the Bible, we read that He was with His Disciples and all this stuff,
but He was also a very alive person.
I remember in one of the churches we visited in Nazareth, there
was a nice – not an icon, it was made with pieces of stone, but it
was not a mosaic. I can't remember the name of it, but it was very
beautiful – Christ as the shepherd. On His shoulder there was a
sheep. For sure you have seen the picture of the Good Shepherd.
What was very beautiful about that particular one, let's call it icon,
was that He was not pictured, as what we usually see, in a long
robe. He instead had a piece of cloth wrapped around and He was
showing His strength.
Then I was talking with the guide and the guide was explaining
about it and I asked him "Do you know who is represented in this
image of Christ?" Of course, you will think it's the Good Shepherd.
Actually, the original picture was of Apollo, which was changed

afterwards into Christ, but it doesn't matter. It shows us that He lived normally; He lived with the people. He was laughing also, not always moody, not always thinking of the Cross.

He had His mission and His mission was and is to spread Universal Love and to make people realise the Kingdom of God. He always said "The Kingdom of God is near," but near

He didn't teach about any dogmas. All that He taught about was about Love.

where? If you shut the mind and stay in your heart through Love, you will see the Kingdom of God inside of you. That's what all these places remind one of – the Love that God is giving constantly to humans, but we have to know how to receive it. If one receives it with an open heart, it will grow always, but if one receives it with only the mind, it will have its limitations.

So remind yourself constantly of opening that heart and finding the Deity inside of you.

You are all pilgrims. This life on Earth is a pilgrimage – a pilgrimage which will end when you have found the Lord, when you have *realised* Him. He has made it so easy and clear. It's not far away; it's just near. Shut the mind, turn it off and open the tap of Love inside your heart. Open it, let it flow and you will see how *near* the Divine is to you. I guess during this trip many have experienced great joy. Of course, it awoke certain things, but it was lovely. Everything is good.

I was talking to somebody today. This person asked me a question last January and of course, I had given him my answer that I had to give him, but he chose to do his way, which is also nice. So today, as I was talking to him on the phone, he was always complaining "Oh Swamiji, I should have listened to you." He was saying all this and that, so much, but I said "Well, look, what is done is done. We can't change it, but there is one thing you can do. You have *learned* a lot from that experience and now you know what you have to do. You could have made it much easier by listening, but you have made experience. You have learned. It was good for your learning." Sometimes, if you just tell somebody something, it is easy, but they will not get anything. It's like when you tell a child "Don't put your hand in fire; you will get burned," but if the child has never burnt himself, do you think he will know what burning is? No, and there will always be this wanting to put a hand in the fire, because he wants to know what burning is. So experience, whether it's good or bad, is a learning process; it's a learning that your soul needs to know. If you attune yourself to the right tune, to the right frequency of your soul, you will learn it very quickly. It's a matter of what you want.

If I ask everybody now "What do you want?" some will say "I want Love", some will say "I want God" or "I want God-Realisation." Well, it's beautiful, but do you really want that? If you really, sincerely want it, then be strong and have faith. Trust! Trust what the Divine is giving to you; trust what you feel inside of you. Like it is said, one has to have faith like a child, no? When you look at children, they are free. They don't think too much. But what happens afterwards? Where is the child gone? The mind has taken over. You think you know more, so you need to reason.

Sometimes you don't need to reason. You just need to sit quietly and feel. Feel and listen, because when you feel of course, it's not just feeling. When you are completely in silence, there is also the voice of God. The voice of God will not talk to you like in ancient times. He will talk to you from within you. Learn to trust this inner voice, and if you still have doubt about it, ask Him questions. Ask Him if it is really like this or like that. Then you test it yourself, so that you can learn to trust this inner voice. It's not that you just hear it and accept it "OK, yes, it's fine. It's good like that." No, you hear, ask certain questions and see if it is really happening this way, then give your full trust to it. This is one way of listening to your inner Self and to make it stronger and stronger.

This example is given by the Virgin Mary Herself. When the angels appeared to Her and greeted Her with "Hail Mary, you are blessed among all the women. The Lord has favoured you that you will bear the Son of God inside of your womb" She didn't say, "OK, cool, I like that." No, She said "How can this be possible? I have never been with a man." So the angels were pleased with it, because this confirmed Her faith. She didn't have doubt, but She questioned it. This is what the angels said "It will be done according to the Will of God. The Spirit shall come over you and overshadow you."

It's important to learn to trust this inner voice, and to know for sure if it is real or if it is just a fantasy of one's mind. You will do that by putting certain questions to that and yet you will be the observer of that conversation. The *atma*, the soul,

> This is the most beautiful thing you can do – to observe how the mind is talking to the Higher Self and what you are hearing inside of you.

will be the observer of that conversation. I will tell you something; this is the most beautiful thing you can do – to observe how the mind is talking to the Higher Self and what you are hearing inside of you.

Like I said to you before, this will happen only when you are in silence. So introvert yourself as much as possible and be in silence, because when somebody talks, talks and talks, like I am doing right now, what happens? Of course it is joyful to talk, but afterwards you are tired. Of course, you will say "When I sit down quietly, I also will get tired," but when the mind is calm, you will not be tired. This is where meditation comes in. Meditation is not only to sit in one place and close one's eyes and meditate, like we know it in the traditional way, but meditation is also every time when you can look inside your heart and see the Divine.

THE PRIMODIAL CREATION OF GOD

Hiranyagarbhalingam Manifestation,
Shree Peetha Nilaya, Germany, 30 November 2009

It's nice that you are all here, firstly because it's Babaji's day and secondly, for you to receive the blessing of the *Hiranyagarbha Lingam*.

Actually, I already talked about the *Hiranyagarbha Lingam* back in 2005 and Babaji wanted the lingam to come and so it came. Normally this Lingam is not manifested just like that, because it's not like a normal Lingam. The *Hiranyagarbha Lingam*, as it is said in the *Vedas,* is the Primordial Creation of God. Actually, it is the Will of God itself and even if it seems so small like this, it has the whole universe inside of it. What we are experiencing now, we are also experiencing inside of it. Even if it seems that we are outside, we are all inside of it.

Why did it manifest now? Probably you have noticed that the past two weeks the world itself is changing. Probably you have noticed, or you have *not* noticed, but there are some changes happening in the world. It has nothing to do with 2012, to make it clear, but these changes reflect what will be a greater change later on. While I was traveling last week, I was saying that I thought people were changing for the better, but actually I realise it's the contrary. Out of the masses of people that are living in this world, only a few are changing really for the better.

So actually, bringing this Lingam into this consciousness, which is low consciousness, will probably help to give a boost to people's advancement. It is not only helping you who are here. It doesn't only reflect on you all, because actually, it reflects on the world itself.

This Lingam has a lot of healing qualities, which means it doesn't heal only the body, but it heals the soul itself. Of course, one would say "Our soul? How can our soul be affected, because our soul is pure and completely into the Divine?" It's true that our soul *is* pure and completely into the Divine, but around it, what suffocates the soul, are all the karmic things that one has accumulated, not only in one life, but also in many lives.

What you're experiencing now, means that for sure, generally speaking, you have done really good things, because it's not often that you see the *Hiranyagarbha Lingam.* Even the *Devas* long for it, because it cannot be created, even by Brahma, Vishnu or Mahesh. It can be created only by somebody who is living, who is embodied. Well... they live somewhere also!

> It's true that our soul is pure and completely into the Divine, but around it, what suffocates the soul, are all the karmic things that one has accumulated, not only in one life, but also in many lives.

Today we are celebrating Babaji's day. You see, Babaji wanted to leave this planet. Then his sister interceded saying "It doesn't make any difference for you whether you are there or here, so why don't you stay?" Actually it's on this day, 1,800 years ago – plus some years – that he chose to keep living here and thus, immortalized Himself here in this world. That's what we are commemorating today. It's like a renewal that he will always be here to help humanity whenever it's needed.

It's time now for the changes to happen. It's time that humanity calls upon him and receives his help. Whether humanity calls him or not, he *will* help, but it's a nice gesture from us to do so. You all get the blessing of the *Hiranyagarbha Lingam*, so I hope all of you will profit. Whoever is in your thoughts and in your prayers will alsoprofit, as well as the whole world.

After the ceremony meditation

You can meditate on the *Hiranyagarbha Lingam*. Meditate and see the Lingam here, on your third eye, then bring it into your heart. Just see the image first in your mind and bring the image to your heart and let the Lingam merge into your heart. You see, it's an equal blessing even to just see a picture of the *Hiranyagarbha Lingam*, so you are blessed to see the *Lingam* itself.

WHY WE DON'T SEE GOD

Darshan, Shree Peetha Nillaya, Germany, 5 December 2009

There is a question that many people have asked "Why don't we see God?". They always ask me this question, but now I reverse the question to you. You tell me what is the reason for people not to see God? Everybody knows that God is omnipresent; everybody knows that He is present in you, in me, in everything. We know it, but why don't we see it? The human mind is so entangled with the sense objects and pride, that it makes it difficult to see God. Actually, we are continuously, always in Him and He is always in us. There is never a moment that He is not present. From day one, before you take birth, He was here inside of you already.

How many times in your life have you said "God is not with me"? Faith is there. As God is there, faith is there. We don't try our best; we don't persevere. Perseverance is important if you try something, but if it's not the same as what you expected, you stop. Then what happens? You will never succeed. You have to keep trying. It is there already. By seeing your effort, He will reveal Himself to you.

There is another question which will arise "But Swamiji, we are so much into the world, shall we leave everything to realise God?" Even today I had this question. No, actually the answer is you don't need to leave anything to realise the Divine. To realise the reality, first say to yourself that you live in the reality and this reality is inside of you. To perceive this reality in your daily life, in your daily actions, you will realise that the Divine is always with you. But if you don't perceive the reality with you, you expect that God will appear in a light and say "Here, cuckoo, I am here". You can wait for some lives! I tell you something: He is patient to wait for you, but you are not patient to wait for Him.

So live in the world, do everything, but do it in the mind-set of surrendering. No matter what action you do, surrender it to the Divine. Know that whatever action you do, whether it is, positive or negative, it is a prayer for and in front of Him. If in this attitude you surrender every action to the Divine, it will be pure always.

In the *Soundarya Lahari*, Sri Adi Shankaracharya wrote about it. He said "Oh, Divine, I give you everything. Let my every action of surrender to You, be a prayer to your Feet. When I am lying down, sleeping, let it be a prostration to your Feet! Be it that every food that I am eating is an offering to Thee." Like that, all the actions that you are doing in daily life, if you do them with the remembrance of the Divine, they will be pure, because the Divine is not limited half as much as we think of Him.

We are limited. We are limited, because our mind, our pride, our ego is so huge, that we live in this world and we get attached to the world. We make our whole life depend on this world. Like the great Sages said "Live in the world, but don't let the world live in you. If you let the world live in you, then God becomes far away."

Like the lotus. Have you seen the lotus flower? Where does the lotus flower grow? In mud – it comes out from mud. All the mud doesn't affect it. Such is the Divine inside of you also. Such is who you are in reality. You live in this world. Don't let the negativity of this world affect you. Be positive firstly. If you are positive, automatically you will be humble. Humility – this is a nice word. Humbleness means acceptance – to accept yourself how you are and to know that what you are looking for on the outside doesn't reside on the outside. It resides here inside of you.

If He has humbled Himself inside of you, why can't you be humble on the outside? Why can't you be loving on the outside? Why?

This has to change. Don't expect that I will change you or God will change you. You have to change yourself. This is the self-effort from your side. We will help you, but make the first effort. Otherwise, it's difficult.

Like Draupadi, when Duryodhana wanted to remove Her clothes, She called for Krishna "Oh, Krishna, come and help me. Whenever people need you, you said, when we call You, You will be there. Come now, I need you." No help. Again she made the same request and no help. She was hanging so much onto her sari for Duryodhana not to take it, but then She let go. She said "OK, you want to take it? Take it off. It doesn't matter". At that moment there was endless sari. Duryodhana could not remove an inch. He was removing, removing, removing. Metres and metres and metres came out from her sari, so that he was not able to finish removing the sari from her. He got tired. He stopped.

> The human mind is so entangled with the sense objects and pride, that it makes it difficult to see God.

So one day Draupadi was with Krishna alone and said "My Lord, I want to ask you something. When I called You, why did You take some time to come?" and Krishna said "Well, you see, when you said *Go-*, I left my palace. By the time you said *-vinda,* I was already there. But when I was there, I saw you clinging so much on the materialistic, on your sari, that I was just standing there and watching you. When you let go of this, then I came to your aid."

The same is for you. Once you make your effort, the Divine will come to your aid. You will see how quickly and how easy it is, but the first effort of letting go, you have to do it. This He can't do for you, and it's not just by merely saying "Yes, I want His love and I am letting go." It's not like that. You really have to let go, you really have to sincerely want it. Once this sincerity is there, you will see. You have everything already, inside of you. When the veil is dropped, the light is seen. Such will be when you make your effort sincerely. When this veil, which covers our eyes and covers our consciousness, is dropped, you shall see the light clearly, even more clearly than this light. So make your effort. Don't just sit down and say "I try this one, I try that one, I try this one." No.

It's like a fisherman who goes fishing. If he just sits in the boat, sits on the side, looks at the lake and says "Oh, there is fish." Every time the fish jumps, he says "There is fish." The fish will not jump from the water into his lap. He has to get the hook, he has to get the line, has to get the bait, throw it and then the fish will come up.

Otherwise, you can sit and wait. There are many examples you can say. If you are thirsty, you must go for water. Water will not come to you. Persevere. Make your effort and the Lord will help you.

THE CHANCE TO TRANSFORM OURSELVES

Darshan, Shree Peetha Nilaya, Springen, Germany 8 May 2010

We have been singing *Jai Ma* as the great feast day of the Divine Mother, the Mother which is seated inside your heart – not the mother who has given you this body, well she is also the mother – but the Mother who has given you this soul, who has given you the spirit, has given you this body to dwell in this world and has given you such a beautiful world to be in.

At the same time a mother wants the child. A mother is always ready to care for the children. How can we make this Divine Mother happy? She doesn't ask too much from us. She doesn't ask that we change ourselves for Her. The only thing that She asks is that each one, by oneself, decides to change not for Her sake, but for their own sake.

I was traveling and I went to a big city, looking at how people were busy on the outside. I asked myself this question "Do they really know that there is something greater than just this life that they are living?" I was asking my *Guru* about it. We can say "Yes." Here, we are all thinking we know there is something greater in the life of man even if you, as a human being, have not realised it, yet you have this sense of feeling that yes, there is something greater and you want to achieve, to attain this.

While walking, I was thinking how many among these people were really living a human life. How many were really knowing that life is not just what they were living? There is much more than that. They can be really eternally happy. They can really find this great

joy, which nothing can take away. How many? I was wondering.
Then a friend said something about a philosopher, a Greek philosopher, Diogenes. He went around during the day with his lamp and of course, everybody would laugh at him. They would laugh at him; they would ridicule him. He didn't bother about anything and one day somebody asked him "Why are you going around in daylight with your torch lit, because it is funny!" His answer was very simple and clear "I'm looking for a human being!" There are many humans, but there are only a few human beings.

If you fully believe in yourself, if you fully have trust in yourself, you will fully believe and trust in God. Then of course, the Divine will always help you.

What is the difference between a human and a human being? An animal can also be counted as a human. It has a body, it breathes, but we call an animal, an animal and a human, a human. The faculty of looking for something greater is only in the human being. But when you go around, as I was singing before in one verse of the song, that illusion, *Maya,* has caught us. *Maya* has caught human beings and she is making human beings play to the tune that she wants.

This is exactly how it is on the outside, until you start to really search for the truth of your Self. When you start searching for the truth of your Self, then you disengage yourself from that grief of *Maya,* but as you know very well, it is not an easy task. It's not something that is very easy to do at all.

Everybody would like to, lots of spiritual people would like to, but only a few succeed. Why? Because their determination is weak. If your determination for the Divine is strong, nothing can move you, but if your determination is weak, then you will be weak, because you make yourself weak, like I said before.

You have the *Shakti* inside of you. You have this power inside of you and if you work on it, you will intensify it, but of course *Maya* will make you more dense. Remembering this is great. When you all remember your Mother, remember also this Divine *Shakti* which is inside of you – the *Shakti*, which, without it, you would not even be here. Without the *Shakti*, without this power, you would not even be able to blink your eyes.

Be grateful for life and really try. I don't say to do it, but try it at least, by yourself to see certain things that you have to transform in your life. Know that you have the power to transform them only when you fully believe in yourself. If you fully believe in yourself, if you fully have trust in yourself, you will fully believe and trust in God. Then of course, the Divine will always help you. There is so much help around, but like this famous saying says "Help yourself; Heaven will help you." You know about this? You have to make the first effort and then of course, you will receive the help.

This reminds me of a story. There was a priest. There was a flood and everything was flooded around. The priest went up on the church and sat there, waiting for God to save him. First a boat came. "Priest, come, we'll save you. Come inside the boat!" The priest said "No, God will save me." Then a second boat came and again the priest refused. The third time, a helicopter came and once again he said "No, God will save me." Finally, he drowned and died. He arrived in front of God very angry. He said "God, I was there. Why you didn't save me?" God looked at him and said "My child, I did come to save you, but you didn't want to save yourself. Look, I sent two boats. I sent a helicopter, but you refused the help that I was giving you. So why are you complaining?"

It's the same for man. Whenever people are on the spiritual path, if they are in tune with the Divine, they will receive help. Accept it and move forward; don't move backwards.

YOU NEED TO BE CONTINUOUSLY IN LOVE

Darshan, Belgium, 6 April 2005

I'm really happy to be among all of you, especially among all the youngsters who are here. It's really beautiful to see that youngsters are moving towards spirituality, and I think this is great in the world today. It's really a grace to be spiritual, and to receive it at such a young age. People don't realise it. I encourage you to carry on in that way and grow more and more, strengthen faith in yourself. Grow in it, also for all of you here, not only for the youngsters. You know there is a saying "Spirituality starts when religion ends."
Real spirituality is in each one of you, in each one of your hearts, whether you believe or not, it's there. God is sitting permanently within you. But to achieve it, this is each one's way, each one's *personal* way. To discover the God without form, God without name, the eternal – to realise that you, all of you, are part of Him. This is the aim of man.
Open up your heart! Love, love unconditionally! Love without limit! Love without expecting anything! Realise this Love is ever flowing, the more you give, the more you receive. Just give for the sake of giving. That is what you are here for. Not to receive anything, not to take anything from anybody. Because what is the difference between you and me? Nothing. But one difference: I realise it, you don't realise it. You can also reach the same level. You need to be continuously in love.
You know how beautiful it is? For sure you know...all of you have fallen in love, isn't it?? (*the audience laughs*)

None of you have answered me. Have you really fallen in love? (*Audience: "Yes, but it was terrible..." laughing*)
You see, as long love is with expectation, it will always be terrible. When you love, when you realise yourself being the source of love, it's not terrible. It's the most joyful thing, the most beautiful thing. Love is just word which I can say to you. It's up to each one of you to experience it, like a small child. If a small child came walking into this room, he would just experience love; he wouldn't bother about anything around.

Now, about our mind, we think before acting. We always think. We think if we give love we will feel hurt. You see, in the mind, you already create the hurt; you create the feeling of destruction, so you don't put love first.

Make the ultimate goal of your life Divine love, and surrender to it. You know what God wants from you? Surrender your mind to Him, continuously. Surrender your mind to the lotus feet of God, to the feet of your Guru, to the feet of any Divine master, and free yourself. Free yourself from the mind, free yourself from all the misery that you created. When you free your mind, you realise the Divine everywhere, in every aspect, in every small thing. Even the clothes you are wearing are divine. Each atom is divine.

If you have divine eyes to look at the world with, you will see that it is just the radiated light of God shining through everything, but as long as you don't come to that realisation, keep trying. Never lose hope. The moment you lose hope, you lose everything. The moment you say "No, I can't do it, I can't do this," you will not be able to do it. Challenge your fear! Keep reminding yourself that you are a part of God. You are in His Divine hands and He will never let go of you. Never! He will be always near to you, even nearer than the breath, the air you are breathing in.

You try to imagine a little bit with the mind, how close God is. It's difficult, isn't it? The mind will never let you imagine that. Only when you start thinking with the mind of the heart – then you can realise the divinity completely.

So, how to think with the heart? This is why meditation is important, when you can sit with yourself in silence. When Jesus said "If you want to pray, run to the darkest corner of your house, close yourself and talk with your Father," he meant, go in the inner chamber of your heart and talk with God, talk with your true Self, you will receive the answer. In this inner chamber – what is there? Just love, nothing else.

There is no power of the mind to stop anybody because you are all equal; you are all the same light, the same energy. Like this lovely chandelier here, it has many lights, doesn't it? It's the same electricity that is lighting all of them. Keep reminding yourself of your purpose of this incarnation and reach it; make sure that you reach it in this life. Don't think of other lives. Now will be the best. It is possible if you surrender, body, mind, and soul completely to God.

> He will never let go of you. Never! He will be always near to you, even nearer than the breath, the air you are breathing in.

Let go of your identity, let go of this "I", this egoism that make you focus only on the outer. When you let go of your identity, the Divine will reveal itself to you. Then you will see the unlimited. You will feel the blissful happiness. Open up – if the mind is still troubling you, take any divine aspect, focus your mind on it and surrender to the divine aspect until you reach the formless. From the form to the formless. Do you want God? Do you want realisation?

(*audience: "Yes!"*)

Is it a "Yes" from the heart or from the mind?

(*laughing... audience: "from the heart!"*)

Don't tell it to me – tell it to yourself and be sincere to yourself. Say "Yes, I want it!" When you say it "Yes I want realisation, I want God!" with such determination, with such strength, such willpower, He will reveal Himself to you. He is accessible twenty-four hours, seven days a week, you know – always. He's not limited to any time, He's not limited to any place, He's not limited to any form. When you close your eyes and drop inside yourself, you access Him. Try it.

Meditation

Close your eyes, sure your mind will trouble you, but don't give much importance to it. The mind is also doing its part to create illusion. Remove all the pressure from your shoulders and travel inwardly. Use your mind to imagine, see your heart, your physical heart. It's a beautiful organ which is pumping the blood in all parts of your body. Look at it, how beautiful it is! You know this.

Deep in this organ there is the greatest thing that has been given to humans! With each beat of the heart it is saying "Let me out!" The Divine is calling from deep within you "Let me out!" You are the one with the key. Open up this heart, make this heart of flesh become the Heart of light, a light that the mind can't comprehend, a light without any form, a light without any colour, the complete beautiful and most majestic light, even brighter than the sun. Then see the light, that

Realise this Love is ever flowing, the more you give, the more you receive. Just give for the sake of giving. That is what you are here for.

is who you really are. Once you see it, once you have it – don't let go of it. Keep it always and radiate this light. At every moment wherever you are, just be the light. Through this light, healing will happen, through this light, pain will be healed. Through this light, realisation will be achieved.

Now you are sitting here with closed eyes. You are feeling something, good. Try to keep it inside you. Take time every day to sit fifteen minutes quietly with yourself, and this fifteen minutes is for yourself. You can open your eyes now.

HOW TO APPROACH DIVINE LOVE

Darshan, Steffenshof, Germany, 18 June 2005

Last week was a great time I hope for all of you it was really enjoyable, wasn't it? So, we will talk about prayer, about Love. Unity is God. We always come to the same point, where we talk about God. We talk about His Love for all of us – this Love that He has without condition. We start our spiritual way because there is something missing in our life, something that this world can't give. This thing, which is missing, you can only discover it inside you. There is a saying – approach Him with Love, reach Him in that Love, meet Him in Love, embrace Him with Love and merge with Him and become eternal Love! I find it so beautiful, because when we start our spiritual way, it's always the approach for the Divine Love.

We start our journey to approaching the Divine. We make our first step, we start searching for Him. This is when prayer starts in our life. Prayer is this essence of realising that there is something greater – whether you call it God, Light, Spirit... The search starts through prayer, and prayer makes the link, makes the first step to this union. Then one will reach the next step by meeting and reaching that Love. By prayer the heart opens up, firstly towards the outside, then towards the inside.

We meet Him in Love. Through the reciting of Divine names, the reciting and singing of God's names, like you are doing, you reach the point where Love is, where everybody is sharing one goal: the achievement of that Love. Then there comes the point of meeting Him in Love. This is happening in meditation, when you sit down and have the connection with your true Self. You meet the Love within yourself and start this discussion, start this communication with the Self, about knowing who you really are. In this meeting we embrace that Love, we become one with it and realise it more and more.

More and more, day by day, you grow. With this Divine Love you will realise that there is no difference between the Love that you knew at the beginning and now. With this Love there is no difference between you, me – anybody. This eternal Love, this eternal Light resides in everything. It's so easy, isn't it? I always recite the same: spirituality is very easy! It's simply that you want it! It's given to you already – inside of your heart. The moment you want it, you will receive it, but humans like complicated things – the more something is complicated the more they like it.

Approach Him with Love, reach Him in that Love, meet Him in Love, embrace Him with Love and merge with Him and become eternal Love!

You come to Swami and Swami says "Don't worry, just love!" You are not satisfied, are you? But if Swami said "Do a mantra ten thousand times", you would be happy with it! These ten thousand times while you were doing this mantra you would lose the consciousness of the mind, you would merge into the consciousness of the Divine, you would become Love. The same thing I would give you much easier – I would give it to you on a plate and you would refuse it! The same God is giving you: Love. The realisation of Love is already in your heart, the moment you are born, it's already there. It's upon to each one of you to let it out. Leave the problems apart, leave your worry apart – be this Love, be this eternal Love, and enjoy it! Love is simple, if you have it inside your heart. Is it difficult? What a simple word, let it flow! Everything is in it, everything – even the Cosmic itself is present in it. So make this your goal: Wanting Love! Want it! First thing in the morning, when you wake up, say it "I want Love, I am Love!" During the day recite "I am Love". And at night, when you are going to bed, recite "I am Love". First you start by reciting it outside to conquer the power of the mind. Then you say it inwardly, quietly, within yourself "I am Love". Then you say it with all parts of your body "I am Love". And at the end - just be Love! Nothing else, just Love.

THE QUICKEST WAY

Darshan, Pacific Palisades, Los Angeles, United States, 3 July 2005

It gives me great pleasure to be among all of you, and especially to share this Divine Love with all of you. As you all may know, the ultimate goal of life is to realise the Self. The soul, the Divine, whatever name you want to call it, is your own Self. In this daily life, with our daily occupations, the mind becomes very busy. We read lots of books and talk about spiritual things. There are many ways of attaining Divine Love. There are many ways of attaining this unity, this realisation of who we really are. Each person has their own way, but all paths are the same. At the end you will experience the same Love, the same happiness. For sure, some ways are longer and some are shorter. Some people like taking a short way, and some people like taking a long way. Do you like the long way or the short way? Of course the shorter way is better. (*laughs*) The quickest way is just to love.

This word 'Love' hides a lot of mystery, hides a lot of secrets given to mankind. This expression of Divine Love, pure consciousness, is who you really are. So many times we forget about it. We try to be separate from it. We have to continuously remind ourselves that we are this Love. No matter what comes on the way, remember that we are this Love. We are here to give and to share this Love, to realise it. So how do we realise this Love? We meet someone and say to the person "I love you." Don't we? How many times in your life have you said to somebody else "I love you?" Many times, but have you ever said it to your own self? "I love myself." When it comes to loving one's own self, people say "It is difficult." It's difficult because you see all the negative qualities of your outer self, forgetting that this true Self, who you really are, is just pure Love. To give love, first you should realise Love with your own Self. Start loving yourself. Not in an egoistic way – some people think loving oneself is very egoistic, but to love the Self is not to love the body. Loving oneself is transcending the physical aspect. Through Love you will develop trust and patience. If you have these three: Love, trust and patience, you have everything else.

This reminds me of a story. Krishna used to stay in Brindavan. He stayed there until the age of sixteen, then he went away. When he left, everybody in Brindavan was sad and always thinking of Krishna. They thought that Krishna had forgotten about them. So, one day, Krishna sent one of his devotees, Uddhava, to tell them that he does care for them. When he arrived there, he met the *gopis* and before he could start talking, the gopis started blaming Krishna, saying "Oh he forgot about us. He has left us. He had given us so much Love and then he just withdrew everything and went away." Uddhava was laughing and said "No, Krishna has never forgotten about you. He thinks about all of you every day. There is not one second that he doesn't talk about all of you. The point is: He had other work to do, and that is why he went." They could not accept it. So they keep on saying bad words about Krishna, but in a more loving way. There was so much Love in it that it didn't matter. Then Uddhava gave the gopis a message that Krishna had given to them. Krishna said "All that is and all that you feel is just a game. I create, I protect and I destroy everything by my own will, and it all goes back to me. Maya, illusion, has created a veil of separation. With this veil, you can't see that you are all a part of me."

That is actually why you are all here, to remove this veil. There are many lifetimes that you keep on playing the same game. You repeat and repeat the same thing, forgetting that the Lord is here, deep inside our heart. We are looking for Him on the outside. We are looking for Him in this world, but we can just drop deep inside of ourselves and find Him. Let go of the mind which is always busy looking on the outside. If we just drop ourselves deep in our heart we can feel this peace and happiness and enjoy it. You will see how great it is, how great it is to love. Not just to say to somebody "I love you." But really to feel it from deep within you — this is the true Love of loving somebody. It is not only for one person but for everybody. Loving unconditionally. When you say "I don't love this person..." "I don't love" means you love this person, but in a different way. The mind of man can't think "No". In words we can say "No", but our mind thinks in pictures, and in pictures, "no" doesn't exist. It is only how we talk about it on the outside. So let go of the power of the mind that makes you feel separate from the Divine, and be one with it. There are different practices to help with this. You can sing the name of God, recite any mantra. Sing the name of Jesus, sing the name of Rama, Krishna, or Allah, it is all equal. All are His names. Become one with this Divine name. That's what the word mantra really means. To merge and become one. Let your life itself reflect who you really are. So, sing with me:

> Each person has their own way, but all paths are the same. At the end you will experience the same Love, the same happiness.

(Everyone starts singing "Om Namo Narayanaya")

Isn't it beautiful to sing the name of God? It's very easy. It's so easy to merge with God. It's so easy to realise His Divine Love. Just take one name and recite it continuously. Make the power of the mind combine with the power of the mantra. Let the mantra take over the mind. Let yourself become the mantra. What is in this name, Narayana, or Jesus, has the capacity to give peace to the mind. It's very simple. Wherever you are, keep singing, keep reciting. It's not limited. Wherever you are, even if you are traveling: you are on the toilet, you are taking a shower… recite the name of God. If you are cooking, you will have better food. Become this mantra. And let your heart open. Let this Love which is inside of you be reflected on the outside. You will become this Divine instrument. Let everybody who is next to you feel this Love so that they will also want it. They will ask "Where does this Love come from?" Some of them will say to you "You look different. You reflect something different." You will answer "It's just the Love of God." It's simple. But you see, sometimes when God gives simple things to man, man is not really happy with it. Man likes to complicate things. The more you complicate it, the more man enjoys it. And the more man complains about it. So, try to be as simple as possible. You will grow closer to yourself, closer to God and closer to the Divinity.

THE 84TH DOOR

Darshan, Encinitas, United States, 12 July 2005

When you are a toddler, when you are still a baby, you are born with full light. When a baby is born, the father, the mother and all the people around it say "Oh the baby is so beautiful, so radiant." Isn't it? Then what happens afterwards? When the child is born it reflects the light of God, but when the child grows up, the light goes deep inside the heart. With the world being how it is outside, it creates a lot of shadows over this light, and the same people who twenty years ago said "This child is full of light," they start saying the child is very bad. How can the same child who reflected the light be the same person in front of you, who now does not reflect the same light? If we look properly with our third eye, we will see that all of you reflect the same light, whether it is a small baby or an adult, but our mind is busy judging. In this judging, our mind enjoys looking only at the negative parts of life. How this person is dressed, or how this person behaves – we tend to see the negative, but behind what we see with our physical eyes is the reality. If we look with our eyes through the heart we will be able to see the reality. First we'll see the reality of our self. We incarnate time after time to attain one thing: liberation. This word liberation is present in all Holy Scriptures. Take the Bible, Jesus talks about it; in the Koran, the prophet Mohammed talks about it; take the Bhagavad Gita, Krishna talks about it. Why does man not achieve it? Why does man not say "It's enough!"?
This reminds me of a small story. There was a blind man who was

taken to a big hole. Some people trapped him in this hole, which had eighty-four exits. Among these eighty-four exits, only one door was open. So they put the man inside and told the man to find this one door. The man stopped, found the first door, tried to push it, but could not, then the next door, the same thing. He reached the eighty-third door, but he didn't know it. He had not been counting. When he was about to push this eighty-fourth door his hand started to itch. He forgot about the door and started scratching his hand. While scratching his hand, he missed the eighty-fourth door.

> You want liberation? Make it strong in your mind; make it strong deep inside your heart.

Likewise, for many humans the door is now here. Don't let the itching of the world get you. You want liberation? Make it strong in your mind; make it strong deep inside your heart. Let it get fulfilled on the outside. You are this light and you all can merge back into this light. You have to want it, and this want has to be very, very strong. It has to be the most important thing in your life. There are many Divine incarnations. They all come, they all teach, they all go. People at different times assimilate it in their own way. But we are living in such an age right now that it is very easy to attain Self-realisation.

We just need to be simple with ourselves. Simple in the mind. When I say simple, I mean just to love. Make this love unconditional. This love that you have inside of you, the source of all things, let it flow. Don't try to stop it; don't put any barrier around it. Now you are putting up barriers. How long can these barriers hold this love? It will overflow one day. So let it overflow, let it flow right now. At the end of life you will say "Oh, I should have done this much earlier. I wasted all my life running after things that have a limit. I am the whole unlimited one which I see in my heart."

Close your eyes, drop inside your heart and feel this fullness. Feel the greatness of yourself, this greatness is you. This greatness is who you really are, without any egoism. Keep concentrating on this greatness inside you. This great love which is emanating from your heart. It passes through each cell of your body. Try to reflect it outside. Isn't it beautiful to see each person as the full light body? Let the eighty-fourth door of your heart open up.

And if your mind is troubling you, sing the name of God. There are so many of them.

Om Namo Narayanaya, Om Namo Narayanaya...

Guided Meditation

I would like to do a small meditation with you. It's a very simple meditation.

We will use our imagination. Like when a child is being a bit naughty, you just give it a game. Give a toy to the child and let the child play. The child is the mind. So, we'll give the mind a game, and we'll let him play his game.

If possible, it's good to dim the lights.

- Try to sit straight, even in a chair. Make sure that your spine is straight.

- Listen to your breathing. Listen to it. With the mind, imagine OM on your forehead. Listen to the beautiful melody of your breathing. Let yourself be drawn deeper and deeper in it. Your mind will think. Let it pass. Don't try to stop it. Don't use force to stop it. Don't give any importance to it.

- Keep your concentration on your breathing. Don't hear anything else other than your breathing.

- To stop the mind, let's use it now. Let's use it to imagine how

God is looking at us. Imagine yourself being God. Imagine the majesty, the hugeness, the purity, the light. See your physical body full of light. See your body radiating this light very brightly. There is so much joy within that is coming out from inside you. So much happiness.

- Now, imagine the people who surround you. Look at all of them. See the same light in them. There's no difference. Visualize the town where we are. Everybody's radiating the same light. See the whole of California radiating light. Imagine the animal kingdom. They also radiate the same light. Imagine the plant kingdom. You see the same light. See the ocean kingdom reflecting the same light.

- See the whole U.S. full of light. See the whole world reflecting this brilliant light. There is no disharmony. There is no hate. There is just peace and love. The whole universe is radiating this beautiful light.

- Now, reduce all this light to one central point which is called the heart. See yourself sitting in all this light around that you have been imagining. See all this light shrinking and entering one point – the heart. In the heart, you feel lots of warmth... happiness... joy...

OM..... OM..... OM.....

BY KNOWING YOUR OWN SELF, YOU WILL KNOW GOD

Darshan, Bad Cannstatt, Germany, 6 August 2005

Often people talk about liberation or freedom. In the mind of man, whenever we talk about freedom, what are the things we think of first? Freedom of country, political freedom, economical freedom. But there is the inner freedom which is the most important among all the different kinds of freedom and that is what mankind really wants to achieve. That is also why each soul has come on earth, to achieve this freedom, this love of God.

This freedom is like, let me try to interpret: If you want something, you shall have it, but you can also detach from this thing by your own will. You see, mankind desires many things, but when they have it they get attached to it. This attachment brings unhappiness. The more you are attached to things which are limited or not eternal, the more you feel miserable. Then you lose this inner freedom. You become limited in the mind, you become limited with your body, which in turn makes your soul limited. To free one's self, one must to surrender the body, mind and soul to God, to the Unlimited. It's true, everybody can't renounce the world and live only for God,

> There is the inner freedom which is the most important among all the different kinds of freedom and that is what mankind really wants to achieve.

but you can continuously try to remember God wherever you are. Remember that the soul inside you is the light of God. The more you think of yourself being part of this light of God, this great love, the more you will reflect this love. The more you think that you are just a normal human being, the more you will just be a normal human being with all of its limited qualities – then you cover all of your divine qualities. Take time every day, just five minutes, to be with yourself. Forget about the world outside, forget everything. Forget about your husband or wife; forget about all your relationships with the outside. Only think of the relationship with yourself.

Do you know what treasure you will find? The biggest treasure of all, a treasure that nobody can steal from you and that's – love. Love is such a big gift! We feel it with our heart, we know it with our mind, but to realise it, to become one with this love, to spread this love, unconditionally — this is the aim of mankind. The more you spread it, the more you reflect it, the more you will discover yourself.

When people say "I want to know God," I answer "Know thyself." By knowing your own self, you will know God, because when we want to know God outside, we automatically create a barrier, we create a limited form. We are this love, we are this light. We are not separate from God, we are part of God. To achieve this we must surrender. Surrender the mind which is always jumping around. Surrender the body, which is the temple of this light and love, and reflect this light always.

ENOUGH IS ENOUGH!

Portugal, 19 November 2005

Today I will not give Darshan. The last three days was a lot for some people, but I will do prayer to all the Deities on the altar. I will ask all of you to join me during the prayer, let your only want, the only desire be for God. Like I said before, the only desire of mankind, the only desire of the Spirit is God.

All others desires are limited. When you desire something, you think you want it. The point is, when you get this thing that you desire, all your feelings are gone. You start disliking this thing, because it is not the Ultimate. It is not the fulfilment of everything. The only desire you will have is God, because He is the unlimited of everything. This want, you will never question, whereas with the other wants, you will always have questions.

For example: if you start a business, the desire is great, you are very happy, because the main thing is to get money. Then what happens? The question arises, how to get the money? When you get the money, it will never be fulfilling, because you will think how to get more, or how you will pay the people who are working with you. How you would buy other things for your business to grow more. So in this game, you will always ask the question "How will I do this?" and you will never really be satisfied and really happy with yourself.

That doesn't mean you should stop your business or should stop your work. It's important that you work, but it's important also that you work with non-attachment. Work, and surrender to the Divine. In the morning, praise the Lord and say "I'm an instrument in your hands. Guide me, be with me!" and at the end, before you go to sleep, say you surrender everything, every action, even if it was not a good action – analyse it and surrender it to the Divine. Be completely detached from whatever you do and focus your mind on the Lord.

There was a great poet, Adi Shankaracharya who said "Bhaja Govindam, Govindam Bhajam Muramate." Meaning, if mankind would realise, how foolish mankind is – we don't realise that the Ultimate of everything is Govinda, is God. If man would realise that everything comes from the source which is God, why not take the source itself? Why just want something that will be finished after sometime?

Even Lahiri Mahasaya, a great Yogi, in one of his previous lives, when he used to live with Babaji, he had the desire to have a golden palace and this desire of this golden palace made him incarnate on Earth again. Because of the grace of Babaji, with his love, and his compassion for everybody actually – He guided him and fulfilled his wish, the life in which he was realised. When Babaji appeared to him, he materialised a very huge golden palace, with lots of diamonds and all the precious stones that you can imagine inside. He was very amazed by everything and then Babaji dematerialized it, the same way he made it appear, he just made it disappear.

When you fall on the feet of Babaji, think of Babaji "You who could create this big palace, you are the source of everything, why do I need just a palace? It's better I take you completely, you are the Ultimate, you are the goal of all life. Let me have you!" In the same way, don't waste your time wanting things which have a limit. Desire the Ultimate, you shall have it. Surrender your body, mind and soul. Focus it on any Divine aspect firstly, then you realise your divinity and remember that God, however you are – even if your advancement is slow or fast, He loves you! He loves you even more than you can think about love, more than the mind of man can think about it. So always trust in this love, always hang on this love, and never let go of this. He is always with you, even if you don't feel Him, even if you don't see Him, but He is there.

There is a beautiful parable, from the Bible, where one man was walking on the beach, you all know about it? There was a man who was walking, and every time he looked behind, he saw two more footprints, like four prints in the sand. He was very happy thinking "God is always with me", he didn't have any fear. Once, in the life of this man, he started having lots of problems. Then he noticed that there weren't four footprints, but only, two footprints of his own. He started thinking, praying to God, saying to God "Why in times of joy you are with me, and I see your beautiful footprints behind me, but in time of pain, you are not with me." and God said "Don't misunderstand my child. These footprints that you see behind you are not yours. They are mine, because in times of trouble, I was carrying you on my shoulders."

> **The more you feed the problem, it will grow. This is your own creation, your own way of feeling it and when it is too much, you say "Enough is enough!"**

God is always with all of His children, even in times of the biggest trouble. The point is, when somebody has troubles, he is focused so much on the troubles that he forgets about everything. Even if the solution of the problem is there, they don't see it. The more you feed the problem, it will grow. This is your own creation, your own way of feeling it and when it is too much, you say "Enough is enough!" Then you realise that what you have always done, you can change, yourself. Then you turn to the Lord and say "Here, I can't deal with this anymore, handle it yourself." Do you think he will not come to your rescue? Directly you will have the solution and you will realise how easy it was. Then you will say to yourself "Oh, if I knew it earlier, I would have changed it." How many times has it happened in your life?

That's why when many problems, many things come on your way, try to analyse them before taking any casual decisions. Try to do it with a calm mind, not excited, because when your mind is already very 'hot', you will not see anything good. Always remember the Divine Love, the Divine help, the Divinity, ultimately within yourself. You are an instrument of this love, an instrument of this joy, bliss and happiness. You have to reflect it, you have to really want that reflection.

It was lovely to spend these few days with all of you. Next year there will be some more of these days for sure. And I hope you practice! Not that when I leave, you forget about what I said – it happens very often! Keep practicing. I would like to have some change, next time I come.

LETTING GO
OF THE LOWER FREQUENCY

Darshan, Shree Peetha Nilaya, Springen, Germany, 26 March 2011

There was a question that arose, "Can we attain eternal bliss? Can someone *really* attain eternal peace and happiness?" The answer is "Yes." One can attain eternal happiness or eternal bliss depending on how much one let's go of the lower frequency. As much as one distances oneself from one's lower nature, is as much as one will rise in higher consciousness.

It's like when things go well in life, when everything is smooth, everything is going very gently, one befriends a lot of people, one has a lot of family. But the wise one knows that all this goodness doesn't last for a long time. Once you are in trouble, what happens to your family, what happens to your friends? They desert you. Is that real happiness? The thing is that there is so much joy in the world, there is so much joy in your life, but very often when the time of testing arises, when the Great Teacher teaches about life, very often one forgets about it.

One longs for this great happiness, yet it's there. It's just that one doesn't see it. When the mind gets in the way, what will you see? The mind fashions the world in a certain way – how and what you want to see – if it is not according to how the mind perceives it, what do you awake inside of you – unhappiness, no? Where is this joy when everything was going well? Does it disappear? No, it doesn't. It stays there forever, but it's up to you how much you want to push it down or how much you want to let it rise. This is

where, when one is on the spiritual path, one doesn't distinguish
– well, at least one tries not to – between sadness and happiness.
As words, it is easy to say, but you have to try to put into practice. I
can't say it's impossible because it is possible.
Very often people consider themselves to be sinners... Like just a
few days ago I heard somebody say "I'm a very great sinner, Swami.
I would not be saved". Well, among great sinners there are great
saints, also. When one realises one doesn't need to dwell in the lower
level, but that one can rise, why not rise? It's like with Valmiki. He
was a great killer and now we are praising him as a great Sage. Saint
Paul, he killed lots of Christians, but when the grace arose, when he
decided to really change his life, what happened to him? He became
a great Saint. Like that, there are numerous Saints' lives which
show that even normal people can change, if they really want. If
you don't really want to change, as much as somebody can tell you
"change, change, change", you will be like a naughty child. You will
do the opposite. You know that very well. Some of the mothers,
they will agree with me, no? (laughter) It is the life experience.
There was once a man in 1500. He was begging. He was a *Brahmin*.
He was begging everywhere. You see, in the Hindu tradition,
Brahmins are considered to be high class and to beg is considered
something very bad for a *Brahmin*. One day the king was passing by.
King Akbar and his counsellor Birbau were passing by. When the
king saw a Brahmin was begging, he was aghast, saying "Oh, he's a
Brahmin. He considers himself as a very high class person, how can
he beg?" He pushed him away. Then Birbau was talking to the king
and the king was talking very badly about the Brahmin. You see,
King Akbar, he was a very good king, but he was always on a search.
Birbau thought to himself "It's not good for a *Brahmin* to be on the
road, so let me go and help him." He went to the *Brahmin* and said
to the *Brahmin* "I don't want you to go begging, but do one thing
for me. I want you to chant five *Gayatri Mantras* for me every day

and for each *Gayatri Mantra* that you chant every day I will give you a gold coin." The *Brahmin* agreed to it and said "Well, five gold coins for five *Gayatri Mantras*, which is so simple, is good." Every day what would he do, he would chant five *Gayatri Mantras* for the Prime Minister of the king, so at the end of the month he would get his money.

After some time of chanting the Divine Names, chanting *Gayatri Mantra* five times, he would sit merged into the mantra and he would feel great peace inside of him just by chanting five Gayatris. He felt this peace and he went into this peace inside of him. After some time the Prime Minister came to visit him and saw him radiating, changed. He said to him "From now on I would like you to chant 108 times *Gayatri Mantra* every day. I will give you more gold coins. The Brahmin said "OK, yes, I can do that." So he started chanting 108 times *Gayatri Mantra*. The more he would chant, the more he would be in the quiet state. He thought

> The thing is that there is so much joy in the world, there is so much joy in your life, but very often when the time of testing arises, when the Great Teacher teaches about life, very often one forgets about it.

to himself and one day he said "Well, this *mantra*, I'm chanting it and it is giving me so much peace and so much quietness that I completely see the world differently." So he started chanting it more and more and he stopped going to see the Prime Minister for the monthly payment.

One day while he was chanting, Gayatri Devi appeared in front of him and said "I'm very pleased with your devotion, but all this time that you have been chanting you have been paid for your chanting, but I would like now, that you stop. I will provide everything for you" and likewise, Gayatri Devi promised him that She would look after his family. So he surrendered completely inside of him. By himself he surrendered to the Divine Mother, to Gayatri Devi. This made the Prime Minister start to think "Where is this man?" He decided to come to search for him. He came to the house of the priest, the *Brahmin* man, and there he saw that the *Brahmin* was sitting in a very peaceful way, radiating lots of light. Lots of people were around him. Lots of people just being in his presence would feel peace, would feel that their worries and problems disappeared. When he saw the Prime Minister, he arose from his seat and fell down at the feet of the Prime Minister and said "Well, because of you I have received the Grace of Gayatri Devi. Because of you I have had Her *darshan,* and because of you I have changed. I am a different person now." Then the Prime Minister said, "But why is it you don't come and get your money? This was our agreement, no?" The Brahmin

> Any mantra has the power to change mankind. It depends not only on the mantra, it depends also on your will. When you will it, God graces you with the strength, but as long as you don't will it, it won't happen.

replied "Well, before I was chanting it because of money or to gain something from it, but now I am chanting it because it brings me great peace and great happiness and my whole life has changed." This is the power of the *mantra.* The *Gayatri Mantra* is considered to be one of the most powerful *mantras,* but any *mantra* has the power to change mankind. It depends not only on the *mantra,* it depends also on your will. When you will it, God graces you with the strength, but as long as you don't will it, it won't happen. The earlier it is, the better it will be. The earlier you change, everything around you will also change. Then you will realise that the real happiness is not outside there. It's within you. You carry it all the time. It's up to you to vibrate it in a higher frequency or in a lower frequency. It's like with a radio, if you want to listen to loud music, what do you have to do? You have to raise the volume. Then you will hear only the music. Probably it's not only the music you will hear. But if you lower it completely onto the lower frequency, you will vibrate in that way. So the first step is up to you and the faster you take the step, the faster you will grow.

REALISING ETERNAL BLISS

Darshan, Kuala Lumpur, Malaysia, 2006

Often there is a question in our mind, a question that almost all the people ask, which is "Why are we here? What is the reason for us to be here?" As your mind keeps thinking, you get drawn to different kinds of answers - some that you like and some that you don't like - but very often your mind leads you to the wrong answer and then you make yourself miserable. You have pain.

The actual and simple answer to this is to Realise the Self. As long as you don't Realise the Self, this question will arise many times. In all Holy Scriptures it's said "Know thyself." We can't know God, but we can know our Selves. By knowing our Selves, we will know God. We will Realise Him and we will Realise the great joy and peace that He brings.

For that, we have to withdraw our mind. We have to put away all negativity that stops us. The first step is to love. We love everybody we love friends, we love our husband or wife, but very often this love doesn't last long. It starts and at the beginning you have great joy and then it fades after sometime. It fades because it is not the Real Love. It is not that for which you have come here. You have come here to Realise this Love, this Eternal Love that you have inside you.

That's why in Hinduism we say "Satchitananda". This is the incarnation of man. Man is the incarnation of the Supreme Cosmic Eternal Bliss. If we think of ourselves as being this bliss and focus on it, we will become this bliss, but by our own effort. Each one of you has to really want it and make this effort. You can't say "I want to Realise God; I want to have Eternal Love" and at the same time, "I want the world." These don't go together.

In God you have everything. God – who is the source of everything – in Realising Him you will realise the limitless quality of mankind, the limitless quality of the true Self. This will be the end of all misery, the end of all pain. However, what man does often is to choose the opposite. People choose to enjoy the world, which brings pain and they like to complain afterwards.

How many times in your life have you wanted something, you desired it so much and the moment you got it you enjoyed it only for some time, then not anymore? Think a little bit. Many times in one's life it happens, because all the other desires have limits, whereas the other desire-if you desire God-it doesn't have a limit, so it will never come to an end. Rather, you will Realise this Oneness with Him, this Oneness of becoming part of Him and feeling Him all the time. So this will remove all the pain, you become ready and Realise really *Satchitananda*, the Eternal Bliss. By doing that you will reflect it

Man is the incarnation of the Supreme Cosmic Eternal Bliss. If we think of ourselves as being this bliss and focus on it, we will become this bliss, but by our own effort.

and you will spread it. This is how God loves his children.

God has sent you all here, not just to stay here, not only to work, He has put you here to Realise the Oneness with Him, to get rid of the shadow that has covered your soul. When this shadow has gone away, the light will shine. The power of the mind will be less, but the power of the heart will be stronger. You will be more loving and calmer and the easiest way to do that is through meditation.

It's only when you take time for you, when you take time and look deep inside you, that you will Realise it.

You can help, you can love, but without loving yourself first, without Realising this love within yourself, it's difficult to really love. So, work first to start loving yourself, trusting in yourself, what you feel, in your intuition. By trusting in yourself you will trust in God. By loving yourself you will love God and you will love everybody without any conditions, without any judgment. It will just be pure Love.

Sit down every day for 15 minutes and lose yourself in the Divine Bliss, which is deep inside you. Forget the world. Forget even your body, but concentrate on the Divine deep inside you.

I will teach you a small meditation, which is very simple. You can practice it anywhere you are.

Meditation

Firstly, I will ask you to sit straight. It is very important that the spine is straight.

- Take a few deep breaths. Breathe in and breathe out – quickly – and when you breathe out, drop your shoulders. Let them relax.
- Now, concentrate on your third eye, in between your eyebrows, on your forehead. Close your eyes. Bring your mind's concentration to your third eye.
- At the same time, listen to your breath. Inhale slowly and exhale slowly. Listen to it.
- Being the creation of God, you have the power to create. So, use this creative power and create with your mind, in the third eye, any Divine aspect that you feel close to.
- With the breath, inhale the name of this Divine aspect and exhale the name of this Divine aspect.

- Look how beautiful this Divine Being is, with lots of light shining through Him.
- Now, you see the Divine Being increasing in size, little by little becoming bigger and brighter. First, it fills your face completely, then the upper part of your body and finally, the whole of your body.
- You feel His love deep inside your heart. You feel an inner peace, calmness. There's nobody else, only you and the Divine – you in Him and Him in you.
- Now, slowly reduce the Divine Being and bring Him to your heart. And let Him merge deep inside your heart. Whenever you need Him, call upon Him.

You can slowly open your eyes. It's relaxing, isn't it?

So, by practicing every day, you will be able to master that. You will be able to Realise this Oneness with the Divine. Of course, at the beginning it will be difficult, because the mind will keep thinking a lot. Often you might try to stop it, but don't stop it and don't focus on the thoughts either. Whenever your mind is thinking, let it think and let the thoughts pass. Don't fight it and don't give it power. Give power to the more essential – to the Divine image that you create. After sometime it will conquer all this negativity of the mind, but this will happen only with practice.

If every day for 15 minutes you sit quietly, forget about everything around you, and do this meditation, it will help you a lot. You will see also, that if you are ill or you don't feel happy, you will develop all these qualities to change this. Illness will be healed. People who are not happy will feel joy, because the inner joy will reveal itself and in this inner joy there is no pain.

YOU ARE FULLY REALISED

Darshan, Springen, Germany, 5 February 2011

I guess most of the people here are familiar with the 2012 things. Some people think that on the 21st of – which month? September? Ah, December? You're sure December? How many are so sure it's December? You see, I just told you, there are a lot of people who are familiar with this.

Some people think that the 21st of December, everybody will become enlightened. Well, it's good to believe that. When I was in Mauritius right now, I heard another theory; that the 31st of May, Jesus will come and take everybody. This was another theory some people were telling in Mauritius. Well, like I told you once probably, this is a subject that I like very much – to see how people believe in all these things. It's nice to believe. It's beautiful, to see how much people have so much trust in all these predictions, which I will say is true, but not the way it is said.

This is one thing; mankind always longs for a higher purpose. The higher purpose of man is to attain the Divine. This is the truth. All religions preach that – one has to attain God. That's why one is born several times, sometimes 800 times as a human, just to attain back the Divine Self. Imagine you get a human body, one time you can attain full realisation, and sometimes you have to take birth 800 times to attain God Realisation or Self-Realisation, whatever you want to call it. That means that if you believe, that on the 21st of December, you will be enlightened, that's good, but the work starts now.

Nobody wants to work for anything, yet they want to get the fruit afterwards. If you don't work there are no fruits. If you sit around not working, would you get your salary at the end of the month? Yes? Well, some who have retired, who have already worked for it, they will get it, but for other people, they have to work for it. It's the same thing, for God-Realisation or rising in your consciousness, it will not be given to you just like that. You have to work for it. You have to deserve it, because still you have to polish yourself. Right now you are a diamond, which is found in nature, a rough diamond, but to have a beautiful shine inside of you, to have a beautiful radiance from yourself, you have to start doing your *sadhana* strongly. Then for sure, 21st of December next year you will be enlightened. Then God will say "Yes, this one *is* ready. Let me give myself to him." It's all about the grace of God giving Himself to mankind.

In the Hindu tradition we believe that God pervades everything, that God is everywhere. All the Hindu people believe that. All the people who are spiritual believe that, that God is everywhere. Am I right? Yes? When you talk to people [about] the way of seeing the Divine, they say "Yes, God is everywhere; God is everything," but within them they don't see God. How come? If you don't see the Divine inside of you, you don't realise it within you firstly, all the theory of the mind, stays only outside.

If you want to realise God, it's something very easy. You have to realise it firstly within your Self, not outside of you. We pray to the Divine outside. We search for God outside, because this is the purpose of man; to search for the divine. At all cost, at all times, throughout lives, is only one thing, to search for the divine, nothing else. All the drama of life, all the illusion that one creates, will stay here only, but it's only this that traps you to come back again and again. If you realise that this is a trap, if you realise that "Yes, I can change certain things in myself, I can really attain the divine and I really can attain, not outside, but within my Self firstly," you will attain Him. But, as long as you see Him separate from you, it's quite difficult. He will always stay separate.

You know when we say... For example, there was one passage in the Bible where Christ talked about; when there were the Pharisees, He was talking and saying "If Abraham will be here and meet me, he will be blessed." You know about this passage? No? You should study the Bible then. This is your culture here. You should know it better than anybody else – even better than me. In this passage Christ mentions it and says "Abraham would be blessed if He were here." Well, then the Pharisees start attacking Him. They asked "Why are you bothering? Why are you talking about Abraham, who was 20 generations before you?" Then

> If you realise that "Yes, I can change certain things in myself, I can really attain the Divine and I really can attain, not outside, but within my Self firstly," you will attain Him.

Christ said "Indeed he will be blessed, because before he existed, I AM." He never said "I was", no? What is this I AM, it means He doesn't identify Himself with the physical body, He identifies Himself as the soul, as a spirit which is everlasting with the divine. The communion of the spirit, your soul itself, is always in communion with God but the mind always likes to separate it. In the Hindu prayer, before we do the *Kalash Puja*, before energising the *Kalash Puja,* we sit and imagine the divine, remind ourselves, of the Divine within our Self. From within our Self we project it to the outside, but first it's here. That's the word also in the Bible, which means, Jehovah. This is in the Jewish tradition. They call it Jehovah. What does Jehovah mean? Nobody knows? It means: I AM. The only thing is that God is, everything – you, me, and everything around, but the way we see it, we separate the divine from the true Self.

That's why for people to really attain God-realisation, they have to go through all this *sadhana* in the outside. *Sadhana* in the outside still only a little bit it helps to realise God. The outside is inside. If you want, on the 21ˢᵗ of December, to realise your Self, start practicing this way of thinking; that God is not outside, God is inside, inside of you. That's what also Christ said "In the future there will be lots of prophets. If a saint would come and say 'Come, I will show you the Kingdom of God; it's this place or that place' don't follow them, because the Kingdom of God is not here and there. It's inside of you." This is the first place where you have to find Him, you have to realise Him. You have not to just say "Oh, I believe in God." For sure, all of you sitting here, all of you say "Yes, I believe in God." I believe very much that all of you believe in God, but believe in God *within* you. Believe in God that the energy, which is given to you to act in this world, is only Him. This is the first step. Once you have this first step, He will manifest Himself through you.

This is the purpose of man; to search for the Divine. At all cost, at all times, throughout lives, is only one thing, to search for the divine, nothing else.

It's not just the energy that you have now. This is just 5 % of the whole energy that you use. There is much more. We say that the divine manifests Himself, no? Of course, He has the power to manifest also on the outside as on the inside. Once you start thinking like that, He will reveal Himself inside of you. In that revelation of the Divine within you, there is the removal of the duality, that you are separated from everything.

This is where the saints always say that they have this deep communion with God and when one has this communion with God, all the duality of the outside disappears, because only the oneness of God consciousness which pervades everything stays. You Realise that you, your Self, from the beginning you are fully realised. Then you realise also how stupid you are, because you have been traveling around and looking for something which is just here, always with you. So let's look forward to the next year, but start now. Like it is said "The future is unborn. The past is gone. The present is reality." It's all now!

THE RICHEST PERSON
IN THE WHOLE UNIVERSE

Darshan, Verona, Italy, 29 May 2011

Often people ask why self-realisation is difficult. You ask yourself also this question, no? How many says it's difficult? Well... (somebody is lifting both hands) and the others say it is easy? What do you say, the others, who did not raise their hands? So-so? *(audience: it is impossible without your grace!)* Everything is grace. *(audience: We make it difficult).* Why? You didn't answer my question. The ones who didn't lift their hand, what do you think – it's easy or not? Actually, it's very simple, very easy. There are so many things people do, to attain the Divine. Where does God reside? Here and everywhere! If He is here, that means you are already realised, no? What is the difficulty about? The mike decides that it's difficult. So, I will tell you because the microphone doesn't want to talk – (maybe you change the mike) you see, we always look at things with logic. In everyday life, we always use our brain, to always put a judgement, whether it's good or not. Same thing in spirituality; some say "We are looking for self-realisation, or God realisation", you are searching, yet we find it difficult to attain Him. We forget that it dwells in every part of our self, it dwells firstly here; before seeing it elsewhere, you have to see inside of you. The Rishis have classified it in two ways; one way, where you can find the Divine completely, and this way is the easiest way. You know how? When your mind is calm. Some are born lucky, from the beginning they are graced with this calmness of the mind and the mind doesn't

bother them. Others are born also lucky, because through the mind they dwell on the outside, but there is no fulfilment; here is not yet that, when we say fully happy and you are happy here (heart), not happy here (mind) – these are two different kinds of happiness. In simple things, if you realise that God is with you, you will attain Him. Can you remind yourself continuously of that? It's very simple, no? Yes, No? You eat every day? Why? Because you are reminded, your stomach is paining. In the same way, if you think of the Divine, try to think of Him all the time. I won't say twenty-four hours you can think of Him but you have many forms which He has given to remind you, that you have to become like Him. If you keep reminding yourself of that, you will see how simple it is. In everything that you do, He is there present. You don't need to make your life complicated. There was once great discourse being given by a great wise man. He was talking, talking, talking; for hours he was talking. Among the public there was a saint with his disciple listening to this man. After the talk was finished, the disciple asked the Saint "Why is he just talking, talking?" At that moment the Saint said "Well, this lecturer, he was looking for Shastra Gyaan, which is the Gyaan from books, that's why he can talk, talk, talk. If he would look for Bramha Gyaan, he would look for the wisdom of God, he would attain the Divine also." You see there is a saying that says 'an empty drum makes more noise than a full one' *(laughter, commotion, wrong translation.)*
You see, just now, to look for a word, how many people, how many words we have heard! The same way, to look for God, people can say so many things, but if one has not yet found the Divine, if one has not seen the Divine within one Self, the Divine has not revealed Himself to that person, how do you know about God? Even Christ when they asked Him about the Father, he said "If you have seen the son you have seen the father." This is the unity of the Atma and the Paramatma, there is no difference. Actually,

this is the realisation, when you realise fully, not just knowing in the mind – "Yes there is no difference, between me and God." Yet you still hang onto your human qualities, you still hang onto all the mind qualities. When we start the spiritual path there are three things that happen – you start saying ko ham; "Who am I?" "Na ham" which means "I am not the mind, I am not what is perceived on the outside." and later on you say "I am Bramhashmi, I am part of the Divine", the Divine reveals itself within you, then all disappears and you see how easy it is. You look backward and say "Oh my goodness I have done so much, but it was just there all the time." When you do your sadhana, you have to *believe* what you are doing. Not just do it "OK, yes I will do my sadhana, I will feel happy afterwards, I will attain God realisation

Make the mind calm, then Love will awaken. It's so simple!

just like that." No. it is not like that. You have to know that you have it. When you programme yourself that you have it, you will not look for it, because you know it is here. Of course this happens with full surrender of the love from your heart.

Without love, nothing exists. Love varies, in different degrees and you have to go little by little. You have a medium degree, which we feel on the outside; then you have a higher degree of love, which consumes everything. That's what you have inside of you. Very often humans deal only with these two qualities of love; the lower love and middle love, yet they want to achieve the higher form of love. Make the mind calm, then love will awaken. It's so simple! You will do it? You will try? You see, when you try, like the Mataji was saying; the grace – it's true, that nothing happens without the grace. Even for you to be here, is the divine grace. Why has He sent you here? There is a reason for that. Trust in that and become an instrument. Then there will be peace in this world. If you just say "Well, we want peace, we want the world to change," but as human beings you don't change, it doesn't help. When *you* change, there will be a change in the world. The objective is very important, if your objective is strong enough, you can do lots of things. But if your objective is so-so well, there is no full trust in it. Then also you will be so-so.

Be clear about what you want in life. Don't be left-right, left-right, just be clear in yourself. Then you will see that whenever you are clear, you will be at peace. Whenever you are at peace, you can make others happy, because you are happy. When you make others happy, you will make change in this world. It starts here, not with the mind but

Without Love, nothing exists.

with the heart. I know in the mind you are all very wise people. In your heart also you are much richer than what you have in your mind. When people come for darshan, they ask me "What do you see, Swami?". I see the beauty that you have inside of you. If you look at it, you would be the richest person in the world, in the whole universe and that beauty, is what you have to see inside of you. When you have seen this beauty inside of you, you will see it everywhere. So keep trying and know that it is there, know that you are there also. It really is simple to do that, it's free.

JUST LOVE 2

GRACE

I am a most noteworthy sinner, but I have
cried out to the Lord for Grace and mercy,
and they have covered me completely.
I have found the sweetest consolation
since I made it my whole purpose to
enjoy His marvellous presence.

Christopher Columbus

THE DEEP PURPOSE OF LIFE

Puja to Narasimhadev, South Africa, January 2010

You don't know how lucky you are to have *Maha Narasimhadev* here so close to you. Actually, all the *Devas* pray to Him to remove their suffering, but you all go around to other temples, leaving the one that all the *Devas* pray to, going around toask for help, when He, Maha Jwala Narasimha is there – the One who destroys all the suffering inside of you and in everybody. Yet, people don't know about it, they don't realise it but it's Him, Maha Jwala Narasimha, who really gives. I am just an instrument, nothing else. All is only through Him of course, you receive the blessing; come pray to Him, show also your devotion and love to Him and then He will show His devotion to you. You know, there's a saying that says 'Come, take one step and I shall take ten towards you.' This is the same thing for the Lord, if you take one step, if you make one move, *sincerely* – this has to come really from your heart. Like I was explaining yesterday, you say one thousand times a *mantra*, but only one part of the *mantra* really comes sincerely from the heart. In the same way, if you make one sincere move, you will see that He will always be with you.

Wherever He is, Maha Lakshmi is present with Him. I know you love money very much, more than you love God, but if you show a little bit that you love Him, you will see that Maha Lakshmi will run to you, also. You see, Maha Lakshmi does not represent only wealth. The Hindu tradition says that Lakshmi, because She is showing that money is coming out from Her hands, is the Goddess of wealth, but wealth for the spiritual people, also means spiritual wealth, which is the best wealth. That's what Christ said "Don't make your bank here on Earth, but put it in Heaven." Maha Lakshmi is responsible for that: to fill your bank in Heaven with lots of good *karma*. Then when you take the next life, you will have a very beautiful life. Otherwise, in your next life you will be miserable. You will be even more miserable! How many people realise that?

You think that you have only one life. You don't have only one life, you have many lives. Like I was saying yesterday, it's a great chance to become a human being. If you can attain Him, through His grace, of course, if you can prove yourself worthy of attaining Him, you will attain Him in one life. That's what is said in the *Bible* "Lord, I am not worthy, but say one single word I shall be purified." That's what it is about – whether you can prove yourself, so that you can receive His grace, so you can receive God's grace.

He's here to give it to you, but you have to really be worthy of it. You have to purify yourself. You have to cleanse yourself through your prayer, through your *sadhana*. It's not about just saying "OK, He will give to me whenever I want or whenever it is time." He can wait for lives. If you ask your higher Self what it wants, you will see that your higher Self will say "You stupid man, you know, wake up! Open your eyes and see the reality! Look around!" You are jumping into *Maya*. *Maya* is playing with you like when you fry something and put it in the pan with oil and everything is frying and you see how it bubbles. You play with it in the same way that *Maya* is playing with you all, but you are letting yourself play. So wake up! Come every Sunday. Come and receive and participate together, so that when the time for you to leave comes, you can say "Yes, I have what I came to this world for. I have achieved it." Otherwise, the greatest regret will come to you when you look back in your life and you see God has given you so much grace to attain Him, but you have refused it. Then life is wasted. The next life will come and you don't know how it will be. A few among you probably will attain Him, but most of you will take birth, again. If you can attain the grace of God in this life, you will be having a lovely next life – also in this life, not only the next life. Try your best to attain His grace, otherwise you will still be in the circle of misery. If you like to jump into that, then carry on the same way, but if you don't want to then change yourself.

Have you ever thought of life? Tell me, are you satisfied with your life? Why not? You all are spiritual, yet you are not satisfied with your life. Still, imagine the people outside. Most of the people in the world are not satisfied with life, because they see life is just a routine. Every day it's the same thing. It becomes boring, no? When you dedicate yourself to the Lord, every day is a new day. Every day you learn new things and every day you will see that there is great learning happening and that you are advancing nearer and nearer

What you have to attain is the Grace of God. Attain the Love, so that it can fill you up fully. You can achieve really the purpose of your life, the purpose of your incarnation here.

to Him. Your heart is opening bigger and bigger and it is filling with so much Love. What you have to attain is the grace of God. Attain the Love, so that it can fill you up fully. You can achieve really the purpose of your life, the purpose of your incarnation here. Start, firstly by praying and chanting the name of God wherever you are. What is chanting? You see, the more you chant the Divine Names, the more you will receive this love and understanding.

Of course, with the mind you will never understand Him, Maha Jwala Narasimha. When you look at Him like that even among you, you say "Oh, my goodness, this is a bit scary, eh?" You have to see that God is not only beautiful. That is the mistake that one always makes. You picture God in the mind saying, "God is the only perfect One", but He can't be perfect if He doesn't have any imperfections inside of Him. That is what makes Him whole, the imperfection and the perfection.

Train your mind, which is full with ignorance. Purify it and transform it, so that when you reach your heart, your spiritual heart, it's fully blossoming so that you can offer the flower to Him. How would you offer the flower to Him? Offering the flower is not just by taking it from here and putting it there, not by taking it and putting it here saying "*swaha*". It's not like that, you know. It's through service that you offer the flower to Him, when you help people who are in need. This is how the more you help, the more you will have satisfaction in life.

Once a doctor went to Ramakrishna and said to Him, "Lord, I am a very successful doctor, but I am very unhappy with my life. Please, tell me what can I do so that I can be happy?" Ramakrishna closed His eyes, asked Ma and She said "Tell him, it's good whatever he is doing. He is very dedicated to his job, but he should one day a week, do it for free, do it for *seva*." Of course, the doctor listened to Ramakrishna and he started, once a week, helping everybody free of charge. After some time Ramakrishna was passing by his town and asked him "Doctor, how are you? You seem much happier." He said "Yes, my Lord, I have taken your advice and I am much happier."

It's true, when you help somebody, it's another form of happiness. It's not just a happiness that "OK, I have helped that person." There are many people who help a lot of people, but they talk a lot afterwards. This is not help, really. Christ said "When your right hand gives, your left should not know. It's better to cut it off and throw it away." It's true: what's the use of helping if you then go around and around hanging onto "Oh, I have helped this; I have done that?" but it's always like that. When you see somebody helping only this much, they talk about helping that much. You know, they come to the temple and put in ten Rand and they go around and talk about it and say "OK, I would have given thousands." That happens very often. This is the ignorance of man, but they will never be free in that way, because the mind will take on what they have given. Don't think they are creating good *karma*. They are creating worse *karma* for themselves.

When you help somebody sincerely, it's a greater joy inside that you feel satisfied with what you have done, but then what happens? You don't hang onto it. You forget very quickly. That's how it has to be in life. Once you have attained the grace of God, once you have opened your heart really sincerely, His grace will just flow, because it's a great fountain inside of you, which is everlasting. The more you take, the more it shall flow. So practice and attain His grace.

He is not only here in the temple. When I say to come here, it's just because when you come together it creates a different vibration – it's stronger. That's why there is a *satsang*, no? It's because everybody comes together. You can pray at home, but very often at home when you pray, you wonder when your prayer will be finished. When you come to a gathering together, everybody has the same motive, the same goal. When you sit there and you are chanting the *mantras*, the prayers, singing *bhajans*, your mind doesn't wander around. You don't allow your mind to jump around. So once a week, it's not much to come for one hour, no?

YEARNING FOR
THE GRACE OF THE DIVINE

Darshan, Vienna, Austria, 27 August 2010

I'm very happy to be here with all of you. I'm very happy Swamiji
Sathyanarayan Das from Vrindavan is also present here.
Somebody asked me a question today "Why do people stay always
in the cycle of birth and death, even if they know that this is misery
and that they have to do everything to attain the Divine? Why life
after life do we come, but we don't realise the purpose?" Actually,
the answer to that is that people don't like to change. Even if they
know they are doing something wrong, they know that they have
to change certain things in life to be really happy, the old habits
catch up. They get caught in the old habits.
If one doesn't take the determination to change now, doesn't take
this resolution, it's very difficult. People would rather say "Later on
we will change." There are always excuses; from childhood they're
learning certain things. They grow up and they think they know
everything. They go around thinking that they know best. Then
it comes to a point where one realises "What am I doing here? I
try everything to be happy, but I'm not happy." Why is that? It's
because whenever one says one wants to change, one has to let
go of certain qualities. You can't change and still carry the same
qualities with you.
It's like if somebody smokes and says "I want to stop smoking." I
come across a lot of people like this, you know. They say "Swamiji,
I've tried my best to stop smoking." It's very difficult. The old habits

catch up again. You see, when you stop smoking, you have to replace it with something. You can't leave the space.

This is where spirituality comes in. If you want to change life, you have to dedicate yourself. You have to develop faith, because if you don't have faith, it's difficult and faith is this yearning. You have to develop not only faith; you have to transcend faith to yearning. You have to yearn for God. As long as there is no yearning for the Divine, there is always emptiness. Into this emptiness, anything from the outside can fill it. That's why you have to guard yourself always, otherwise the old one, the old you, will be back.

In somebody who lives in the world, you see it very clearly. You see that somebody who lives in the material world, when they don't have much they complain. They have a little bit, yet they are not happy. They always long for more. This is how the world, the material world functions. It never gives you real happiness, because the more you have, the

> You have to develop not only faith; you have to transcend faith to yearning. You have to yearn for God. As long as there is no yearning for the Divine, there is always emptiness.

more you will want to have. So having more, you will still not be happy.

This reminds me of a story. There was a man who was passing under a tree and he heard a voice. The voice said "Do you want seven pots of gold?" He looked around, could not find anybody. He said, "OK, let's try it." He heard the voice again and the voice said "Go home. Your seven pots of gold are waiting for you." He reached home very happy and he saw seven pots. He approached and he looked inside. They were full with gold. Six of them were completely full with gold and the seventh one was only half full. He said "What is that? Why is this one only half full? I have to fill this up."

What did he do? He took all his savings, changed it into gold and put it in the seventh pot. In spite of doing that, the pot was not full, so he sold all his utensils. He sold all his furniture. Still the pot was half full. He started working, slaving himself, working very hard night and day to fill the seventh pot. He worked, starving his family. His wife and children were starving, because he tried to fill up the seventh pot with gold. He was getting depressed.

He was working at the king's palace, and one day the king said "What's your problem?" He said to the king "I would like that you increase my salary. I'm not so happy." The king said, "Alright, we'll increase your salary, because you are a good person." In spite of increasing the salary for a few months, the king saw that he was still unhappy. One day the king called him and said "Tell me, when your salary was low, you were happy, you were content, you were joyful. Now your salary is double, but you look more depressed. You look unhappy. What's your problem? Have you met the *yaksha*, the demon of the seven gold pots?"

He was shocked that the King could know about that, because he had kept it secret. Then he said "Well, yes." and the king said, "Well, that's a big mistake you have made to accept the seven gold pots, because this will never bring happiness, but only sadness and unhappiness. It will bring only misery to your life. Go quickly and return them."

Well he went and returned them. When he returned it, the seventh pot was still only half full. This pot can never be full. You can't fill it up and it brings misery. When he returned the seventh pot, he lost everything. All his savings, all the money that he had put inside the pot, all was lost, but that's what humans often do. Life after life, they want to fill the pot of misery. In spite of knowing that this pot will bring their own ruin, they like to play this game, but when you realise that this is bringing misery to you, do you like to play this game, or do you want to change something? You change your life, because you realise that the world we see outside will never bring happiness. Only your spiritual path will bring you this real happiness. On the spiritual path one has to yearn for the Divine. You have not to be superficial, because if you are superficial, you will get only superficial things. When you are sincere from within yourself, you know, with yourself you are sincere and call the Divine, He can't refuse you. He will run to you. That's why it is said "Have faith; have faith like a child," because when the mother says to the child "That's your sister," the child, without asking a second question, will believe that. You should believe and have no doubt.

That reminds me of another story. There was one little boy living with his mother in the forest. To go to school he had to cross the forest, to get to the school in the town. Every day when he returned back from school, he said to his mother "I have so much fear, I'm scared when I'm walking toward the school or when I'm returning." The mother was very

If you want to change life, you have to dedicate yourself. You have to develop faith.

sad, because only the mother and the son were there, the father having died. So the mother said to the child "Well, you should not be scared, because in this forest you have your brother who lives in the forest. Whenever you need him – his name is Gopal – call him, he will come to you."

The next morning, the mother brought the child to the door and the child started to walk. As he was walking in the forest, he was very scared and he started calling "Gopal, Gopal, Gopal, my brother, where are you? Why don't you come?" This call was so much from his heart that the Lord could not resist coming. Like that, every day he went to the school and returned, Krishna would be with him.

One day, the headmaster said that his birthday was the next day and that everybody had to bring him something. Everybody brought something, but this boy didn't have anything to bring for the headmaster. He asked Gopal, saying, "Gopal, you know, today is the birthday of my headmaster. I don't know what to give him." So Krishna gave him a pot of butter.

He brought this pot to the school and gave it to the headmaster and the headmaster said "Well, distribute it to everybody" and as much as they would distribute, it would never get empty. The headmaster said "Where did you get this pot? It's a magic pot." Then the boy said to the headmaster "My brother gave it to me" and they said "Your brother? You don't have any brother." He said "No, I have a brother. His name is Gopal and He lives in the forest." They said, "You are lying. Let's go and see."

They went in the forest and they saw him talking to Gopal, to Krishna, but nobody else could see and they said to him "You are lying." He said to Krishna "Please, they don't see that I am talking to you. Why don't they see?" Then Krishna said "They lack faith inside of them. That's why they can't see." But as the boy was crying and sincerely asking Krishna "Please

The world we see outside will never bring happiness. Only your spiritual path will bring you this real happiness.

show Yourself to them, so that they can believe that You do exist, You are my brother and You are here with me", out of this sincerity, out of this yearning, this love, Krishna said "OK, fine." Krishna revealed Himself to the headmaster and to all the children.

That's what faith makes happen. That's what this yearning for the Divine makes happen. That's why it has to grow more and more. It's not that you ask for something and you don't get it, so you say "OK, I will change." Until you are pure at heart, keep trying. Then one will ask the question "How will I know if I am pure at heart?" Well, when you are pure at heart, you will notice the change inside of you. Your attitude, the way you look at things, will be more loving and calmer, because the old you will have disappeared completely. Keep asking the Divine to give you this Grace and He will.

WHEN GOD CALLS YOU

Darshan, Capetown, South Africa, January 2011

It is lovely to be here with all of you. On my way to come here – as you know there is lot of traffic – I was having a nice discussion with Kalindi. I will just talk about that in short. You see, mankind thinks that when they become spiritual it is just a coincidence, or it is just a way of living happiness. Actually it's not like that. When God called you onto the spiritual way, it doesn't matter in which religion, he called you through his grace for different levels of spirituality, because the mind wants to understand certain things. Firstly, the mind wants to understand where it comes from. The soul holds the secret, but humans are bound by the intellect, the mind and the senses, which make it difficult. Why does somebody search for things? One can say "Yes, I am happy." One can say "I am happy in whatever religion I am." Again, "I am happy however I am." Often it is not the case. One wants to be happy, but they are not happy, because the soul longs for something else. What does our soul long for? Have you ever asked this question to yourself? What does the soul long for? Does the soul long for the world outside? Yes, does it? No, it doesn't. The soul longs for something greater. This thing which is greater is very difficult for the mind to understand, because the mind, the intellect and the senses have grabbed man and have made him focus only on the outside. As long as one is focusing on the outside, one is limited to the outside. That is not the goal of why you are here. The goal of why you are here is to fully realise yourself. It's something which is easy from my point of view, I can say it is also easy for everybody. Many among you here will not agree with that. It is normal, because the power of the mind in the level the soul state one is, will make you perceive certain things accordingly. If the soul is in the kindergarten level, it needs a kindergarten level of understanding, which is the basic level. The more you rise in spirituality, the more you rise within you, what happens? The more your way of understanding grows, things change. The more the way of how you see things changes, the Divine grace pours upon you. Call for God, awaken this longing, this urge to know more things.

Actually it is not a knowing here (pointing to the mind), it is to receive the wisdom of the soul. In reality, your soul has everything. Don't forget that in reality, your soul is part of God, all religions say that. God blows Himself into man and infuses man with his divine power that is the beginning of the bible. The same thing, the Shastras say how man was created: God infused himself, God from Himself manifested as human, created the first man and first woman. Like that our soul has never forgotten about its true reality. But through karmas of previous lives, one can say one is further or one is nearer, depending on how much karma one has. The *samskaras* which one has worked out through previous lives carry on, until one completely dissolves everything. Through the help of the Teacher, the Master or the Spiritual Guide, God sends different levels of understanding. The first level of understanding one has when one realises one's spiritual path, when one finds one's spiritual path, one has this great... Love. This is only when you have found the way. Once you have found your path, there will be a great Love, which will awaken inside of you. According to that great Love, the Divine is calling you. It is calling your soul to be again one with Him, to realise itself, the soul is exploding with this Love, like it's suffocating within you, to know more and more, to reach Him more and more, then the Divine manifests itself in the form of the teacher. In that aspect of the teacher, he helps you to awaken this unconditional Love. That's why the Guru in that aspect is called *Premaka*. Because Premaka is awakening the *prem*, the love inside of you once the love is awakened, you know how it is. Love is something which is always thirsty for more and more, the opposite of love is?(audience: hate?) No, no, not hate.. envy! When one has envy or avarice one wants more and more, the same quality is with Love also, because when pure Love awakens it will want more and more, because it is like a volcano where when there is a small hole in the earth, what happens? All the magma, all that is inside, which is burning with so much power, wants to come out, no? When it finds a small hole it pushes through with its force and strength, comes out and explodes. That's how you get a big volcano explosion, but the same explosion happens inside of man, when one finds one's path and one realises this Love, the explosion happens inside more and more and more. This is at the heart level here (pointing to the heart), still then it is bound by the mind. The mind wants to understand what is happening, because the Divine knows what is happening to its creation, what is happening to your soul. Your soul longs! But your mind is stopping

> Your soul has everything. Don't forget that in reality, your soul is part of God, all religions say that.

it, and that's why many people start on the spiritual path and half way through they say "Oh my goodness, I am tired" you know that, no? They get diverted.., they let the mind take over, but if they are patient and wait.., what will happen? The Divine, the Master will take another aspect of Himself, which is called *Svatchaka*. In this aspect of the Divine in this aspect of the teacher, it helps to... What is *Svatchaka*? (audience: "to slap" – laughter) No, not to slap, it is to clean! You know like a mirror, a mirror is very beautiful, but you will not see yourself in it until it is... clean! Then you say "Wow, look how beautiful I am!" You then ask the mirror "Mirror mirror, who is the most beautiful?" Like that the Master takes the aspect of *Svatchaka* to clean all the doubt, to clean all the negativity from the mind. The mind is something which is holding very much onto negativity. For example, when something good happens in one's life, it is very easy for one to forget about it. But if something bad happens in one's life, you will probably remember about this your whole life, right, no? This is how the mind is, so with all this, because of the mind's power, the Master has to take the aspect of cleansing. This is where the Master gives a test to the disciples to make them ready. What is a test? You go to school, no? You learn for a year, and at the end of the year you have a big exam where you will either pass or fail. If you fail you repeat it, if you pass you carry on. The law of nature is the same thing and also it is the same thing with the cosmic law.

When the soul is calling, the tests come, and a test is not something bad or something terrible. It's actually to strengthen yourself, to make yourself ready to receive that which is greater and about to come. In the form of this aspect of the teacher, the soul is growing and cleansing itself of all negativity. When the cleansing of negativity happens, the trust awakens, and when the trust is awakened, the Guru takes the aspect of *Vachaka*, where the Guru infuses the disciple with wisdom. I didn't use the word knowledge now because knowledge is limited. The knowledge that we are talking about just now is limited. The power of word, not the cosmic word, but the power of word that we utter through the mouth is limited.

It has great limitation, and that's why when I sit in front of Him (God) whenever I visit Him or meet Him, we don't speak like word-to-word with an open mouth, but we just talk inside, because the limitation of the word outside is for the kindergarten stage. It would only be good to awaken the love and the longing to search. Then in *Vachaka*, the Master infuses one with divine knowledge; the knowledge of the soul. In these three aspects He gives you the Love, helps you in realising to cleanse all the negativity of the mind, and infuses you with Divine Wisdom. Then you grow. Then the Master takes another aspect which is to free oneself completely from everything.

Janardhaneshwara, this is another name of Krishna. When one has wisdom, one sees only one thing, which is the reality. Everything around which we can describe in words outside for the mind, is an "illusion", yes. Behind this illusion there is one reality which is hidden, there is one reality which is giving strength of power to all and this reality is also inside of you. That's why the way a Teacher or Master sees things is not the same as people see it, because there is no judgement. Man is bound by judgement through the mind. Through the heart one can see just love, only love, but unconditional love. These are, in short, the steps of how the soul progresses, how the soul receives help and how the soul is tested. Actually, that's why I said at the beginning that it is not a coincidence that you are all on the search, because your soul has manifested it, your soul has already through many lifetimes burned certain *sanskaras*, and is now advancing; until you attain your true Self completely, until you radiate who you are, not as individuality but as unity, as the oneness. In this short time it sounds very easy, but it takes its time. For some it takes years, for some it can take just a few seconds or a few minutes. How long depends on how much one is looking at things with the heart. I was just telling to Kalindi: Paramahansa Ramakrishna used to say "The

> When pure Love awakens it is like a volcano where when there is a small hole in the earth.

ones who consider themselves wise, are not wise, and the ones who consider themselves not wise are the wisest." You see, you have to understand the truth that is behind this.

Let's take for example Moses himself. He didn't have knowledge of anything, but he had the grace of God. Through the grace of God his mission was revealed to him, his dharma was revealed to him. Through the grace of God his way was revealed to him and through the grace of God he attained a very high degree of spirituality. Similarly, know one thing, that whatever happens in your life, you can make an effort, yes. But count not on your effort, count always on the grace of God. Like that, all that you will do will be blessed. All that you will do will be perfect, because it is not you who will do it, not as you in the form of pride and ego. This is how very often when men are focused, they try their very best. They try their maximum, but yet nothing happens without the grace of God. This is one little hint for you that will help you in releasing your pressure that you put on yourself. For example, there are so many great saints, great yogis, ascetics, which are meditating from morning until evening, they meditate in the Himalayas, no? They have become great ascetics through many years of penance, through many years of prayer and chanting divine names, and yet, they are still far away, whereas a simple person from a village, Moses for example, who comes from nowhere, He just takes him and says "OK, you will do this mission for me." Like that, if you look at the life of Saints, they were not knowledgeable people, but they had the grace of God with them. Through that they have complete trust in the Divine that whatever the Divine is doing for them is for their own benefit and is for their own good. So if God has called you on to this way, if God or your soul has revealed your path to you and you feel this love, this unconditional love inside of you, then hold tight, no matter what, hold tight, be strong! When you make yourself strong, the Divine will give you more energy so that you become even stronger.

But if you make yourself weak you will fall down completely. So never cease to practice, never cease to ask the Divine for help. Make yourself ready, and remind yourself always of the love for God – wherever you are, whatever you do. Like that you will become Love. What is someone who is enlightened? We talk about enlightenment, no? Or self-realisation, what is that? Can somebody tell me? Tell me please, don't be shy! (someone: "Remembering who we are.") Yes, remembering who you are. Not only remembering, realise who you are! What is this word "realising" who you are? Enlightenment, who is the light? The Divine, no? Enlightenment means you are radiating the Divine Light, when you start radiating the Divine Light, you become enlightened. When the mind is in a calm state, when the mind doesn't bother you, and the pride is not there, you are like a white cloth, no? The Divine is like a golden cloth.

What happens when the white cloth is brought closer to the golden cloth? Automatically the white cloth will start to reflect the golden cloth, no? The golden colour, the same thing, the more you advance towards the Divine, the more you do your effort to advance towards the Divine, the more the Divine will move closer to you. The closer he moves to you, the more his reflection will be on you. Then you become also Divine, then you realise this Divinity – the Divinity which you are already. Then you start to radiate it, you start to reflect it, you start to let it go into action. So whenever tests come, don't fall into them, be strong. Whenever you feel you are down, know that you are not alone. The Divine is much closer than you think.

JUST LOVE 2

JUST LOVE 2

GLOSSARY

Abhayahasta: *Abhaya* means helping and *hasta* means hand; a gesture of encouragement. Sri Swami Vishwananda has said it is "a blessing received from the Guru. ... You go to the Master, you bow your head, you offer the *sahasrara (crown chakra)*, and the teacher touches you on the head, no? He gives you the blessing that says not to worry, the Divine will look after. (Gurupurnima, Shree Peetha Nilaya 25ᵗʰ July 2010)

Abishekam: Form of veneration of the Divine through ritual bathing (water, milk, yoghurt, ghee, honey, sugar) and the offering of fruit, flowers and incense. Every external part of the ritual and each substance involved have a symbolic meaning.

Ahobhilam: The temple is dedicated to Lord Narasimha, the lion form of Lord Vishnu. It is believed that Lord Narasimha manifested himself on the natural rock cave.

Amrita: The nectar of immortality that emerged from the churning of the Ocean of Milk. (see Churning of the Milk Ocean)

Asana: A body posture or pose that is done as part of a spiritual system called Yoga.

Asura: Demon (*a-sura = without light*)

Arjuna: A hero in the *Mahabharata* war in the Bhagavad Gita; the archer in the chariot with Sri Krishna who humbled Himself to be Arjuna's charioteer and teach him about his *dharma* and *Bhakti* Yoga.

Ashram: Spiritual hermitage, often a monastery.

Atma: Soul that is supreme and super conscious; the individual soul, known as the living entity; Jivatma.

Atman: The individual Self or eternal soul; true Self.

Atma Kriya Yoga: *Atma* means Self, *Kri* means action and *ya* means awareness, thus a series of yogic techniques given by Mahavatar Kriya Babaji to his disciple, Sri Swami Vishwananda, who has given it to the world, that helps one Realise one's True Self – Divine Love. Techniques in this Kriya Yoga system include the OM Healing technique, asanas , japa, meditation, mudras and pranayama.

Avatar: A fully realized being sent back to Earth by God to help redeem souls and bring them back to their Eternal Home.

Ayodhya: An ancient city described as the birth place of Rama. It was capital of the ancient Kosala Kingdom.

Bhagirath: A great king in Hindu mythology who brought the River Ganges to Earth.

Bhakti: In Hinduism Bhakti is a term for religious devotion, understood as active involvement of a devotee in divine worship.

Bhakta: One who practices bhakti is called a bhakta.

Balaram: The elder brother of Krishna who incarnated with Sri Krishna and was carried in the womb of Vasudeva's, first wife, Rohini, much to her surprise, since she was beyond child-bearing age when He appeared there. He was so powerful that He single-handedly, at a very tender age, killed the great demon, Asuradhenuka, who had the form of an ass.

Baptism: Baptism is a sacrament (sacred secret) common to all Christian traditions. Practiced by religious traditions worldwide, it became associated with the early Christian movement following the baptism of Jesus of Nazareth by John, called the Baptist or the Baptizer. Jesus would later issue a Great Commission to his church: Go ye into all the world and preach the Gospel, baptising them in the name of the Father, the Son and the Holy Spirit. (Matthew 28:19) [1]

Batti: A kind of bread.

Bhagavad Gita: In it's own words, the Gita is described as "the scripture of yoga and the science of God-Realisation" (brahmavidyayam yogashastre). *Bhagavad Gita* means *Song of the Spirit...* and consists of 700 verses in which Bhagavan Krishna's intent in the dialogue between Him and Arjuna is to overthrow the usurping psychological forces of the body-bound ego and material ignorance and reclaim his eternal spiritual identity – one with Spirit." [2]

Bharata: Second brother of Lord Rama whose mother wanted him to rule in Lord Rama's place, so their broken-hearted father acquiesced to her wishes, because of a promise he had made to her. Bharata was mortified when he came back to Ayodhya and found this out and tried to persuade (to no avail) his brother, who was devoted to Dharma, to return from exile in the forest to his rightful rule of Ayodhya.

Brahman: According to the Vedantins, the *Brahman* is both the efficient and material cause of the visible Universe, the all-pervading soul and spirit of the Universe, the essence from which all created things are produced and into which they are all absorbed at dissolution. The *Brahman* is not generally an object of worship, but rather, it is an object of meditation and attaining it is the ultimate aim of knowledge. [3]

Bible: A collection of writings that comprise the main Christian teachings.

Buddhism, Tibetan: A type of Buddhism whose main Buddha is Padmasambhava.

Buddhism, Zen: A type of Buddhism that is practiced extensively in Japan and includes the incorporation of Taoism.

Buddhism: A religion or philosophy founded on the teachings of the Indian teacher Siddhārtha Gautama.

Chakras: Chakra = wheel. "The seven centres of life force and consciousness in the spine and the brain that keep the physical and astral body of Man alive. The seven centres are divine exits or entrances through which the soul has descended into the body and through which the soul has to ascend, again, by meditation. The soul reaches cosmic consciousness through seven consecutive stages. By consciously ascending through the seven opened or awakened cerebrospinal centres, it begins the path to infinity – the true path, which finally leads to confluence with God." [4]

Chanting: Repetition of a mantra or Divine Name.

Christianity: A religion in which followers see Jesus as the Christ, the Son of God.

Churning of the Ocean of Milk: It is said [in the Vedas] that the demigods and the demons assembled on the shore of the Milk Ocean that lies in the celestial region of the cosmos. The demigods and the demons made a plan to churn the Milk Ocean to produce the nectar of immortality. They then agreed to share the nectar equally once it was produced.
For the task of churning the Milk Ocean the Mandara Mountain was used as the churning rod and Vasuki, the king of serpents, became the rope for churning. As the churning began the Mandara Mountain began to sink deep into the ocean, at which

time Sri Vishnu incarnated as a great tortoise [Kurma Avatara] and supported the mountain on His back. With the demigods at Vasuki's tail and the demons at his head, they churned the milk ocean for one thousand years.

At last Dhanvantari [Sri Vishnu Avatara, physician of the gods and father of *Ayurveda*] appeared carrying the pot of nectar of immortality in His hands. Seeing Dhanvantari with the pot of nectar, both the demigods and demons became anxious. The demigods, being fearful of what would happen if the demons drank their share of the nectar of immortality, forcibly seized the pot.

Wherever the demigods went with the pot of nectar, fierce fighting ensued. ...In an endeavor to keep the nectar from falling into the hands of the demons, the demigods hid it in four places on the earth, Prayag (Allahabad), Hardwar, Ujjain, and Nasik. At each of the hiding places, a drop of immortal nectar spilled from the pot and landed on the earth. These four places are since believed to have acquired mystical power. Eventually, the demons overpowered the demigods and took possession of the nectar of immortality. To rescue the demi-gods from the hands of fate, Maha Vishnu incarnated as a beautiful woman, Mohini-murti, and approached the demons. ...While the demons were thus bewildered by Her beauty, Mohini-murti seized the nectar and returned it to the demigods, who drank it immediately. [5]

Dakshina: Dakshina is typically used to mean an offering usually an "Offering in gratitude to the Guru." Dakshina is also a Vedic Goddess, who represents discrimination. Discrimination is one of the faculties of Truth Consciousness, and is the capability to differentiate between truth and falsehood.

Darshan: literally *sight* or *seeing*. *Darshan* is the sight of a holy being as well as the blessing received by such a sight.

Dasharatha: The father of Lord Rama.

Devi / Deva: (sometimes called a Demi-God) Literally, shining one. A Divine Being, a celestial. [3]

Devaki: Birth mother of Bhagavan Krishna and wife to Vasudeva (see Vasudeva), who had done much tapasya (penance) to have the boon of being Sri Krishna's mother. Sri Swami Vishwananda has said: "...Narayana... chose the right time and manifested Himself into the womb of Devaki. ..... in one of their past incarnations, Devaki and Vasudeva had been a king and a queen who had wanted so much to have God as their child. They had done penance for thousands of years. Mahavishnu was really pleased with them and had promised to them: Whenever I will incarnate myself next time, it will be through you." (*Krishna Janmashtami*, Shree Peetha Nilaya, Springen, Germany, 13th August 2009)

Devotee: One who is ardently given (devoted) to a Guru or Master.

Dhanvantari: In the *Hindu* tradition, an incarnation of *Narayana*. He appears in the Vedas and *Puranas* as the physician of the Gods (Devas) and the giver of *Ayurvedic* medicine.

Dharma: The eternal rules of righteousness that keep up the whole universe; the innate duty of man to live in harmony with these principles. [4]

Dhoti: Cloth worn by men around the waist and covering the legs.

Diksha: Initiation given by a Guru.

Disciple: A devotee who is completely surrendered to his or her Guru.

Divali or Diwali: The Indian "festival of lights", celebrated annually around mid-October or November. Divali is a festival of the light which dispels the darkness of our ignorance. The name "Diwali" is a contraction of "Deepavali" which translates into "row of lamps". Diwali involves the lighting of small clay lamps (*diyas* or *dīpas*) filled with oil to signify the triumph of good over evil. During Diwali, everyone wears new clothes and shares sweets and snacks with family members and friends. Most Indian business communities begin the financial year on the first day of Diwali. Diwali commemorates the return of Lord Rama, along with Sita and Lakshmana, from his 14-year-long exile and vanquishing the demon-king Ravana. In joyous celebration of the return of their king, the people of Ayodhya, the Capital of Rama, illuminated the kingdom with earthen *diyas* and burst firecrackers.

Divine Mother: Devi is the Divine Mother of Hinduism. Her name means goddess. All Hindu goddesses may be viewed as different manifestations of Devi. In some forms she is benign and gentle, while in other forms she is dynamic and ferocious, but in all forms she is helpful to her devotees. Her main Scripture, adored by Hindus, is the *Devi Mahatmyam* (also known as *Chandi Path* and *Durga Saptashati*), in which an allegorical telling of the binding force of *Maya* and ego is represented through devotional stories about the Divine Mother slaying demons which afflict the world.

Divine Names: The Names of God.

Draupati: The wife of the five Pandavas (see *Mahabharata*).

Durga Devi: *Durga* in Sanskrit means "She who is incomprehensible, invincible or difficult to reach." Goddess Durga is the warrior aspect of the Divine Mother (Shakti) worshiped for Her gracious as well as terrifying aspect. Mother of the Universe, She represents the infinite power of the universe and is a symbol of a female dynamism. Durga, a beautiful warrior seated upon a lion or a tiger and maintaining a meditative smile, was the first appearance of the Great Goddess. The circumstance of her miraculous arrival was the tyranny of the monster-demon, Mahishasur, who through terrific austerities had acquired invincible strength. The Gods were afraid of this shape-shifting water-buffalo bull, because neither Vishnu nor Shiva could prevail against him. It seemed that only the joint energy of *Shakti* was capable of vanquishing Mahishasur, and so it was the eighteen-armed Durga who went out to do battle. She introduced herself saying She was the form of the Supreme Brahman who had created all the Gods. They did not create Her; it was Her lila that She emerged from their combined energy. The Gods were blessed with Her compassion. Durga slew Mahishasur and hence, She is also known as Mahishasurmardhini—the slayer of Mahishasur. Durga manifests fearlessness and patience, and never loses Her sense of humor, even during spiritual battles of epic proportion. Kali is considered to be an aspect of Hers.

Duryodhana: The eldest of the Kauravan brothers who was the enemy of the Pandavan brothers in the *Mahabharata* war see.

Ganga Devi: The name of *Ganga* appears only twice in the *Rig Veda* and it was only later that Ganga assumed great importance as a goddess. According to the *Vishnu Purana*, she was created from the sweat of Lord Vishnu's Lotus Feet. Hence, she is also called *Vishnupadi* - the one flowing from the foot of Vishnu. According to *Devi Bhagavata Purana*, Sri Vishnu has three wives, who constantly quarrel with each other, so that eventually, he keeps only Lakshmi, giving Ganga to Shiva and Saraswati to Brahma.

Gadha: Mace

Ganesha: The elephant-headed son of Parvati Who is the remover of obstacles; Lord (Pati) of the Ganas (spirits that always accompany Shiva); God of wisdom; the granter of success is spiritual and material life. In pujas and yajnas he is worshipped first and is, therefore, known as Adideva, the First God.

Ghee: Clarified butter.

Gopis/gopas: "Bhagavan Krishna's childhood companions, who with Him tended the village herds of cows in the sylvan environs of Vrindavan and who shared with him the purity of divine Love and friendship that bears no taint of carnal expression or desire." [2]

Govinda: One of the names of God, often assigned to Lord Krishna.

Guru: *Gu* means darkness and *ru* means the act of removal; the teacher, the Spiritual Master one who dispels darkness (ignorance) of the mind (ego/personality).

Guru Mantra: A sacred, potent vibratory chant given by one's Guru that helps the disciple to purify his thoughts and actions when done according to the Guru's guidance.

Gurudeva: "Divine Teacher"; a customary Sanskrit term of respect used in addressing and referring to one's spiritual teacher.

Hari, Lord: *(Om) yam brahma vedanta-vido vadanti, pare pradhanam purusham tathanye. vishvodgateh karanam ishvaram va, tasmai namo vighna-vinashaya* meaning Obeisances unto Him who is the destroyer of all obstacles, who the knowers of Vedanta describe as the Supreme Brahman, and who others describe as the *pradhana*, or totality of mundane elements. Some describe Him as the supreme male person, or *purusha*, while others describe Him as the Supreme Lord and the cause of the creation of the universe." (Vishnu Purana)

Hanuman: Sri Swami Vishwananda has said about Hanuman:

"Hanuman is considered to be the model of *bhakti*. ...As you know, Hanuman is an incarnation of Shiva. When Rama came down, all the Deities manifested Themselves in the form of Monkeys – *Vanara Sena*. And Hanuman is Shiva Himself, actually. .....You know, Hanuman is considered as the Ocean of Wisdom..." (*Hanuman Jayanti*, Shree Peetha Nilaya, Springen, Germany, 30 March 2010)

Hinduism: With about 900 million followers (over 13 % of the world population) Hinduism is, after Christianity and Islam, the third biggest religion on Earth and it has its origin in India. The followers are called Hindus. Hinduism is composed of different streams that influence each other and sometimes overlay each other, but have differences in the Holy Scriptures, the dogma, the Gods and rituals.

Hindu-Trinity: Creator-Brahma, Preserver/Sustainer-Vishnu, Destroyer-Shiva

Hiranyagarbha Lingam: The golden womb; God, the immanent spirit of the universe; God the Father, transcendent reality.

Hiranyakashipu: Hiranya = gold; Kashipu = soft feathers or bed; the one who loves gold and soft beds. He is a demon (*asura*) who was slain by *Narayana* in his *Narasimha* (man-lion) incarnation and who was the father of Prahlad.

Holika: "Holika is the sister of *Hiranyakashipu*... and she was blessed for so many years of penance with a shawl. If ever she wore this shawl, fire couldn't burn her."* She tried to use this shawl to keep herself safe from the fire in an attempt to burn Prahlad for her brother. *(Sri Swami Vishwananda, *Gaura Purnima* at Shree Peetha Nilaya, Springen, Germany, 2 March 2010.)

Hrdaya Mudra: *Hrdaya* means heart; a *mudra* for opening the heart (see *Mudra*).

Incarnation: When a Deity or soul takes an earthly form.

Indra: Indra is the king of the gods and ruler of the heavens. Indra is the god of thunder and rain and a great warrior, a symbol of courage and strength. He leads the Deva (the gods who form and maintain Heaven) and the elements, such as Agni (Fire), Varuna (Water) and Surya (Sun), and constantly wages war against the opponents of the gods, the demon-like Asuras. As the god of war, he is also regarded as one of the Guardians of the directions, representing the east.

Islam: A religion in which there is one God, Allah, and in which Mohammad is seen as the main prophet or Saint.

Jai: Sanskrit word meaning "hail" or "victory"; used in the same way that "ave" is used in Christian chants.

Jai Gurudev: A greeting meaning "victory to the Divine Guru".

Janmashtami: Birthday.

Japa Mala: Chanting the Name of God or a mantra is Japa. A mala is generally a 108 beaded necklace used to count as one chants which collects the vibration produced by one's chanting the sacred mantra of Divine Name of God, hence it becomes a source of healing, so should always be kept safe in one's Mala bag.

Jaya: Victory; hail; salutations.

Jesus: Son of God, Christ, who came to redeem the world and bring new ways of seeing it.

-Ji: Suffix added to a name or a title, denoting respect.

Jivan Mukta: *Mukti* means release; a liberated sage living in the world but being not of the world.

Judaism: A religion whose main teachings are found in the Torah and whose worshippers, the Jews, are descendents of Abraham.

Kalash Puja: A *kalash* is a copper pot and *puja* means worship or a ritual in honour of the Gods; a coconut is placed on top of the *kalash* during the ritual representing the heart of the Deity; the kalash, also, represents the perfection of the devotees' heart.

Kalki Avatara: The future tenth incarnation of Maha Vishnu in the form of a rider on a white horse who will restore *Dharma*. He will come to end the present age of darkness and destruction known as Kali Yuga. The name Kalki is often a metaphor for eternity or time. Further meanings are destroyer of foulness, destroyer of confusion, destroyer of darkness or annihilator of ignorance.

Kali Ma: Kali, the Dark Mother, is one such Deity with whom devotees have a very loving and intimate bond, in spite of her fearful appearance. In this relationship, the worshipper becomes a child and Kali assumes the form of the ever-caring mother. Kali is the fearful and ferocious form of the Mother Goddess. She assumed the form of a powerful goddess and became popular with the composition of the Devi Mahatmya, a text of the 5th - 6th century AD.

Kamsa: Brother of Devaki (see *Devaki*), who imprisoned her and Vasudeva (see *Vasudeva*), her husband, "because an *Akashvani*, a celestial announcement, had said to Kansa that the eighth child of Devaki would kill him." (Sri Swami Vishwananda, *Krishna Janmashtami*, Shree Peetha Nilaya, Springen, Germany, 13th August 2009.)

Karma: From Sanskrit *kri=to do*. Effects of previous actions from this life or preceding lives, the redeeming law of *karma* is, according to the scriptures of the Hindus, the law of action and reaction, of cause and effect, of sowing and reaping. The natural justice causes that each human being becomes the creator of his fate by his actions and thoughts. [4]

Kauravas: Descendents of Kuru; refers to the descendants of the legendary King Kuru who was the ancestor of many in the Mahabharata war (see *Mahabharata*).

Kirtan: Devotional chanting, singing the Names and praises of God.

Krishna: Krishna is the eighth incarnation of Narayana and was born in the Dvapara Yuga. He is the embodiment of Love and Divine Joy who destroys all pain and sin. He is the protector of sacred utterances and cows. Krishna is an instigator of all forms of knowledge and born to establish the religion of Love. Sri Swami Vishwananda said about Sri Krishna: "...the most beautiful of all the incarnations of the Divine...is Sri Krishna Himself. The Name, Krishna, just by reciting this beautiful Name, one awakens peace and love. The Name means the one who attracts everyone. Krishna is the one who destroys all the sin, who cleanses and purifies everybody. Actually, His life is a mystery itself. It's one of the greatest mysteries, because His life deals with our spiritual life, to attain Him." (Krishna Retreat, Los Angeles, California, USA, December, 2007)

Kurma: (literally turtle) Is considered in *Hinduism* as the second incarnation of *Narayana*. According to several *Puranas*, the old books about the *Devas*, Maha Vishnu incarnated after his form of a fish (*Matsya*) in the form of a turtle. Kurma lifted the mountain, Mandara, onto his back out of the mystical ocean during the Churning of the Milk Ocean by the *Devas* and *Asuras* in search of the *Amrita*.

Lakshmana: Lakshmana is the twin brother of Shatrughna and third brother to Lord *Rama*. In *Puranic* Scripture Lakshmana is described as the incarnation of Anata Shesha, the thousand-headed Naga upon whom rests Lord *Narayana* in the primordial Ocean of Milk, Kshirasagara). He is said to be an eternal companion of Sri Vishnu in all incarnations.

Lakshmi: The consort of Narayana; the Goddess of wealth and prosperity, good fortune and spiritual abundance.

Lakshmi/Narayana: Like Shakti/Shiva, an expression of the female and male principle of God; Goddess of spiritual and material abundance. *Narayana* is the One who pervades all things. Literally, God in humanity.

Lanka: Sri Lanka, formerly Ceylon, where the demon *Ravana* took *Sita* after he kidnapped her from Lord Rama.

Lila or Leela: Divine play; the cosmic play; the concept that creation is a play of the Divine, existing for no other reason than for the mere joy of it.

Lingam: Represents the universal masculine principle which in human nature manifests through such qualities as strength, determination and wisdom.

Lord Chaitanya: As prophesied throughout the Vedas, Lord Krishna descended again in the person of Sri Chaitanya Mahaprabhu (1486 - 1534) in the holy land of Mayapur Sridham (Bengal, eastern India). He inaugurated the Sankirtan Movement, the universal glorification of the Lord by spreading the mass chanting of the Hare Krishna Maha-mantra, as the prescribed process of self-realization for everyone in this age. ix

Mahabharata: India's great epic poem made up of eighteen books recounts the history of the descendants of King Bharata, the Pandavas and Kauravas, cousins whose dispute of a kingdom was the cause of the cataclysmic war of Kurukshetra." [2]

Mahashivaratri: The great night of Shiva; dedicated to the worship of Lord Shiva. Devotees sing bhajans in honour of Shiva, recite Sanskrit shlokas (verses) from scriptures, offer prayers in the morning and evening; some fast for the whole day. The prayers and worship go on throughout the night.

Mahavatar Kriya Babaji: Maha means great, Avatar means Divine Manifestation and *babaji* means revered father; around 5000 year old yogi from the Himalayas and *Paramguru* who has given Kriya Yoga to the world.

Manasa Puja: Written by Adi Shankaracharya in the form of a prayer by a devotee who offers puja with the mind, showing the importance of faith and intention.

Manifest / unmanifest: *manifest=obvious, cognizable.* The manifest universe is absolute and as perfect as the non-manifest, because it comes from the non-manifest. The appearance of the manifest from the non-manifest does not influence the wholeness and perfection of the non-manifest.

Matrika: In Sanskrit, refers to the 14 vowels.

Master: A great spiritual guru.

Mata: Sanskrit word for mother.

Matsya: In his first incarnation, Maha Vishnu has the lower part of his body like that of a fish (Matsya) and the upper part like that of a man. He has four arms. With two he holds a conch-shell and a *chakra*, while the other two are holding a lotus and a mace or are in the protection and boon giving mudras.

Maya: Illusion, that which prevents us from realising our true Self. Sri Swami Vishwananda said about Maya: "Maya Devi is very powerful, because She traps everything. .... Once you step in the world, you get trapped in the grip of Maya and it's quite difficult to get out of Her grip. Her grip is so strong that once She grabs you it's only by chanting the Name of God that you can get yourself released; only by saying, truly from your heart '"God I want you. I surrender completely to you. Do what you have to do with me."' Then She will let go of you." (Darshan, Kiel, Germany, December 2006.) Paramahansa Yogananda wrote: "The Sanskrit word Maya means *the measuring one*; it is the magic force which is innate in creation, which causes in the unlimited and undividable, virtual limitations and fissions. [4]

Mecca: A holy city in Saudi Arabia that is the most important pilgrimage site for Muslims.

Meditation: Practices that help one to control the mind. Sri Swami Vishwananda had said it is: "...something, which is very simple, for attaining this state of Bliss. .... It's through meditation that one can really come to the power of complete fulfilment. .....when one is concentrated, when one is focused on God, when one is in deep meditation, one is not affected by anything around, by any noise, by any touching." (*Darshan*, Mumbai, India, 10th February 2006)

Mohammed: The main prophet in the Islamic religion.

Mohini: In *Hindu* mythology the name of the only female incarnation of Maha *Vishnu*. Mohini is mentioned in the narrative epic of the *Mahabharata*. Here she appears as a form of *Vishnu*, which acquires the pot of *Amrita* (elixir of immortality) from thieving *Asuras* (Demons), and gives it back to the *Devas* (demi-gods), helping them retain their immortality.

Moksha: Liberation from the cycle of birth and death.

Mount Meru (Mount Kailash): A mountain of supreme height on which the Gods dwell or the mountain on which Shiva is ever seated in meditation; the centre of the world, supporting heaven itself; the Olympus of the *Hindu* gods and goddesses, *Mount Meru*, or sometimes Sumeru or Mandara is, according to the *Mahabharata*, a golden mass of intense energy. Brahmā's golden city is at its summit. It is the *axis mundi* for both Hindus and Buddhists. [6]

Mudra: A gesture usually done with the hands that focuses and directs energy. Twenty of these ancient mudras have been given by Sri Swami Vishwananda to his disciples and are available through His teachings to all who wish to learn them.

Muni: A sage, seer, saint, ascetic, monk etc.

Murti: Hindu image (statue) in which the Divine Spirit is expressed.

Namaskar (also Namaste): Indian greeting gesture consisting of a small bow while holding the palms together in front of the body. In Hindu view, Brahman dwells in the heart of each being as the individual self. The joining of hands symbolizes the idea that in the meeting of two persons, the Self actually meets Itself. Joining hands also symbolizes humility. Thus when a Hindu joins his hands and says *namaskar*, he actually says in humility, "I bow to God in you; I love you and I respect you, as there is no one like you."

Nanda: Foster father and uncle of Sri Krishna.

Nada Kriya Yoga: *Nada* means sound. A meditation focused on sound that is one of the *Atma Kriya* techniques.

Nadi: Within the human body there is a network of channels along which energy of the subtle body flows, called nadis. In the Yoga tradition there are said to be 72,000 nadis. Each nadi deals with a specific function and energy. The three main nadis are the Sushumna – rising straight up through the center of the spine and the Ida and Pingala nadis which run on either side of the spine.

Narad Muni: Spiritual Master and son of Lord Brahma's Mind who was directly initiated by Lord Brahma, who eternally sings hymns, prayers and mantras to Sriman Narayana and who is always traveling throughout the Three Worlds; author of Pancharatra, the Vaishnava "Vaishnava Sanskrit texts dedicated to the worship of Sriman Narayana.

NARAYANA, SRI; MAIN INCARNATIONS: (see also *Vishnu*) Is said to have manifested himself in various incarnations, called Avatars, for the destruction of evil or restoration of faith and justice in the world. These incarnations have been in the human form, in the animal form and in the combined human-animal form. Though popularly believed to be ten in number, the Bhagavat Purana mentions twenty-two such incarnations with innumerable more to follow.

    The ten main avatars are:
    1. Matsya
    2. Kurma
    3. Varaha
    4. Narasimha
    5. Vamana
    6. Parasurama
    7. Rama
    8. Balarama
    9. Krishna
    10. Kalki (yet to come)

Narasimha: Nara=man, Simha=lion, the fourth incarnation of Maha *Vishnu*, whose form is half-man and half-lion. The *Puranas* tell about the demon king *Hiranyakashipu*, who once was reigning almost over the whole universe, but who finally was killed by Sri Vishnu in his form of Narasimha. Lord Narasimha is the fiercest incarnation of Maha *Vishnu*. He came to protect His pure devotee *Prahlada* against the tortures of his evil father Hiranyakashipu. While He is feared by the demons and non-devotees, He is worshipped with love and reverence by His devotees.

Navaratri: Hindu festival of worship to the Divine Mother. From the Sanskrit: Nava – Nine and Ratri – nights. During these nine days and nights, nine forms of Shakti i.e. female divinity are worshipped.

Nrsingadev / Lord Narasimhadeva: (nara + simha = human + lion) Is the fiercest incarnation of Maha Vishnu. He came to protect His pure devotee, Prahlada, against the tortures of his evil father, Hiranyakashipu. While He is feared by the demons and non-devotees, He is worshipped with love and reverence by His devotees.

Padma: Lotus flower or Padma, held by the lower right hand of Sri Vishnu, represents spiritual liberation, Divine Perfection, purity and the unfolding of Spiritual Consciousness within the individual.

Panchabhuta: A Sanskrit word meaning five elements or constituents. According to ancient Indian philosophy, the universe is composed of panchabhutas. Even the body and food is derived from this. Prithvi (earth), Apa (water), Tejas (fire), Vayu (air), and Akash (ether) are the five elements of panchabhuta. These elements are kept in a certain balance in the universe and the body. The variation in this balance ends in natural disasters, and diseases in the body. In India, there are temples devoted to the Panchabhuta called 'Panchabhuta Kshetras,' each of which represents one of the Panchabhuta. vii

Panchamrit: A mixture of five foods used in Hindu worship and puja, usually honey, sugar, milk, yoghurt and ghee.

Pandavas: The sons of Pandu; Arjuna and his four brothers who, with their allies, formed one side in the Mahabharata war (see *Mahabharata*).

Parampara: Literally "proceeding from one to another"; "guru parampara" refers to the tradition of guru-disciple passing on wisdom through the ages. (see also sampradaya)

Paramatman: The supreme Being; *the Brahman*.

Paramguru: *Param* means supreme and *guru* means remover of darkness; the guru's guru.

Parashurama: Rama with the axe – Sri Vishnu in a human form, the sixth incarnation of Narayana.

Parvati: Consort of Lord Shiva. "Parvati is the Mother of the Universe. She is *Parashakti*.'" Sri Swami Vishwananda, *Kartik Purnima*, Springen, Germany, 2 November 2009.

Pentecost: It is the day when the Holy Spirit came upon the Disciples after Christ Jesus had resurrected. It is now celebrated 50 days after Easter Sunday.

Prahlad: A great devotee of Krishna even from birth, having been taught by Sage Narada while still in the womb of his mother. As a small boy of five he would preach about Sri Vishnu to his school friends any time the teachers left the room. This preaching infuriated his father, Hiranyakashipu who was determined to deny Sri Vishnu's existence.

Premaka: When the Divine manifests itself in the form of the teacher. In that aspect of the teacher, he helps you to awaken unconditional Love. Swami Vishwananda says "That's why the Guru in that aspect is called Premvatha. Because Premvatha is awakening the prem, the Love inside of you once the Love is awakened, you know how it is."

Puranas: A classic set of sacred stories and legends written in simple Sanskrit; belonging to the past, ancient; an ancient story or legend.

RadhaKrishna: "It is Krishna Himself in the form of Radharani. When we talk about Radha, we always put Her first and then Krishna. We say *Radhe Krishna, Radhe Shyam*, because She is the *Shakti* of Krishna." Sri Swami Vishwananda, *Radhastami*, Springen, Germany, 27 August 2009.

Ramakrishna: (1836-1886) Great Indian Saint born near Calcutta who taught the universality of religions; a great *Bhakta* who worshipped Divine Mother in Her form as Maha Kali.

Ram, Rama: According to the teachings of Hinduism, the seventh incarnation of Sri Vishnu. He is described as educated, beautiful and endowed with all royal qualities. His story is told in the heroic epic Ramayana. It deals with Rama's banishment to the woodland solitude and the victory over *Ravana* after he had kidnapped his wife, *Sita*, to Lanka. An essential helper in this battle was the greatest devotee of Lord Ram, *Hanuman*.

Ravana: Evil demon King who abducted Lord *Rama*'s wife *Sita* and took her to *Lanka*.

Reincarnation: When the soul is born again in a new body; the cycle of birth, death and rebirth; reincarnation ceases when one's karma is resolved.

Rishi: Great seers who revealed the Vedas; *Rishis* can speak only truth and have provided much knowledge to the world.

Sabari: Great devotee of Lord Rama. "...she waited her whole life for Rama. Every day she would chant Ram names continuously. Deep inside of her, she knew that one day she would meet her Rama." Sri Swami Vishwananda, *Darshan*, Steffenshof, 2nd May, 2007.

Sadhana: A Sanskrit word, literally "a means of accomplishing something" – is spiritual practice. It includes a variety of disciplines in Hindu, Sikh, Buddhist and Muslim traditions that are followed in order to achieve various spiritual or ritual objectives.

Sadhu (Saddhu): A Hindu ascetic holy man or wandering monk. The *sādhu* is solely dedicated to achieving *moksa* (liberation), the fourth and final stage of life, through meditation and contemplation of *brahman*. *Sādhus* often wear ochre-colored clothing, symbolizing their *sanyāsa* (renunciation).

Sage: A wise person venerated for experience, judgment and wisdom.

Saint: One who lives in God or the eternal; custodian of super divine wisdom, spiritual powers and inexhaustible spiritual wealth who is free from egoism, likes and dislikes, selfishness, vanity, lust, greed and anger, who is endowed with equal vision, balanced mind, mercy, tolerance, righteousness, cosmic Love and has Divine Knowledge.

Samadhi: A yogic trance (state) where the mind has withdrawn from limited working activities into freer, higher states of God; a state where the seeker and the process of seeking merge into one single continuum and no separation remains between them; when applied to worship, the state where there is no difference between the devotee, God and worship.

Sampradaya: In Hinduism, a sampradaya can be translated as 'tradition' or a 'religious system'. It usually refers to the tradition or established doctrine of teaching from master to pupil through the ages. (See also parampara)

Sannyasin: One who has given up a normal or worldly life to become an ascetic.

Sanatan Dharma: Literally, The Eternal Religion. This term describes the codex of different Vedic sciences, which was called Hinduism after the Greeks had called the people at the banks of the Indus River Indus or Hindus (see also *Dharma*). [4]

Shankha: Conch, conch shell horn.

Shastras: Order, teaching, instruction; any sacred book or composition that has Divine authority.

Saraswati: Goddess of knowledge and the arts, represents the free flow of wisdom and consciousness. She is the Mother of the *Vedas* and chants to her, called the *Saraswati Vandana* often begin and end *Vedic* lessons. It is believed that Goddess Saraswati endows human beings with the powers of speech, wisdom and learning.

Satguru: *Sat* means true; guru the true teacher; highest spiritual teacher; ones primary or main spiritual teacher (see also Guru).

Satsang: Sat means literally "being", hence "essence; reality"; sanga means "association or fellowship". Satsang is a gathering of spiritual seekers for meditation, prayer and devotional singing in order to uplift each other to the divine goal of Self-realization of union with God.

Self: The Atma; who one truly is – Divine Love.

Self-Realisation: Transcending the misidentification with the mind and body that happens to the embodied *Atma* here in the *Maya* and becoming aware of one's true nature; Union with the Divine.

Seva: Selfless service.

Shakti: "...the whole universe is governed by these two cosmic energies, which are the female energy and the male energy. That is what makes everything into manifestation. ..... you can call it Shiva Shakti,..." Sri Swami Vishwananda, The Significance of the Two Hiranyagarbalingams, Shree Peetha Nilaya Temple, 2nd March 2011, Springen, Germany.

Shiva: Part of the Hindu trinity; aspect of Dissolver and Liberator.

Sita Rama: Shakti (see Shakti) and consort of Lord Rama; "Sita Devi is a manifestation of Lakshmi." Sri Swami Vishwananda, Ram Navami, 24th March, 2010, Shree Peetha Nilaya, Springen, Germany.

Soundarya Lahiri: The Soundarya Lahari meaning "Waves Of Beauty" is a famous literary work in Sanskrit believed to be written by Adi Shankaracharya. Its 103 shlokas (verses) eulogize the beauty, grace and munificence of Goddess Parvati / Dakshayani, consort of Shiva.

Spirituality: Latin, *Spiritus, spirit, breeze, or spiro, I breathe,* spirituality in a specific religious sense stands for the idea of a mental (spiritual) connection with the transcendent or infinity.

Sri Adi Shankaracharya: Sri Adi Sankaracharya was the greatest exponent of the doctrine of Advaita Vedanta. Adi Shankara stressed the importance of the Vedas, and his efforts helped Hinduism regain strength and popularity. Many trace the present worldwide prominence of Vedanta to his works. He travelled on foot to various parts of India to restore the study of the Vedas. He lived probably circa 788 to 820.

Srimad Bhagavatam: (Bhagavata Purana) This purana (storybook) is the most important sacred book of stories in India, arranged in twelve so-called cantos and is comprised of 335 chapters with about 18,000 verses that stress the prime importance of the maintaining (preserving) aspect of God personified by the transcendental form of Sriman Narayana, Lord Vishnu.

Sri Lahiri Mahasaya: A householder and spiritual Master who was the first person to receive Kriya Yoga from Mahavatar Kriya Babaji who then shared it with other householders.

Sri Shirdi Sai Baba: A great Master (1838-1918) from India whose teaching combined elements of Hinduism and Islam. He constantly chanted *Allah Akbar* and was known for many divine miracles.

Sri Yukteshwarji: A disciple of Lahiri Mahasya and the guru of Paramhansa Yogananda.

St. Panteleimon: 284-305 A.D from Nicomedia; Physician and Patron of midwives and doctors and one of the fourteen Holy Helpers. Known for miraculous healings. An incarnation of Dhanvantari, physician of the Gods and Father of Ayurveda. (see Churning of the Milk Ocean); one of the patron saints of the chapel at Sri Swami Vishwananda's international Ashram Shree Peetha Nilaya, Germany.

Surdas: 15th century devotional saint of Lord Krishna; a poet, saint and musician who taught *Bhakti*.

Subhadra: Sister of Sri Krishna.

Surrender: In spirituality meaning giving everything completely to God. Sri Swami Vishwananda has said:"... to surrender means to say to God, "Lord, I give myself, my body, mind and soul completely to You. ..... So this is complete surrender where God can do whatever He wants with you, whenever He wants, as He wants. And for that you don't need to be scared, you know, you have just to give yourself. And who is your Self in reality? It's just Him! In the *Gita,* Krishna said: Everything is me." (*Darshan* in Lisbon, Portugal, 12 April 2008)

Svatchaka: Swami Vishwananda says "Svatchaka means to clean. When the Master takes the aspect of Svatchaka it is to clean all the doubt, to clean all the negativity from the mind."

Swaha: Sanskrit for "I offer", used in a yagna fire ceremony.

Swami: Literally "lord"; one who has achieved mastery of himself; also a title commonly given to sannyasis (renunciates); a swami is a member of the monastic Swami Order, reorganized by Swami Shankara in the 8th century.

Tulsidas: 16th century great devotee who, also, wrote the *Ramacharitmanas,* an epic poem devoted to Lord Rama.

Tulsi Devi: See *Vrinda Devi.*

Upanishads: Meaning the inner or mystic teachings; refers to over 200 texts which are considered to be an early source of the Hindu religion.

Vachaka: Means utterance, passing of instruction and knowledge. Swami Vishwananda says "it is rather when the Guru infuses the disciple with wisdom. I didn't use the word knowledge because knowledge is limited."

Vaikunta: The celestial abode (*loka*) of Sri Vishnu and His Devotees.

Valmiki: A sage and poet told by Narad Muni to write the

Ramayana.

Vamana: Is described in the texts of *Hinduism* as the fifth
incarnation of Mahu Vishnu and the first incarnation of the
Second Age or the Treta Yuga. He is the first incarnation of Sri
Vishnu which appears in a completely human form, though it
was that of a dwarf Brahmin. He is, also, sometimes known as
Upendra.

Varaha: In Hinduism the third incarnation of Sri Vishnu in the form
of a boar. In the form of Vahara he fulfills his reputation as the
preserver of the world. According to the Varaha Purana, when
a new age had begun the Earth was sinking in the primordial
waters. Like a mother who does not hesitate to jump after her
child when it has fallen into the water, Sri Vishnu's first thought
was to preserve the world. He took the form of a boar, the
mightiest swamp animal, and dived into the Primordial Ocean.
There he killed the dangerous Demon *Hiranyaksha* (the brother
of *Hiranyakashipu*), lifted the Earth up with his colossal tusks
and saved Her from drowning in the primordial chaos.

Vasudeva: The son of Shoorsen of the Yadu and Vrishni dynasties,
husband of *Devaki* and father of Sri Krishna and his sister,
Subhadra. Vasudeva was a partial incarnation of Rishi Kashyap.
According to *Harivansa Purana*, Vasudeva and *Nanda*, Sri
Krishna's foster father, were brothers.

Vasuki: The King of the Serpents. He assisted at the churning
of the Milk Ocean. In one of the most famous episodes in the
Puranas *(Bhagavata Purana, the Mahabharata* and the Vishnu
Purana), the Devas (Demi-Gods) and the Demons (Asuras) had
lost their immortality at that time. According to Sri Vishnu's
advice, they bound the snake, Vasuki, around the mountain and
started – Gods at one side and Demons at the other side – to

pull back and forth on the snake. In that way they churned the Milk Ocean in order to gain *Amrita*, the nectar of immortality. In memory of that a festival is celebrated in a major way every twelve years known as Kumbha Mela.

Vedas: Ancient Indian texts and the oldest Sanskrit literature written in Vedic Sanskrit and compiled into four sections by Krishna Dvaipayana Veda Vyasa, a sage considered in some Vaishnava traditions as an Avatar of Maha Vishnu who later incarnated as Sage Kapila to teach the Bhakti Yoga of the Shrimad Bhagavatam written by Sage Vyasa at the suggestion of the son of Brahma, Rishi Narada.

Vibhishana: Ravana's younger brother (see Ravana). Although half-demon he was against the kidnapping of Sita and advised his brother to return Sita to her husband Rama. Ravana exiled Vibhishana and he joined Rama's army. Later, when Rama defeated Ravana, he made Vibhishana king of Lanka.

Vijaya: Victory

Vishnu: Literally, all-pervading; God as the Preserver; part of the Hindu Trinity.

Vishwamitra: Was the first saint to have received the *Gayatri Mantra* and who, subsequently, taught it to his Disciple, Sri Rama, who then used it to defeat the great *asura*, Ravana, and rescue His wife, Sita, from the demon; an author of the *Rigveda* known for enduring many austerities and who underwent many trials.

Vrindavan: Vrindavan (also Brindavan) in Mathura district, Uttar Pradesh, India, is a town on the site of an ancient forest where Lord Krishna spent his childhood days and where He was cared for by His foster mother, *Yashoda*, and His foster father and uncle, *Nanda*. It lies in the Braj region about 15km away from Mathura, the city of Lord Krishna's birthplace, near the Agra-Delhi highway. The town hosts thousands of temples dedicated to the worship of Radha and Krishna.

Vrinda Devi: (*Vrindavana*) "The Sanskrit word *vana* means forest. *Vrindavana* is the name given to the forest where Srimati Vrindadevi (Tulasidevi), grows abundantely."

Vyasa: Often regarded as an Avatar of Vishnu, he is sometimes referred to as Veda Vyasa, the compiler of the Vedas; composed *Puranas* and the poetic work *Mahabharata*.

Yagna: Sacrifice of pride and ego; a fire ceremony where one gives up the self, what one wants for the benefit of others getting rid of pride and opening the heart through mantras and offering back what the Divine has given us.

Yamuna: Like the Ganges, the Yamuna, too, is highly venerated in Hinduism and worshipped as Goddess Yamuna, throughout its course. In Hindu mythology, She is the daughter of Sun God, Lord Surya, and sister of Yama, the God of Death, hence, also, known as Yami. "Vasudeva entered the water of the Yamuna carrying the baby Krishna and, as he was going deeper and deeper into the Yamuna River, Yamuna wanted so much just to touch the feet of the Lord. And the moment the feet of the baby Krishna touched the water of Yamuna, she became very calm." Sri Swami Vishwananda, *Krishna Janmashtami*, Springen, Germany, 13 August 2009.

Yantra: A symbolic representation of aspects of divinity. It is an interlocking matrix of geometric figures, circles, triangles and floral patterns. Each deity is said to have a Yantra, a specific geometric shape that represents the nature of the deity. The Yantra is worshipped and charged with the corresponding mantra. It is treated like the deity, and is worshipped as the deity.

Yashoda: Foster mother of Sri Krishna and wife of His uncle, *Nanda*, his foster father. "So as Narayana had said to Maya Devi 'Incarnate Yourself in the womb of Yashoda', Maya Devi manifested Herself inside of Yashoda. On the same night she was born in Gokul, Narayana was born in Mathura [as Sri Krishna]. ...Bhakti, in the form of Yashoda and Nandadev enjoying the Lord." Sri Swami Vishwananda, *Bala Krishna Retreat*, Los Angeles, California, USA, December, 2007.

Yoga: The word "yoga" means union. The union of the individual soul with Spirit; also the method of attaining this goal.

Yogi: One who practices yoga.

Yudishtira: The eldest Pandava; also known as Dharmaraja – the righteous king (see *Mahabharata*).

Yuga: Yuga refers to a large unit of time, era, or epoch. There are four Yugas that happen sequentially, and the four of them collectively loop, creating an endless loop of time.

Zamzam: A well in Mecca where Ishmael, Abraham's infant son, cried for water and kicked the ground and God responded by generating water.

[1] Douglas, J. D., ed. The New International Dictionary of the Christian Church. Grand Rapids, MI: Zondervan Publishing, 1974.

[2] From *The Yoga of the Bhagavad Gita* by Paramahansa Yogananda published by Self-Realization Fellowship, Los Angeles, California, USA in 2007

[3] Srimad Bhagavatam 10th edition English translation by Smt. Kamala Subramaniam, Bharatiya Vidya Bhavan, Kulapati Munshi Marg, Mumbai, 400007 India, glossary pg. 762

[4] Paramahansa Yogananda: The Eternal Search of Man. Collected Talks and Essays – To Realise God in Daily Life. Volume 1. Self-Realization Fellowship Publishers. Printed in USA 2005.

[5] hindupedia.com

[6] Oxford Dictionary of Asian Mythology

[7] india9.com

[8] advaita.org.uk

SRI SWAMI VISHWANANDA

Sri Swami Vishwananda is a spiritual master from the island of Mauritius. For some years he has been visiting numerous countries in Europe, North America, Africa and Asia to convey his message of universal Divine Love.

Swami Vishwananda inspires people to open their hearts to the Love of God. He teaches to go beyond the boundaries of religions and to experience the all-connecting unity behind the conceptual differences. He encourages people to deepen the individual path to God and supports them in their personal beliefs and religious heritage.

I no longer have any great desires,
beyond that of loving till I die of Love.
Nothing is sweeter than Love;
nothing stronger, nothing higher,
nothing more generous, nothing more pleasant,
nothing fuller or better in heaven or earth:
for Love proceeds from God,
and cannot rest but in God,
above all things created.

Saint Therese of Lisieux

The Essence of Everything

is just

LOVE

Made in the USA
Lexington, KY
20 December 2013